Contents

BOXES

Roma in an Expanding Europe: Breaking the Poverty Cycle

By
Dena Ringold
Mitchell A. Orenstein
Erika Wilkens

THE WORLD BANK
Washington, D.C.

Library of Congress Cataloging-in-Publication Data

Ringold, Dena, 1970–

    Roma in an expanding Europe : breaking the poverty cycle / Dena Ringold,
Mitchell A. Orenstein, Erika Wilkens.
    p. cm.
    Includes bibliographical references and index.
    ISBN 0-8213-5457-4

    1. Romanies—Europe, Eastern—Social conditions. 2. Romanies—Europe, Central
—Social conditions. 3. Poverty—Europe, Eastern. 4. Poverty—Europe, Central. I.
Orenstein, Mitchell A. (Mitchell Alexander) II. Wilkens, Erika, 1970– III. Title.

DX210.R56 2004
305.891′49704′091717—dc22   2004053003

Cover photo courtesy of Dusan Guzi from the Slovak Republic. See the work of
Mr. Guzi at www.fotoagent.sk.

FIGURES

TABLES

Foreword

Roma have suffered from severe poverty and exclusion throughout European history. For many Roma in Central and Eastern Europe, the period of transition from communism has been especially dire. Low education and skill levels, compounded by discrimination, have led to widespread long-term unemployment and deteriorating living conditions. Even in some of the new member states of the European Union and those countries on the brink of accession to the European Union, Roma are likely to live in poverty and lack access to education, health care, housing, and other services.

Their plight has not gone unnoticed. Over the past decade, governments, civil society, and the international community have actively supported initiatives to keep Roma children in school, expand access to jobs, and overcome discrimination. Many of these interventions have helped, and the time is right to scale up. Lessons from these projects can make policies more inclusive and expand their reach. This study calls for an inclusive approach to overcoming Roma poverty, based on increased Roma involvement and participation in society and respect for their diversity.

There is reason for optimism. The European Union's recent and ongoing enlargement has focused attention on the need to address Roma exclusion at the national level and has highlighted common European challenges. Most importantly, a small but growing core of experienced and dedicated young Roma leaders now can work both within their communities and with governments to advocate for change.

This study was prepared for the conference "Roma in an Expanding Europe: Challenges for the Future" in Budapest, Hungary, June 30–July 1, 2003. This event catalyzed an ongoing dialogue between the new Roma leadership and the wider policy community, which aims to improve the living conditions and future opportunities of Roma over the long term.

James D. Wolfensohn
President
The World Bank

Acknowledgments

This study brings together analysis done by teams of researchers in different countries. The authors benefited from the guidance and inputs of peer reviewers Christine Jones and Ana Revenga. Useful comments and contributions at various stages were received from Ziad Alahdad, Asad Alam, Warren Bass, Tünde Buzetzky, Ian Conachy, Mukesh Chawla, Armin Fidler, Richard Florescu, Clare Gillsater, Boryana Gotcheva, Daniela Gressani, Richard Hirschler, Franz Kaps, Alexandre Marc, Veronica Nyhan, Alexey Proskuryakov, Michal Rutkowski, Ana Maria Sandi, Merrell Tuck-Primdahl, Nick van Praag, Julius Varallyay, and four anonymous reviewers. Maureen Lewis and Annette Dixon provided feedback, support, and overall guidance throughout.

The main data sources and contributors are as follows:

Chapter 3: The third chapter draws from analysis by Ana Revenga, Dena Ringold, and William Martin Tracy using a three-country household survey of poverty and ethnicity. Iván Szelényi and his team at the Center for Comparative Research at Yale University's Sociology Department made the dataset available.

Chapter 4: Iveta Radicova of the SPACE Foundation, along with Michal Vašečka of the Institute for Public Affairs (IVO), and Michal Šebesta of the Department of Political Science, Faculty of Arts, Comenius University, led the team of Slovak researchers who conducted the qualitative study of Roma settlements in Slovakia. Helen Shahriari and Dena Ringold led the work at the World Bank and wrote the final report. Imrich Vašečka was a consultant to the team, and Marián Babitz at the SPACE Foundation was the project assistant. The listing of the field research team can be found in the full report: "Poverty and Welfare of Roma in the Slovak Republic," available at www.worldbank.org/roma.

Chapter 5: Romanian researchers Cosima Rughinis and Marian Preda conducted the qualitative study of Roma communities in Romania. Liliana Proteasa of the Ministry of Education and Research provided comments.

Chapter 6: A team of Hungarian researchers led by János Zolnay conducted the project inventory and case studies. The team included Gábor Bernáth, Angéla Kóczé, József Kolompár, Katalin Kovács, and Zsolt Zádori. Richard Hirschler edited the project case studies.

Chapter 7: Francisco Alvira Martin in Madrid and Bronwyn Alsop in Washington compiled the information used in the case study of Spain. The authors also thank the Office of the Publisher.

Abbreviations

AFDC	Aid to Families with Dependent Children
ASGG	Asociación Secretariado General Gitano (Spain)
CIDE	Centro de Investigación y Documentación Educativa (Spain)
CEDIME-SE	Center for Documentation and Information on Minorities in Eastern Europe – Southeast Europe
CoE	Council of Europe
CSCE	Council for Security and Cooperation in Europe
ECOHOST	European Centre on Health of Societies in Transition
ECRI	European Commission against Racism and Intolerance
ERDF	European Regional Development Fund
ERRC	European Roma Rights Center
ESF	European Social Fund
EU	European Union
FCNM	Framework Convention for the Protection of National Minorities
FSGG	Fundacion Secretariado General Gitano (Spain)
IRIS	Institute for New Homes and Social Integration (Spain)
IVO	Institute for Public Affairs
MSG	Minority self-government (Hungary)
NEKH	Office for National and Ethnic Minorities (Hungary)
NEVI	National Institution for Health Prevention (Hungary)
NGO	Non-governmental organization
NMSG	National Minority Self-Government (Hungary)
NPDR	National Program for the Development of Roma (Spain)
ODIHR	Office of Democratic Institutions and Human Rights
OECD	Organisation for Economic Co-operation and Development
OFA	National Foundation for Employment (Hungary)
OMC	Open Method of Coordination
OSCE	Organization for Security and Co-operation in Europe
OSI	Open Society Institute
PER	Project on Ethnic Relations
PPP	Purchasing power parity
RCRC	Roma Communities Resource Center (Romania)
Sf.	Saint (St.) (Romania)

SSP	Self-Sufficient Program (Canada)
STDs	Sexually transmitted diseases
TANF	Temporary Assistance to Needy Families (United States)
UN	United Nations
UNICEF	United Nations Children's Fund
UNDP	United Nations Development Programme

Overview

Increasingly severe poverty among Roma, or "gypsies," in Central and Eastern Europe has been one of the most striking developments since transition from socialism began in 1989. Although Roma have historically been among the poorest people in Europe, the extent of the collapse of their living conditions is unprecedented. Whereas most Roma had jobs during the socialist era, there is now widespread formal unemployment and poverty among Roma communities. The problem is a critical one. Because of higher birth rates, the Roma population's relative size is increasing across the region. A minister of education in one of the new European Union (EU) member states recently noted that in his country, every third child entering school is Roma. Policies to address Roma poverty therefore need to be an integral component of each country's economic and social development strategies.

WHO ARE THE ROMA?

The Roma are Europe's largest and most vulnerable minority. Unlike other groups, they have no historical homeland and live in nearly all the countries in Europe and Central Asia. The origins of Roma in Europe are widely debated. Historical records indicate that they migrated in waves from northern India into Europe between the ninth and fourteenth centuries. Roma are extremely diverse, with multiple subgroups based on language, history, religion, and occupations. While Roma in some countries are nomadic, most in Central and Eastern Europe have settled over time, some under Ottoman rule and others more recently under socialism.

Size estimates of the Roma population differ widely. Census data are intensely disputed, as many Roma do not identify themselves as such on questionnaires. By most estimates, the share of Roma has grown to between 6 and 9 percent of the population in Bulgaria, FYR Macedonia, Romania, and the Slovak Republic (Slovakia). These shares are likely to increase in the near future because of high population growth among Roma and decreasing fertility among the majority populations. Romania has the highest absolute number of Roma in Europe, with between 1 million and 2 million. Large populations of between 400,000 and 1 million also live in Bulgaria, Hungary, Serbia and Montenegro, the Slovak Republic, and Turkey. Western Europe's largest Roma populations are found in Spain (estimated at 630,000), France (310,000), Italy (130,000), and Germany (70,000). In total, about 7 million to 9 million Roma live in Europe for a population equal to that of Sweden or Austria.

Why has attention to Roma issues increased so sharply over the past decade? Following the collapse of the iron curtain in 1989, political liberalization allowed for increased international and domestic awareness of the situation of Roma, including emerging human rights violations and humanitarian concerns related to deteriorating socio-economic conditions. National governments have a large stake in the welfare of Roma, for human rights and social justice concerns, but also for reasons of growth and competitiveness. In countries where Roma constitute a large and growing share of the working-age population, increasing marginalization of Roma in poverty and long-term unemployment threaten economic stability and social cohesion. Important priorities are understanding the nature and determinants of Roma poverty and taking policy action.

ROMA POVERTY

Roma are the most prominent poverty risk group in many of the countries of Central and Eastern Europe. They are poorer than other groups, more likely to fall into poverty, and more likely to remain poor. In some cases, Roma poverty rates are more than 10 times that of non-Roma. A recent survey found that nearly 80 percent of Roma in Bulgaria and Romania were living on less than $4.30 per day (see figure 1). Even in Hungary, one of the most prosperous accession countries, 40 percent of Roma live below the poverty line.

WHY ARE ROMA POOR?

For several interwoven reasons, Roma poverty is rooted in their unfavorable starting point at the outset of the transition from planned to market economies. Low education levels and overrepresentation among low-skilled jobs led to labor market disadvantages, which were compounded by discrimination and the low expectations of

FIGURE 1 POVERTY RATES, 2000
(Percentage of population living below $4.30/day[a])

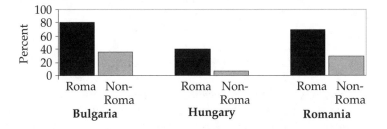

[a] Adjusted to purchasing power parity (PPP) to allow for price comparisons across countries.
Sources: Yale dataset; Revenga et al. 2002.

employers. As a result, Roma have had more difficulty re-entering the job market than other groups and have become caught in a vicious circle of impoverishment. Additional barriers include a lack of access to credit and unclear property ownership. Combined with an over-dependence on welfare, these factors create a poverty trap that pre-cludes many Roma from improving their living conditions or starting their own businesses. Persistent disadvantages in education, includ-ing low school attendance and overrepresentation in "special schools" intended for physically and mentally disabled children, make it highly probable that without policy interventions, the next generation of Roma will remain in poverty. Moreover, very few Roma are active in local or national politics, which mutes their political voice.

Growing needs and tight fiscal constraints are further limiting access to social services in Eastern Europe's transition period. These conditions have brought formal and informal charges for previously free services and eroded service quality. The increasing barriers to access have hurt Roma in particular because they are at a higher poverty risk and are often geographically isolated.

Similarly, because Roma frequently live in settlements where prop-erty ownership is unclear, or in remote areas, they may lack the doc-umentation necessary to enroll in school and claim social assistance or health benefits. The high prevalence of Roma in informal sector employment—such as petty trade and construction—also limits their access to benefits based on social insurance contributions, including health care and unemployment benefits.

In addition, social and cultural factors affect access and inter-actions with service providers. Because of language barriers, Roma may have difficulty communicating with teachers, under-standing doctors, and maneuvering through local welfare offices. Poor communication and stubborn stereotypes of Roma and non-Roma breed mistrust and reinforce preconceptions on both sides. Moreover, the overall absence of Roma personnel involved in policy design and delivery of public services means that few individuals can bridge the cultures.

REGIONAL CONTEXT

Roma issues have gained increasing international attention over the past decade because of emerging evidence of human rights violations and seriously deteriorating socio-economic conditions within many Roma communities. These developments have caught the attention of international organizations such as the United Nations Development Programme (UNDP), the Council of Europe, and the Organization for Security and Co-operation in Europe (OSCE), as well as non-governmental organizations (NGOs), including the Open Society Institute (OSI), Save the Children, and the United Nations Children's Fund (UNICEF). Perhaps most significant Roma issues have been an integral part of the EU enlargement process; in 1993, the EU adopted attention to Roma issues as part of the Copenhagen criteria for accession. At the international level, Roma NGOs such as the International Romani Union and the Roma National Congress have become increasingly active.

CONTEXT AND CONTENTS

The Role of the World Bank

In 2000, the World Bank published the first cross-country report on the poverty and human development challenges that Roma face in Central and Eastern Europe (Ringold 2000). Unlike prior analyses that had largely focused on human rights questions, the Bank report addressed Roma issues from an economic and social development perspective. This study updates and expands that work, incorporating new survey findings and, for the first time, publishing some background studies that were included in the 2000 report. Policymakers, the Roma and NGO community, and a wider audience concerned about Roma issues showed a strong interest in more detailed information on the conditions in Roma communities and policy responses.

This study responds to that demand, but does not quench it. The surveys and case studies included are still incomplete. Further work is needed to examine the particular circumstances of Roma living in Albania, Moldova, Russia, Ukraine, and the former Yugoslavia, among other countries. Health, housing, and the situation of Roma women are issues that need further attention. These gaps stem from a lack of information and measurement challenges. Despite the severity of Roma poverty, the limited information on their living conditions and challenges is often unreliable and frequently anecdotal. The analyses presented here are intended to fill these gaps—and to stimulate further action.

Contents

The chapters draw on both quantitative analyses of household surveys and qualitative, sociological case studies that document the experiences of Roma communities in different countries, focusing on Bulgaria, Hungary, Romania, and Slovakia and drawing on examples from other countries. Chapter 1 provides background on the Roma, their characteristics, and their origins. It also discusses contrasting policy approaches that have shaped the position of Roma in Europe over time.

Chapter 2 looks at Roma poverty—its nature and characteristics—using quantitative data from household surveys, including a cross-country Roma household dataset. It examines the correlates of Roma poverty, including poor housing conditions, education, and health.

Chapters 3 and 4 report the results of detailed field studies by Central and East European sociologists on diverse Roma communities in Romania and Slovakia. The studies draw directly from interviews with Roma and non-Roma to provide a better understanding of the interrelated challenges that Roma face in accessing markets and services. One of the strongest findings was that access to public services and labor markets is compounded by the geographic isolation of some Roma settlements. Often, these isolated settlements originated from past exclusionary policies. Today, the geographic isolation of Roma settlements limits their access to education, health care, and waste collection, and thus increases poverty over the long run.

Other causes of Roma poverty are interrelated as well. For instance, the choice of Roma parents to enroll their children in "special schools" that are intended for the mentally and physically disabled is sometimes driven by discrimination that Roma experience in regular schools. Roma parents sometimes feel they are protecting their children by sending them to special needs schools with other Roma children, but the education that they receive ill prepares them for life, again exacerbating the long-term risks of poverty and exclusion.

Chapters 5 and 6 look at the experience of projects in Hungary and compare the Central and East European experience with that of Spain, a West European country with a large Roma population. Chapter 7 reports the survey results of Roma projects in Hungary and shows that despite the proliferation of such projects since 1989, it remains difficult to evaluate their impact. Case studies of several projects identify several important factors, including the quality of project leadership, local economic conditions, and monitoring and evaluation.

While this study aims to pull together as comprehensive a picture as possible of poverty and human development among Roma in Central and Eastern Europe, it does not attempt to be comprehensive in its coverage of Roma issues more broadly. Critical topics, such as the human rights situation of Roma and their political participation, are central to the agenda of improving the welfare of Roma in Europe, but are outside the scope of the study. There is also a full agenda for future research and analysis on Roma issues, which is discussed further in chapter 8, including more in-depth analysis of the determinants of poverty and exclusion and greater understanding of the internal organization of diverse Roma communities, including their origins, language, and social structure.

Methods and Approaches

This volume draws from both quantitative and qualitative methods to paint a fuller picture of Roma living conditions. Both approaches have distinctive benefits and drawbacks. Quantitative methods are useful for illustrating where Roma stand relative to non-Roma populations in individual countries and for comparing Roma populations across different countries. On the other hand, data on Roma are notoriously unreliable and difficult to attain. Even basic population figures are subject to dispute. Since Roma often do not self-identify as Roma, survey-based research has serious limitations. Still, quantitative data offers useful comparisons of welfare measures that can improve policy analysis and responses.

Although quantitative research shows that Roma poverty is distinctive, it does not provide an adequate basis for understanding the particular dynamics that underlie Roma poverty. Here, qualitative research has the greatest impact. Qualitative research can identify social processes, mechanisms, and relations between variables that are difficult to discern by looking at numbers alone. For example, the empirical analysis presented in chapter 3 shows that much of the gap between Roma and non-Roma welfare is likely due to factors such as discrimination and exclusion, which cannot be assessed empirically. Therefore, qualitative research provides a sharper picture of Roma living conditions in different communities and emphasizes the diversity of Roma populations, allowing for a better understanding of interconnections between causes of poverty. Carefully constructed qualitative surveys conducted by researchers in Central and Eastern Europe are the primary source for this analysis. This qualitative research highlights how Roma perceive their poverty situation in their own words.

Yet qualitative research has drawbacks as well. It tends to provide a snapshot of a single area, emphasizing certain factors over others with biases that may reflect the researchers' specific concerns. This is particularly important for this study, as different research teams in each country conducted the qualitative studies with different foci and depth. While these caveats should be kept in mind, the combination of quantitative and qualitative analysis provides a complementary set of perspectives and a better starting point for analysis and policymaking.

The Policy Development Environment

Policies to ease Roma poverty need to be designed with three key factors in mind: (i) the multidimensional nature of Roma poverty and its interconnected roots, (ii) the diversity of Roma in Central and Eastern Europe, and (iii) the European integration process.

The Multidimensional and Interconnected Roots of Roma Poverty

This study's central insight is that Roma poverty has multiple and interrelated causes. The causes tend to reinforce one another in a vicious cycle of poverty and exclusion and require a multifaceted approach. Roma often have poor labor market access because of low education levels, geographic isolation, and discrimination. Low education levels result from constraints on both the supply and demand side. Roma often face discrimination in school and feel that schools ignore their culture and language. In addition, Roma sometimes lack sufficient food or clothing to support school attendance. Thus, attitudes, experiences, and social conditions conspire to reduce Roma education levels and labor market performance. Because of these interconnected roots, one cannot adequately address Roma poverty by focusing on a single aspect. Rather, a comprehensive approach is needed.

For example, researchers found that poor housing conditions, in part, contributed to Roma poverty in several countries. In many cases this is because Roma were left out of the property and land privatization processes that occurred during the early 1990s. Information was scarce about how to navigate the bureaucratic procedures for property ownership, and Roma were less likely than others to do it successfully. Hence today Roma disproportionately live in unregistered dwellings, contributing to poverty in complex ways. According to one man interviewed in Kyjov, a segregated Roma settlement in the town of Stará Lúbovňa, Slovakia, "We built our house with a building permit, but there are still problems with the site, although it was officially given to us during socialism. But today the land is not ours, therefore we can not install any water, gas, or sewage pipes." This example shows that Roma poverty is rooted in incompatibilities between Roma social practices, dominant state behaviors and norms, limited political representation, and geographic exclusion. It also shows how economic reforms may have missed Roma.

Diversity

While demonstrating the distinctive nature of Roma poverty, this study also emphasizes the diversity of Roma populations in Central and Eastern Europe—ethnic, occupational, religious, and economic. The proportion speaking Roma language dialects differs greatly from country to country, as does the proportion living in cities, integrated neighborhoods, or segregated rural settlements. These differences have a major impact on welfare status. Efforts to create, define, or represent a single Roma community will similarly founder on the rocks of internal cultural diversity. Roma tend to have distinctive problems of integration and access, but the situation of different communities and individuals varies immensely and cannot be reduced to a single, simple set of answers or policy responses.

Illustrating this diversity is a study of nine Roma communities in Romania that is included in chapter 5. Each of the nine communities consists of different combinations of Roma subgroups, with different languages, religions, and occupations. The Bucharest Zabrauti neighborhood contains a mosaic of Roma ethnic groups, varying from the quite traditional Sporitori, who speak the Roma language, to more integrated Roma, who speak primarily or only Romanian. The Babadag urban community has three main Roma groups, the largest of which is Muslim. However, in the Iana rural community, most Roma are active Orthodox Christians. Other communities are relatively homogenous. Primarily Hungarian-speaking Roma lived in an urban and a rural community in Romania. Populating another rural community were relatively well-off Caldarari Roma, who speak the traditional Roma language; they work primarily in trade, after being laid off from a large state-owned enterprise. Such diversity complicates any approach to reduce Roma poverty, since the root causes may also differ dramatically.

The European Dimension

Policies to address Roma poverty must also be framed in the context of the Central and East European countries' drive for EU membership. The timing of the publication of this study and other reports on Roma is not coincidental. The EU's expansion on May 1, 2004, to include eight countries of Central and Eastern Europe and to acknowledge the candidacy of Bulgaria and Romania, focused attention on the Roma issue through the adoption and monitoring of the Copenhagen criteria for EU accession. Based on these criteria, those countries have built institutions and legislative mechanisms to address Roma issues. However, this is only the beginning. Addressing Roma poverty will require a long-term approach that is part of each country's overall economic and social development program.

Interactions between Roma policy and the EU accession process can be seen most vividly in Hungary—the first Central and East European country to apply for EU membership and also the first to make a substantial policy effort to address Roma issues. Hungary passed the Minorities Act in 1993, which granted considerable cultural, educational, and linguistic rights to Hungary's 13 recognized minorities, including Roma. The act created a system of national and local minority self-governments that let minorities initiate social, educational, and development projects. Approximately half of these are Roma self-governments.

Hungary has also established the national Office for National and Ethnic Minorities, an independent minorities ombudsman to oversee minority rights and protections, and the Roma Office under the Office of the Prime Minister to coordinate Roma policy across the government. Together, these offices enable Hungary to comply with EU norms, in part through the implementation of a "medium-term package" of measures aimed at the Roma's social inclusion. Hungary's extensive experience with Roma institutions and projects provides an important example for other new EU member states and aspirants.

POLICY IMPLICATIONS AND APPROACHES

While the plight of Roma in Central and Eastern Europe has not gone unnoticed, many lessons need to be drawn and new policy approaches pursued. In the past decade, governments, NGOs, and international organizations have launched numerous initiatives to address various aspects of the Roma issue, from combating human rights violations, to addressing racial stereotyping in the media and promoting education and employment. The activity level varies significantly across countries. With EU enlargement, a more systemic policy-oriented approach is needed to address gaps in Roma economic and social development. Project lessons from the 1990s can be used to inform policy interventions in key areas, such as education, health, social assistance, and the labor market.

Together, the multidimensional and interrelated roots of Roma poverty, the diversity of Roma communities, and the differences in European background constitute a unique context for policy. This report outlines a number of policy implications. First, a comprehensive approach is needed to address the multiple, interrelated causes of Roma poverty simultaneously. Second, primary emphasis needs to be placed on furthering the social inclusion of Roma in European societies. In identifying policy approaches, useful lessons can be drawn from other countries with similar experience. Finally, greater attention needs to be paid to policy implementation and evaluation and the central role of Roma in these processes.

Links with Systemic Reform

Improving Roma conditions is inherently linked to the overall success of each relevant country's economic and social development strategies. Each country must implement policies that promote and sustain growth, while improving social welfare outcomes and the inclusiveness of policies for all populations. However, macro-level policies will not be sufficient to reach all Roma, so targeted interventions are needed to address unique exclusion problems and ensure that Roma are able to work and participate fully in public services.

Related to this, better access to quality social services for Roma is linked to the overall effectiveness of each country's education, health, and social protection systems. In many ways, the inherited systems were ill suited to the reality of a market economy, and one way that they have proven ineffective is in their inability to reach all vulnerable groups, including Roma. Throughout Central and Eastern Europe, countries have embarked on systemic reforms to improve the efficiency, equity, and relevance of public services. These measures are making a difference. Addressing systemic issues and improving access and quality of social services will improve conditions for the entire population. Again, interventions designed to reach Roma need to accompany these system-wide measures.

Toward an Inclusive Approach

As Roma poverty is rooted in broad-based social exclusion—economic, social, and geographic—addressing it calls for an inclusive approach that aims to expand and promote Roma involvement and participation in mainstream society while maintaining cultural and social autonomy. Only policies that allow Roma to take advantage of opportunities in national and European labor and housing markets, education and health systems, and social and political networks have a chance of reducing poverty over the long term. Policy mechanisms include those that make existing policies more accessible to Roma and identify areas where targeted initiatives will specifically reach Roma. An emphasis on inclusion policies would complement rights-based approaches by tackling the economic and social barriers that Roma face.

A central policy goal should be the multifaceted inclusion of Roma into institutions and mechanisms that create economic and social opportunities. Emphasis should be placed on providing incentives, rather than forcing compliance. Interventions that reduce the isolation and exclusion of Roma can help improve living conditions over the longer-term. An inclusive approach also needs to rely on the greater participation of Roma, particularly of Roma women, in the projects and programs that affect them. A number of successful projects use Roma mentors as liaisons between Roma and non-Roma communities. For example, Roma teachers' assistants who work with parents or peer advisors who assist with job placement can facilitate integration, while strengthening the Roma community.

Addressing exclusion and the wounds of segregation also involves overcoming divisions between Roma and non-Roma communities. This helps build trust and social capital within communities. Such measures need to involve both Roma and their non-Roma neighbors. In most cases, policies should target communities at large, rather than Roma in particular. However, there may be exceptions where explicit attention to ethnicity would be appropriate, such as overcoming language barriers. Critical vehicles for overcoming cultural barriers are multicultural education and a curriculum that includes the history and culture of Roma and other minorities. Training teachers, local government officials, and other personnel working in social services can address discrimination in public services. Finally, public information campaigns can promote multiculturalism and raise awareness about discrimination.

Policies need to balance three related sets of objectives: first, increasing economic opportunities by expanding employment participation; second, building human capital through better education and health; and third, strengthening social capital and community development by increasing Roma empowerment and participation. In this vein, options include the following:

- Reducing housing segregation, particularly by alleviating the problems associated with, or providing alternatives to, isolated rural settlements;
- Integrating Roma students into mainstream education systems through preschool programs and provision of food and clothing to enable attendance;
- Increasing outreach to Roma communities through social service providers, including health and social workers;
- Involving Roma as liaisons between communities and public services; and,
- Providing relevant job training and programs that increase Roma participation in formal labor markets.

Learning from Examples

When considering future policy directions, a key source of ideas and experiences may be found in the minority policy experiences of other countries and regions, particularly in the West. North America and South America provide interesting counterpoints to Europe's experience, in part because the histories of African and indigenous peoples in the Americas offer more parallels to that of Roma than other national minorities in Europe. While all ethnic groups have distinct features, minority-majority relations share important similarities everywhere, and much can be learned from the policy experience of other countries that have confronted these issues over centuries.

What is distinctive about the Roma in Europe is that they have endured centuries of exclusionary and assimilationist policies without being absorbed into majority societies. They remain stateless and have founded no statehood movement because they lack a historic homeland. These general characteristics underline the challenges facing an integration-oriented approach to Roma poverty. However, they also focus attention on the stakes involved in getting policy right. Policymakers need to approach Roma poverty issues from a long-term perspective, with a clear idea of objectives and tradeoffs.

Learning from Evaluation and Implementation

Developing a comprehensive national policy response to Roma poverty entails attention to monitoring and evaluation. The wealth of Roma projects in Central and Eastern Europe provides a great deal of implementation experience, but very few initiatives were evaluated or monitored, making it extremely difficult to identify lessons learned for future interventions. It is still important, however, to examine this body of experience to distill lessons for future work. Mechanisms for monitoring and evaluation should be built into new and ongoing initiatives, as should opportunities for exchanging information within and across countries.

A first step is to increase the availability and quality of information about Roma. To address this, countries need to examine their statistical instruments—for example, censuses and household surveys—and administrative data to assess how they can better capture policy-relevant information on Roma and other minorities. Multilateral coordination, advice, and guidance can be important for ensuring data comparability. More information on international practices is needed, particularly in addressing the privacy issues involving ethnic identification. The outcomes of targeted public policies and NGO initiatives also require close monitoring. Program evaluations should be used for ongoing policy development. Mechanisms should be in place for disseminating lessons across regions and countries.

Privacy concerns about data collection must be respected, but up-to-date information is critical for policymakers to make decisions about program design and to monitor outcomes. Such data collection should benefit Roma in the long run through better-designed and targeted interventions. By making ethnicity declarations voluntary and by using periodic sample surveys rather than national administrative data to collect information on specific topics, privacy concerns can be respected. It is extremely important to involve Roma groups in survey development, implementation, and analysis. This was an emphasis of recent censuses in Bulgaria and Slovakia. Qualitative assessments can also provide valuable information for project design.

It is vital to build monitoring and evaluation mechanisms into projects and policies. Monitoring should be an integral part of all projects to ensure accountability. Equally important are evaluations to assess project impacts and outcomes. These require collecting baseline data at the outset of projects for comparison with data once the projects have been completed and experiments with controls that compare the project to outcomes in the absence of the project. For example, an intervention designed to improve school enrollments should measure enrollments prior to the project and assess whether participants stay in school during the project and afterwards. The time horizon for outcome evaluation should also be long enough to assess longer-term impacts. Again, in the case of education, the evaluation should assess not just whether children are in school at the project's end, but what they have learned, whether they graduate and continue their education, and how the project affects their chances in higher education and the labor market.

Ensuring Participation

Regardless of whether programs and policies are explicitly designated for Roma, Roma participation is essential. The success of the inclusive approach outlined earlier rests on the ability of the Roma to contribute to the development processes that affect them. The experience of policies and programs directed at Roma during both the socialist and transition periods showed that it is essential to involve the Roma in program design, implementation, and evaluation. The recent past is littered with projects and programs that, however well intentioned, failed because they were designed and implemented without the involvement of the future beneficiaries.

Ensuring Roma involvement in policy and project development rests on the existence of effective participatory mechanisms that recognize the diversity of Roma communities. While Roma have been increasingly involved in civil society and various aspects of policy-making, significant challenges remain to ensure effective communication and involvement. Some have been discussed in this chapter, including low education levels and illiteracy, which diminish the potential pool of Roma leaders and voters, and lead to mistrust and prejudices between Roma and non-Roma. It is essential to continue expanding opportunities for Roma to participate in civil society at the local and national levels and to increase contacts with non-Roma. The example of Slovakia presented in chapter 4, in particular, highlights the perils of separation and segregation. Lacking opportunities for interaction with wider society, including other Roma communities and non-Roma, Roma are cut off from society. Increasing partnerships between non-Roma and Roma will facilitate inclusion and address the mistrust and miscommunication that limit the progress of local and community development.

CONCLUSIONS

Poverty among Roma remains one of the most pressing issues for the Central and East European states as they move toward EU integration and sustained economic development. Using a variety of sources and approaches, this report examines the nature of Roma poverty—a multifaceted challenge that can only be addressed by a policy approach that attends to all dimensions of Roma social exclusion and focuses on the potential contributions Roma can make to social and economic development. Since the dominant policy approach in the years after socialism has tended to rely on a fragmented set of projects, often delivered by local NGOs with limited assistance from the state, the opportunity to make a difference through comprehensive change is significant and bright.

The current level of activity and interest in Roma issues in Central and Eastern Europe provides a promising start. The next step is to integrate the lessons learned into policy. The mechanisms to facilitate this are in place. Most countries have formulated strategies to improve the conditions of Roma and of established institutions to develop, coordinate, and administer policies and projects. However, the agenda is complex, and improvements will not come overnight. Indeed, poverty among Roma communities in some West European countries highlights the scope of the challenge. Effective policy responses will require a multilayered approach involving cross-country partnerships among Roma and international organizations, national and local governments, NGOs, and communities.

Box 1 In Their Own Words

Interviews with Roma throughout the region highlight the range of their experiences and living conditions across and within countries. These snapshots illustrate this diversity. The challenges they face are explored further throughout this volume.

Education
Many Roma children do not attend school. Some parents are unable to send their children to school because they lack basic supplies or even clothes. Other children are excluded because of social and cultural factors, such as language.

"We can't afford to send them to school in the winter. We have no sneakers, no proper shoes for snow. They can't go to school in slippers. They don't have jackets or warm clothes either. We can't afford anything—copybooks, pens. . . . Children have no money for meals. That's why they don't go to school," said a parent in Bulgaria.

"Children from segregated Roma settlements do not master the Slovak language and do not understand their teachers. The teachers do not speak the Roma language, so they communicate by using gestures," a school director in Slovakia stated.

While demand for education is low in some Roma communities, other parents express a strong interest in their children's education and recognize its importance for their future success.

A grandparent in Slovakia noted, "My grandson is a first grade student. We sent him to kindergarten and hope in the future that he will put more importance on education than we did."

"I waited for my daughter to return from school every day and asked her what happened at school. I sat beside her when she was writing up her homework. I would not let her go out until I saw that she had finished. I would not allow anyone at home to touch her and make her do some other housework. . . . [I] do not know what will happen to her after she completes her education, but whatever that is, it will be better. She can become a doctor, a teacher. She will go higher than us," explained a parent in Bulgaria.

Employment
Formal unemployment in some Roma settlements can reach 100 percent. Many Roma face severe obstacles in finding a job because of their limited education and low skill levels and discrimination on the labor market.

"Who is going to give me a job? I have no education, no skills, and am Roma. Even in my neighboring village nobody wants to give us any work," said a 35-year-old father of five in Slovakia.

A Roma in Bulgaria stated, "If his Bulgarian name is Angel or Ivan or Stoyan or Dragan, he'll get all the application forms and be asked to

(*continued*)

Box 1 *(continued)*

come in. As soon as they realize he's Gypsy, Roma, he's turned down, they lower their voices and tell him to come some other time. When your name is Bulgarian and they see you are a Gypsy, they throw you out!"

Roma Identity

In Hungary, experiments with alternative education for Roma high school students that include Roma language, culture, and history in the curriculum have sparked interest in Roma identity among young people.

A student in Hungary noted, "My grandmothers spoke the Roma language, and my parents can understand it. I do not speak the language, but I would very much like to learn it."

Another student in Hungary added, "I would like to know more about the origin of my people and our values."

Chapter 1
Introduction

Increasingly severe poverty and exclusion of Roma in Central and Eastern Europe have been among the most striking developments in the region since the post-socialist transition began in 1989. Although Roma have historically been among the poorest people in Europe, there has been an unprecedented collapse in their living conditions in the former socialist countries. While most Roma had jobs during the socialist era, formal unemployment is now widespread. Even in the new EU member states and leading candidate countries, the levels of poverty are striking. Roma poverty rates range between 4 and 10 times that of non-Roma in Bulgaria, Hungary, and Romania. Because of higher birth rates, the relative size of the Roma population is increasing across the region.

As a result, confronting poverty among Roma is one of Europe's most pressing development challenges. While living standards have declined for many during the post-socialist transition to market economies, conditions for Roma have deteriorated more severely than for others, and Roma have been poorly positioned to take advantage of emerging opportunities in the economy and society. Poverty among Roma is a complex and multidimensional phenomenon related to poor health and education status, limited chances in the labor market, discrimination, and unique aspects of Roma social organization, which together contribute to their social exclusion. At the same time, Roma are extremely diverse, with different subgroups experiencing different degrees of poverty and different development challenges.

The diverse and multidimensional nature of Roma poverty and social exclusion raises three interrelated questions:

1. What distinguishes Roma poverty from poverty among other groups in the transition countries of Central and Eastern Europe?
2. How have countries in the region attempted to address Roma poverty during the transition?
3. What lessons have been learned, and how can these be applied in the future?

In answering these questions, this study draws on quantitative analyses of household surveys and qualitative, sociological case studies that document the experiences of Roma communities in Bulgaria, Hungary, Romania, and Slovakia, and brings in examples from other countries. This approach is intended to provide a more nuanced picture of Roma poverty and its determinants, as well as of policy experience. Identifying the unique factors that underlie Roma poverty helps to explain why the transition has been harder on Roma than others and what interventions are needed to expand their opportunities, within the context of economic and social development for the population as a whole.

This chapter provides background on Roma in Central and Eastern Europe, their characteristics, and origins. It also discusses contrasting policy approaches that have shaped the position of Roma in Europe over time. Chapter 2 looks at the nature and characteristics of Roma poverty using quantitative data from household surveys—including a new cross-country dataset. It examines the correlates of Roma poverty, including housing conditions and educational and health status.

Later country chapters on Hungary, Romania, Slovakia, and Spain explore aspects of Roma poverty through qualitative methods. Sociological field studies enrich the picture of living conditions in Roma communities. In Chapter 3, case studies of Roma settlements in Slovakia highlight the relationship of Roma poverty to social exclusion. Chapter 4 examines conditions in nine Roma communities in Romania and reveals substantial diversity in access to social services. Chapter 5 focuses on policy lessons, drawing from the case of Hungary, where more projects to address Roma issues have been undertaken than in any other country in Central and Eastern Europe.

Chapter 6 focuses on Spain and provides a counterpoint to the case studies from Central and Eastern Europe, illustrating the commonalities and differences between Roma in the East and West, while drawing policy lessons. These lessons form the basis of the discussion of policy recommendations in the final chapter. Examples of programs and policies from other countries are included where possible. Together, these multiple approaches provide a striking picture of Roma poverty with policy implications for the future.

WHO ARE THE ROMA?

The Roma are Europe's largest and most vulnerable minority. They have no historical homeland but live in nearly all countries of Europe and Central Asia. The roots of the Roma are widely debated. Historical records indicate that they migrated in waves from northern India into Europe between the ninth and fourteenth centuries. Roma constitute an extremely diverse minority, with multiple subgroups based on linguistic, historical, and occupational distinctions. While some Roma groups are nomadic, the vast majority of Roma in Central and Eastern Europe have settled, some during the Austro-Hungarian and Ottoman empires and others under socialism.

Size estimates of Europe's Roma population range from 7 million to 9 million, similar to the total population of many smaller European states. Approximately 70 percent of Roma in Europe live in the coun-

FIGURE 1.1 ESTIMATED ROMA POPULATIONS IN SELECTED
EUROPEAN COUNTRIES

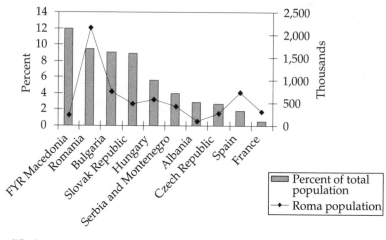

Sources: Wheeler (1999); Liegeois (1994); total population data: World Bank Atlas (1995).

tries of Central and Eastern Europe and those of the former Soviet
Union; nearly 80 percent of this population lives in countries that joined
the EU in 2004, or are in accession negotiations. Roma are estimated to
make up between 6 and 11 percent of the populations of Bulgaria, FYR
Macedonia, Romania, and the Slovak Republic (see figure 1.1).

Why has attention to Roma issues increased so sharply over the
past decade? The fall of the iron curtain in 1989 increased international awareness of Roma. Subsequently, concern over human rights
violations and seriously deteriorating socioeconomic conditions for
Roma gained attention from international organizations and international NGOs, such as the Council of Europe, the OSCE, various United
Nations (UN) agencies, the Open Society Institute, and western news
media. Many international organizations have issued major reports on
Roma issues in recent years, including a recent UNDP Human Development Report on Roma.[1] Most significantly, attention to the rights
and living conditions of Roma were incorporated into the EU accession process, under the political criteria.

Paying attention to Roma issues is squarely in the interest of
national governments. The severe deterioration of their living standards has raised humanitarian concerns and called attention to human
rights issues. Countries also cannot ignore the growth of Roma long-
term unemployment and poverty, which will undermine competitiveness over the longer term. In countries where Roma constitute a large
and growing share of the working-age population, their increasing

marginalization threatens stability and social cohesion. It has become a priority to understand how Roma poverty differs from poverty generally in the transition countries to overcome it.

POVERTY IN TRANSITION

Changes in the socioeconomic status of Roma in Central and Eastern Europe over the past decade are closely linked to the economic transition's effects. The shift from planned to market economies has led to an increase in poverty and lower living standards across the region.[2] However, regional figures mask considerable diversity across and within countries. Poverty in the new EU member states—including the Czech and Slovak Republics and Hungary—remains substantially lower than in the poorer countries of the region—such as Bulgaria and Romania (see figure 1.2). This difference is due to many factors, including the slower pace of economic reforms in the latter two countries in the early 1990s (World Bank 2000b).

Deep pockets of poverty distinguish the profile of poverty in many of the leading EU accession countries. Even in the more prosperous countries, significant poverty persists within some segments of the population. In the transition countries of Central and Eastern Europe, the unemployed, the poorly educated, rural populations, and children are more likely to be poor. In Slovakia in 1996, the national poverty rate was 10 percent—low by regional standards—while the poverty

FIGURE 1.2 POVERTY RATES IN SELECTED TRANSITION COUNTRIES (Percent living under $4.30 PPP per day)

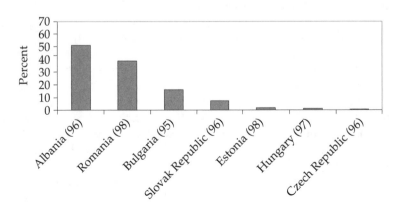

Source: World Bank 2000b.
Notes: Poverty line is adjusted using PPP for comparisons across countries. Household surveys differ across countries, refer to source for details.

rate for those with only primary education or lower was 14 percent, or 40 percent higher than the national average (World Bank 2001b). Even worse, poverty rates for households headed by an unemployed person were nearly four and a half times the national average. Roma represent one of the main poverty groups. They are both poorer than other population groups and more likely to fall into poverty and remain poor. Poverty therefore has a substantial ethnic dimension.[3]

HISTORY

The roots of Roma in Europe have long been a controversial subject (Hancock 2003). According to records, Roma arrived in Europe from northern India, although the reasons for their migration are unknown. Linguistic evidence and the limited documentation suggest that Roma came first through Persia and the Caucasus, through the Byzantine Empire and into southern Europe (Fraser 1995), although some Macedonian legends place Roma in Europe at the time of Alexander the Great, as early as the fourth century B.C. The first detailed references to Roma in Central and Eastern Europe are found in twelfth-century records from the Dalmatian Coast and Hungary, which is now the Slovak Republic (Crowe 1994).

The subsequent history of Roma in Europe is as varied as the countries to which they migrated. However, marginalization and discrimination have been common (Bárány 2002). During their first centuries in Europe, Roma were valued for their skills in metalworking, armaments, and music. They were also subject to prejudice and persecution. As early as the fifteenth century, Roma were traded as slaves in the Moldavia and Wallachia principalities (currently Romania). Draconian anti-Roma policies were adopted throughout Europe. A scholar notes that "[h]ad all the anti-Gypsy laws which sprang up been enforced uncompromisingly, even for a few months, the Gypsies would have been eradicated from most of Christian Europe well before the middle of the sixteenth century" (Fraser 1995).

In Central and Eastern Europe, the policies of the Austrian Empire, the Hungarian Kingdom, and the Ottoman Empire had a significant role in shaping Roma communities. In the latter half of the eighteenth century, under Empress Maria Theresa, Habsburg policies aimed to eliminate the Roma's nomadic lifestyle and encourage assimilation. While these restrictions were loosened with the end of Maria Theresa's reign, they were the first step toward settling Roma; this feature still distinguishes Roma in Central and Eastern Europe from those living in Western Europe. Under the Ottoman Empire, policies toward Roma were more relaxed, on the whole, and mostly allowed for free movement across borders, despite occasional attempts at forced settlement, including an initiative against Serbian Roma in the 1630s (Fraser 1995).

The Nazi era marked the darkest period of Roma history. Like Jews, Roma were targeted with discriminatory legislation and subsequently extermination. During the course of the "Devouring," as Roma call the Holocaust, approximately half a million Roma from across Europe were executed or killed in concentration camps. The largest population losses were among Roma from Hungary, Poland, Romania, the Soviet Union, and Yugoslavia (Fraser 1995; Lewy 2000).

The Socialist Period

Soviet bloc policies adopted toward Roma in Central and Eastern Europe left a legacy that affects the socioeconomic status of Roma today. Although the extent varied, socialist governments made a concerted effort to assimilate Roma and minimize ethnic differences. Communist parties issued decrees and adopted policies that aimed at socioeconomic integration by providing housing and jobs for Roma.

These measures were frequently culturally repressive, though their stringency varied. Among the most repressive campaigns were movements in Bulgaria and Czechoslovakia that sought to erase ethnic divisions completely. In contrast, in socialist Yugoslavia, Roma were granted official nationality status in 1981 (Poulton 1991).

In Czechoslovakia in 1958, the government proclaimed that Roma were not a separate ethnic group and embarked upon a violent campaign against nomadism. The regime planned a "dispersal and transfer" scheme to resettle Roma from areas with large Roma communities in eastern Slovakia to the Czech lands. However, this program was never fully implemented, and conditions were relaxed somewhat during the Prague Spring reforms of 1968. During this time, Roma language teaching was introduced in schools. However, assimilation programs were imposed with new vigor following the Soviet crackdown on the reformists (Fraser 1995).

In Bulgaria, all ethnic minorities, including Bulgarian Turks and Roma, were targeted with "Bulgarization," as the regime attempted to suppress cultural identities through forced assimilation. Minorities were forced to change their names to Bulgarian names and could lose access to social services for not complying. In Romania, President Ceauşescu mounted an aggressive "systematization" program across the country in the 1980s, resettling entire villages and urban neighborhoods. While the campaign was not explicitly targeted at Roma, both Roma and non-Roma settlements were destroyed (Crowe 1994).

Assimilation efforts under socialism transformed Roma communities. Policies forced Roma into the mainstream economy by providing employment, housing, and education. The impact of these efforts was mixed. Major strides were made in enrolling children in schools. In Czechoslovakia, a campaign increased kindergarten enrollment rates for Roma from 10 percent in the early 1970s to 59 percent by 1980. At the same time, the share of Roma finishing compulsory education rose from 17 to 26 percent, and literacy rates rose to 90 percent among adults. In Poland, an education initiative enrolled 80 percent of Roma children in the late 1960s. Some school promotion initiatives, such as a Hungarian effort in the late 1980s, attempted to increase Roma school attendance by experimenting with Roma language teaching (Fraser 1995).

However, these gains were tempered. In many cases, socialist education policies helped only to perpetuate earlier inequities. In the push to increase enrollments, Roma were often channeled into segregated schools intended for children with mental and physical disabilities. For example, Hungary's education campaign was initiated in the 1960s and focused on creating "special classes . . . within the national school system for retarded or difficult children" (Crowe 1994). A disproportionate number of Roma were enrolled in special classes and schools. Similar practices were followed in other countries, including Bulgaria and Czechoslovakia. The practice of pushing Roma into special schools has continued following the transition.

Employment programs were also a mixed blessing. Some attempted to formalize traditional Roma trades. For example, the Polish government set up cooperative workshops to support traditional artisans such as coppersmiths. However, these low-paying and physically demanding jobs were in less demand and did not attract Roma workers (Fraser 1995). Because of their low education levels and skills, Roma were often employed instead in state-owned enterprises and on collective farms, frequently in the most onerous, unskilled positions. A 1995 study of the Hungarian labor force found that half of Roma workers were unskilled, in comparison with 12 percent of the Hungarian population (Crowe 1994).

As a whole, socialist policies did improve conditions for Roma by increasing access to education, employment, and housing. However, these initiatives also created new divisions between Roma and the state. The forced and often repressive assimilation campaigns fomented mistrust and tensions between Roma and service providers. The absence of participatory processes, authentic self-government, and Roma involvement in policy development and implementation further reinforced this strain. Paternalistic state provision of "cradle to grave" jobs, housing, and other benefits also created a culture of dependency. The transition, employment losses, and growing poverty have left many Roma, as well as others, feeling abandoned and alienated.

Roma in the Transition Period

The democratic transition to market economies has presented new challenges to Roma in Central and Eastern Europe. On the one hand, Roma have greater opportunities to organize politically and express themselves culturally; on the other, they have also proven more vulnerable than other groups. There are four broad sets of reasons for this.

First, as Roma generally have less education and skills than others, they have had difficulty competing for jobs in the new market economies. Roma were often the first laid off from state-owned industrial factories, mines, and agricultural cooperatives. As a result, they face significant hurdles to labor market reentry and have depended instead on poorly funded public assistance, insecure jobs in the informal sector, or work abroad.

Second, the transformation exacerbated numerous social problems facing Roma, including low educational and health status. Third, the transition has had a profound impact on Roma housing. Roma were historically not landowners. As a result, they have generally not benefited from land restitution and privatization policies. Fiscal constraints during the transition have meant fewer state resources for maintaining the public housing where many Roma live. Finally, political transformation has been accompanied by rising discrimination and violence against ethnic minorities, including Roma.

Addressing Roma poverty is therefore a multifaceted problem, related to a complex mix of historical, economic, and social factors. Although the region's other vulnerable groups face similar circumstances, with the lack of social capital among some Roma communities and the added discrimination barrier, the challenges loom large. Aspects of Roma culture and living conditions also reinforce stereotypes by limiting communication between Roma and non-Roma and contribute to a vicious circle of isolation and marginalization.

Moreover, access to social services has been threatened by an increasing need for services and tight budgets. Formal and informal charges now accompany previously free services, as does eroding quality. Roma are particularly affected by increasing barriers to access because they are at a higher risk of poverty and face unique circumstances that limit their access to services. Geographically isolated Roma communities may lie far from social service facilities and personnel. Similarly, because Roma frequently live in remote areas or illegal housing, they may lack the documentation necessary for enrolling in school and claiming social assistance or health benefits. The prevalence of Roma in informal sector employment also limits their benefits based on social insurance contributions, including health care and unemployment benefits.

Political liberalization has proven to be a mixed blessing. The transition brought new opportunities for ethnic minorities to express their identity and participate in society. In most countries, minorities were once again recognized as distinct ethnic groups. For example, the new Declaration of Basic Human Rights and Freedoms that the Czechoslovakian Federal Assembly adopted in January 1991 allowed for the free determination of ethnic identity. Roma political parties emerged in some countries, as did a range of Roma NGOs. However, the transition also brought new civic challenges and hardships. Political liberalization let extremist parties onto the political scene and opened other avenues for public expression of hatred against Roma. Anti-Roma violence was documented in the 1990s in all the Central and Eastern European countries. Hence, designing and implementing programs to address the exclusion of Roma requires attention to the unique issues of diversity, culture, and social exclusion.

ROMA DIVERSITY, CULTURE, AND SOCIAL EXCLUSION

Diversity

A defining characteristic of Roma is their diversity. Researchers refer to a "kaleidoscope" and "mosaic" of Roma groups (Liegeois 1994; Fraser 1995), with numerous crosscutting subgroups, including family clans and religion. Many Roma groups have little or no contact with each other (Beissinger 2001). Because of their varied history in Asia and Europe, Roma also participate in many different religions. There are Roma of different Christian denominations, as well as Muslim Roma. In Bulgaria, Roma have traditionally been Eastern Orthodox or Muslim, although in recent decades many have begun to attend Protestant and Pentecostal churches (Iliev 1999). There are also geographic and historical groups, such as the Slovensko Roma from Slovenia, and subgroups based upon occupational categories, including former cauldron makers (Kalderashi) in Bulgaria and Romania, and bear trainers (Ursari) and basket makers (Kosnicari) in Bulgaria.

Roma may have multiple affiliations, such as with an extended family group, as well as a geographic and occupational subgroup (Liegeois 1994). The densest concentration of different Roma communities is found in southeastern Europe, where there is greater variation in religious affiliation, dialect, and occupation (Fraser 1995). The degree of assimilation also varies notably across subgroups, depending on "the amount of time they have lived . . . in the proximity of the dominant population, the size of the Gypsy community, familiarity with the majority language, the presence of (an)other . . . strong minority, and the history of interethnic relations" (Bárány 2002). In

Hungary, the most integrated are the Romungro Roma, who speak Hungarian.

The Roma language is still prevalent among some Roma communities, and there are numerous dialects. In Bulgaria, half of the Roma speak the Roma language at home.[4] In Hungary and the Slovak Republic, much less of the population does so. However, in both countries, it has been found to limit some children's school participation and performance (Ministry of Labor 1997; Radó 1997).

The diversity of Roma creates significant challenges for researchers and policymakers. Information on Roma living conditions and poverty is scarce, fragmented, and often anecdotal. In addition to the difficulty of drawing generalizations about such a diverse group, measurement challenges include undersampling in censuses and household surveys; privacy legislation in many countries, which prohibit data collection by ethnicity; and the reluctance of many Roma to identify themselves as such. These challenges are addressed through a multimethod approach combining quantitative and qualitative sources, but still there are limitations in the face of poor data.

Culture

Given the striking diversity of Roma communities, generalizing about the nature and characteristics of Roma culture is extremely difficult. The literature paints a fragmented and sometimes contradictory picture. However, it is clear that aspects of Roma social organization and values affect the interactions of Roma and non-Roma, the dynamics among Roma subgroups, and many aspects of their welfare. Cultural factors can influence the level of integration of communities, participation in civil society and political institutions, demand for public services, and household behavior.

Despite the complexity of the topic, there is consensus concerning the importance of the relationship between Roma and the *gadje*, the Roma word for non-Roma. Roma define themselves as distinct and different from gadje. This helps explain how Roma have maintained a separate identity across centuries, despite repeated pressures for integration:

> Their ethnicity was to be fashioned and remoulded by a multitude of influences, internal and external, they would assimilate innumerable elements which had nothing to do with India, and they would eventually cease to be, in any meaningful way, Indians; their identity, their culture would, however—regardless of all the transformations—remain sharply distinct from that of the gadze [*sic*] who surrounded them, and on whom their economic existence depended (Fraser 1995).

This distinction continues to influence Roma integration, participation in civil society, and use of public services. To varying degrees, Roma communities have remained insular and separate. While some Roma communities have integrated, more traditional Roma communities and extended families are close knit, providing both security and protection from the outside world (Wheeler 1999). This division between the Roma and gadje worlds has reinforced stereotypes and mistrust on both sides. Roma may be reluctant to send their children to state schools because of fear of losing their cultural identity. This concern likely influences other aspects of life, including employment preferences and use of health services. The distance between Roma and non-Roma communities breeds mistrust and misunderstanding among non-Roma and reinforces negative stereotypes and discrimination.

The socially heterogeneous nature of Roma society also influences the integration level of various Roma communities, their political participation, and relations among different Roma groups. For example, traditional Roma groups may distrust or reject more integrated Roma. In Hungary, the more traditional Vlach Roma have few interactions with the Romungros Roma, and in Bulgaria, the Kalderashi relate little to the poorer Ierlii, whom they believe have abandoned their traditions (Stewart 1997; Iliev 1999). Little is known about the complex hierarchy among Roma groups, which is based not only on their adherence to Roma traditions, but also to the prestige of clans and occupational groups, religion, and other divisions. These factors may correlate strongly with poverty and social exclusion.

Social Exclusion and Discrimination

A defining aspect of poverty among Roma is its relationship to social exclusion. Social exclusion and discrimination severely affect Roma access to employment opportunities, education, and public services. Social exclusion refers to a process of social separation between individuals and society (Rodgers et al. 1995; Silver 1994; Brady 2003). Exclusion can have multiple dimensions, including economic, political, socio-cultural, and geographic. In economic exclusion, individuals cannot participate in market activity, including employment, access to credit, and land. Political exclusion refers to limitations on participation in democratic processes, such as voting, participation in political parties, and other associations within civil society. Socio-cultural exclusion encompasses separation based upon linguistic, religious, and ethnic grounds. Geographic exclusion involves various types of spatial differentiation. Moreover, different facets of exclusion often reinforce each other. For example, geographic exclusion in housing can lead to economic exclusion if people are unable to find jobs where they live or attend mainstream public schools there.

For Roma, social exclusion from majority societies in Europe has mainly taken the form of ethnic discrimination. Roma have been shunned throughout European history, and ethnic tensions have intensified in the transition period with revival of nationalism in some countries. Discrimination, both explicit and implicit, permeates many aspects of life, including education, employment, and housing. Roma have been barred from restaurants and hotels in Central and Eastern Europe. Documented racial violence, including skinhead attacks and police violence, has also been on the rise during the transition period.[5]

Stereotypes of Roma continue to be widespread throughout Central and Eastern Europe. UNDP Human Development Reports for Bulgaria and the Slovak Republic quoted opinion surveys that found deeply negative perceptions of Roma to be pervasive. In Bulgaria, nearly 80 percent of the population surveyed in 1999 said that they would not want to have Roma as neighbors, a figure far higher than for any other ethnic or social group, including former prisoners (UNDP 1999). Similar results have been reported from surveys in other countries in the region.

The roots of such sentiments are difficult to trace, but undoubtedly stem from a combination of factors, including history, difficult economic conditions, and feelings of social insecurity. As mentioned earlier, aspects of Roma culture and living conditions have reinforced stereotypes and spurred marginalization. Self-exclusion of some Roma can breed misunderstanding and mistrust among non-Roma. Similarly, the poverty of many Roma communities contributes to resentment, as Roma are perceived as dependent on welfare benefits and burdens on the state.

POLICY APPROACHES AND DEBATES

Historically, European states' policies toward Roma have either aimed to further exclude Roma from majority societies—through expulsion, forced ghettoization, and denial of services—or to fully assimilate Roma into the majority society, often through coercive measures. Policies of exclusion and forced assimilation, though different in many ways, share one important goal: both seek to reduce the visibility of Roma communities—on the one hand by forcing them to the margins of society, on the other by forcing them to assimilate. Both deny Roma communities and individuals the right of their own culture.

While the legacy of exclusionary and assimilationist policies lives on in Europe, current policy approaches to Roma are built on different foundations, emphasizing individual and group rights for ethnic minorities. This section discusses historic and current policy approaches

TABLE 1.1 A TYPOLOGY OF ROMA POLICY APPROACHES IN EUROPE

	Coercive	Rights-Based
Roma Treated as a Separate Group	Exclusion	Minority Rights
Roma Treated as Individual Members of Broader Society	Assimilation	Integration

toward Roma within a conceptual framework that helps to understand the influences and trends that shape current policy development.

Roma Policy: Four Approaches

Policy approaches that European governments have taken in modern times fall into four broad groups: policies of exclusion, assimilation, integration, and minority rights (see Marko 2000 for a similar typology). These approaches reflect different responses to two basic questions about Roma policy: whether Roma should be treated as a distinct group or as individual members of a broader society, and whether Roma policy should be pursued through coercive measures or with respect for Roma rights. Table 1.1 shows that these policy approaches reflect different answers to these fundamental questions.

In this discussion, Roma policy refers to both explicit governmental policies toward Roma, as well as other state policies that affect Roma and other social groups but may have a different effect on Roma. In addition, this discussion also considers how official state policies set the tone for the unofficial attitudes of non-state organizations, enterprises, and associations that have practices toward Roma that also relate to their social status and poverty. As with any typology, these definitions are ideal types; some policies will not fit neatly into one or another of these categories, and some may be explicitly geared at blurring lines of distinction. Because of the diversity of Roma, the impact of government policies may be different for different groups or may have unintended consequences. Nonetheless, this typology captures the broad logic of policies toward Roma in Europe over time and reflects enduring differences in how societies attempt to address Roma issues.

Exclusionary Policies

As noted above, exclusion of Roma from majority societies in Europe results partly from the beliefs, attitudes, and behaviors of Roma themselves. However, self-marginalization of many Roma is related to a long legacy of European policies that sought to reinforce Roma exclusion. Policies of exclusion seek to exclude Roma from the majority society along economic, political, socio-cultural, and geographic dimensions.

Why have European governments often sought to exclude Roma? The rationale is usually based on a racial and nationalist perspective that holds Roma to be inferior and separate from the majority. Contact and intermarriage between Roma and the majority community are seen as harmful. Exclusionary policies are usually enacted to protect the majority from perceived threats and are often pursued coercively. Lack of regard for Roma rights and interests is justified by the view that Roma are not members of the majority community but as dangerous parasites. Therefore, the majority community has no obligation to concern itself with the welfare of Roma individuals or communities. While policies that reinforce social exclusion are widely rejected in international law today, their legacies persist.

One of the most important of these legacies is housing segregation—a form of geographic exclusion. Socio-cultural exclusion of Roma in Europe has long been underpinned by housing policies that shunt many Roma into separate settlements or ghettos. Under the Ottoman Empire, urban neighborhoods, or *mahalas*, were organized along religious and ethnic lines. As a result, many Roma neighborhoods in the Balkans—such as the large Roma enclave of Suto Ozari, in Skopje, FYR Macedonia—have their roots in long-standing policy legacies. In Slovakia, policies enacted during and after World War II forced Roma to settle on the outskirts of towns, leading to the creation of a large number of Roma settlements. Roma also live in ghettos on the outskirts of cities in Western European countries, such as Italy (ERRC [European Roma Rights Center] 2000).

More recent policies in Central and East European countries have—both directly and indirectly—led to continued geographic marginalization. In one notorious case, Czech authorities erected a wall around a Roma settlement in the town of Usti nad Labem. The wall was later torn down after protests from Roma, the international community, and Czech political leaders. As seen in the study of Slovakia in chapter 3, geographic exclusion of Roma powerfully reinforces social exclusion of other kinds, including access to employment and state services.

Beyond geographic exclusion, current policies at the national and local levels continue to exclude Roma from public services, such as health and education. Such policies may have a critical impact on Roma poverty. The OSCE has documented extensive evidence of continued discrimination in the justice system, housing, education, and other areas (OSCE 2000; OSCE ODIHR [Office of Democratic Institutions and Human Rights] 1997). Roma children often are excluded from education in mainstream public schools in Central and Eastern Europe and instead relegated to schools for the mentally handicapped.

Roma in Central and Eastern Europe also have been stripped of fundamental political rights, including citizenship. A notorious law enacted after the division of Czechoslovakia forced non-Czech citizens to reapply for Czech citizenship and included provisions that prevented many Roma originally from Slovakia from winning Czech citizenship (Orentlicher 1998). Lack of citizenship can prevent people from acquiring property, voting, working, and receiving education, health care, and social assistance. Political rights are also important for allowing Roma to assert their economic interests.

Economic exclusion of Roma in Central and Eastern Europe often results not from official state policy but from the actions of other actors, particularly businesses and social associations. Many firms in the transition countries do not hire Roma, compounding the labor market woes of a population with low skills and education levels. Governments may foster employment discrimination by not acting effectively to prevent it.

Other exclusionary acts toward Roma are similarly outside the direct control of the state, such as barring Roma from restaurants and clubs, skinhead attacks, and the portrayal of Roma by the press as "the most problematic section of the population, disturbers of the social order" (PER [Project on Ethnic Relations] 1997b). In these areas too, the government's failure to take firm action can reinforce exclusionary social practices by signaling their acceptability.

Such signaling almost undoubtedly occurs through the expression of anti-Roma sentiment by state officials in public. As Save the Children found, "There are few, if any, other population groups in Europe against which regular racist pronouncements and actions still pass largely unremarked" (Save the Children 2001a; OSI 2001). Such outbursts rarely cost the officials their jobs. Reinforcement of exclusionary norms by public officials is an unofficial policy of exclusion.

Forced Assimilation Policies

Unlike exclusionary policies, forced assimilation policies aim to eradicate differences between Roma and non-Roma, by making Roma adopt mainstream norms, values, and behaviors.

Like exclusionary policies, assimilationist policies are by definition coercive. However, assimilationist policies tend to be undertaken not to harm Roma but to help them. Assimilationist logic asserts the benefits of belonging to the majority culture and participating in economic life, and takes the view that all individuals would be better off if they were elevated to full membership of this culture. Assimilation is often conceived as a "civilizing mission," helping marginal or outside groups win greater prosperity and culture. Opponents of assimilation argue that assimilation often entails repression, losses to minority groups and cultures, and disproportionate benefits to the majority group. However, assimilated individuals are often granted nearly full rights in the majority society.

Assimilationist policies have been common in Europe for centuries. The Austrian Empire and Hungarian Kingdom adopted an assimilationist policy approach under the modernizing rule of Empress Maria Theresa (Bárány 2002). Maria Theresa issued four "Gypsy decrees" between 1758 and 1773 that

> ordered all Gypsies to settle, pay taxes, and do mandatory service to churches and landowners . . . prohibited their leaving the villages to which they were assigned without permission . . . mandated compulsory military service . . . eliminated the authority of Romani leaders over their communities, banned traditional Gypsy dress and the usage of Romani language . . . forbade marriages between Gypsies and ordered Roma children over age five to be taken away to state schools and foster homes. (Bárány 2002)

Empress Maria Theresa did not shy away from coercive measures to promote assimilation.

Assimilation was also the predominant Roma policy of socialist regimes in post–World War II Europe. Following Karl Marx's lead, socialist regimes believed in advancing "common interests of the entire proletariat, independently of all nationality" (Marx 1985). In practice, this meant promoting cooperation between different ethnic groups and nationalities, with the goal of forging an undivided, classless socialist society. Policy toward Roma was therefore guided by an effort to merge the population into the proletarian mainstream.

Thus in the 1950s and 1960s, most socialist regimes in Europe engaged in a strong, multipronged policy initiative to assimilate Roma (Ulč 1991). "The fundamental goal was to assimilate them and transform them into productive, cooperative, and supportive socialist citizens" (Bárány 2002). This was to be achieved through improved housing, higher educational enrollment, and guaranteed employment. However, many of these policies were pursued with a heavy hand. Settlements were broken up, housing was assigned, and work was made mandatory under threat of imprisonment. Roma generally were not given the opportunity to participate in decision making or in the administration of these policies (Bárány 2002).

Neither the exclusionary policies nor the forced assimilation policies allow room for individual choice or individual rights. They are often pursued, at least in part, through official coercion. However, with the rise of a liberal democratic international order during the latter half of the twentieth century, both of these models of minority policy began to be discredited, at least in the eyes of international law and organizations such as the UN, OSCE, and EU (Wippman 1998). These trends opened the way for two rights-based policy approaches to emerge: integration policies and minority rights.

Integration Policies

Since the Second World War, minority policies in Europe have been heavily influenced by rights-based approaches, as part of a reaction to coercive policies of exclusion and assimilation that were seen as contributing to the causes of war. Rights-based approaches seek to elevate state protection for minority individuals and groups by providing basic civil and political rights. Rights-based governance is believed to contribute to international peace and thus forms a key part of many international conventions.

Policies of integration and minority rights are both rights-based policies, but they differ on whether rights are accorded primarily to individuals or to groups. Integration policies focus on bringing individuals into society as full members. In integration policies, Roma individuals may choose to retain their cultural identity while adopting much of the dominant society's lifestyle and practices. Minority rights policies place a higher value on maintaining traditional lifestyle and practices of groups.

Critics of integration warn that it shares the flaws of assimilation, since both approaches aim to subsume Roma in the broader society and to downplay the importance of ethnicity. However, integration policies genuinely differ from those of assimilation. They do not require that individuals completely assimilate before being granted rights, for instance. Instead, they are inspired by modern, liberal values that "favor broad political participation of all those within the geographic boundaries of a given state, regardless of their ethnic identity" (Wippman 1998). Integration policies also typically respect individual rights and individual choices about how to integrate, leaving room for continued ethnic identification. Assimilation policies do not.

Integration policies seek to integrate Roma, without coercion, into the majority society while protecting their individual rights. As Pace expresses it, "[a]ssimilation refers to the absorption of a minority group into the host or majority society, with consequent dissolution of the cultural features of the group. . . . Integration means that an ethnic group tries to maintain some or all of its cultural characteristics, while seeking to minimize the practical problems inherent in adapting to the dominant society" (Pace 1993).

Philosophically, integration policies are based on a belief in progress, individual rights, and equal opportunity. Proponents of integration tend to believe that modern society is better than traditional society, providing forms of human development unavailable in the past. Members of more traditional groups, such as Roma, can benefit from integration if it facilitates individual growth and well-being. Proponents of integration also argue that no individual should be discriminated against and that all individuals should be allowed to progress in society to the best of their abilities.

Integration has been the dominant European policy paradigm toward ethnic minorities since the 1970s (PER 1997a), except in the former socialist states. It has also been the dominant paradigm in international law (Wippman 1998). Some examples include integrating Roma into school systems, banning labor market discrimination, increasing access to social services, addressing housing discrimination, and reducing ghettoization. All these policies seek to provide individuals with equal rights and the same opportunities for empowerment as members of the dominant society.

Minority Rights Policies

Starting in the 1990s, European and international policies toward minorities have increasingly emphasized group rights (Wippman 1998; Pejic 1997; PER 1997a; Save the Children 2001b). This reflects "a growing acceptance of the legitimacy of group consciousness" in Europe—and, indeed, the world (Basurto 1995). This minority rights approach differs from the integration approach, since it advocates the establishment and protection of group, rather than individual, rights as the basis of minority policy.

The minority rights approach stresses the importance of cultural preservation as a means of improving the condition of minority groups. Minority rights advocates suggest that the situation of socially marginalized groups, such as Roma, will not be improved simply by integrating individuals into the majority society. Instead, their welfare will be secured best by enhancing opportunities for group empowerment and cultural self-determination. Community and group empowerment have become increasingly viewed as essential ingredients for improving the welfare of the poor. Empowerment in this context refers to the capacity of the poor to "participate in, negotiate with, influence, control and hold accountable institutions that affect their lives" (World Bank 2001a).

The last two decades have seen a growing international concern for the rights of minorities globally and in Europe. Intergovernmental organizations such as the OSCE, EU, and the Council of Europe have taken a particularly active role in establishing minority rights. The result is an emerging "common European standard" for minority policy, grounded primarily in international commitments undertaken by European states (De Witte 2002). These include the European Convention on Human Rights,[6] the Copenhagen Document (1990),[7] the Framework Convention for the Protection of National Minorities (1995),[8] and the new European Community Treaty's Article 13, established within the 1997 Amsterdam Treaty (the first treaty provision to explicitly include anti-discrimination measures relating to ethnic minorities), and the EU Charter on Fundamental Rights (2000).[9]

On the basis of these emerging European standards, the 1993 Copenhagen Summit of the European Commission included "respect for minorities" as one political criterion for the accession of new member states. These political conditions were determined during the European Council meeting of June 1993. According to the concluding document, "membership requires that the candidate country has achieved stability of institutions guaranteeing democracy, the rule of law, human rights and respect for and protection of minorities" (Conclusions of the Copenhagen European Council 1993). This has shaped policy toward Roma in the accession states.

Both the OSCE (formerly the Council for Security and Co-operation in Europe, or CSCE) and the Council of Europe have been actively engaged in constructing a framework for policy on minorities, including Roma. Over 40 years ago, the CSCE led the way in taking on the issue of minorities in Europe. The Roma question was explicitly addressed in a series of Human Dimension meetings held in the 1990s. In 1995, the OSCE created the Contact Point on Roma Issues within the ODIHR to focus on Roma rights and protections in general. In 1998, the Contact Point's mandate was extended to "oversee, coordinate and advise on legislative and policy developments affecting Roma (and Sinti) both at the European and state levels" (Kováts 2001a).

The Council of Europe has demonstrated a concern for minority issues for many years, including the development of a convention on linguistic rights and protections for Roma.[10] In 1993, a council resolution declared Roma to be "a true European minority" and established a Specialist Group on Roma/Gypsies. Together with the OSCE High Commissioner for National Minorities, the Specialist Group produced the Guiding Principles for Improving the Situation of Roma in candidate countries. Adopted by the EU in 1999, this document has been influential in shaping EU relations with post-communist countries regarding the Roma issue, as well as marking a convergence in Council of Europe, OSCE, and EU approaches to Roma policy. Over the years, the council has undertaken various initiatives and has had an indirect influence on Roma through its work in the field of minority and linguistic rights.

The European Union—founded to build economic cooperation in Europe—historically has not engaged directly in minority policies. As a result, through the principle of subsidiarity, education, culture, and language have predominantly remained the policy concerns of member states, not the community. Nevertheless, the Treaty of Maastricht, signed in February 1992, established the EU as an economic and political union. It also opened the door for the EU to include within its scope some actions pertaining to culture, providing that the European Community shall "contribute to the flowering of the cultures of the Member States, while respecting their national and regional diversity." In the minority rights context, this article recognizes the existence of diversity within and between its member states, as well as the importance of EU and member state support for preserving this diversity.

Most Central and East European countries have, at some level, accepted the importance of protecting national minority rights. As of March 2001, 33 states had ratified and entered into force the Council of Europe Framework Convention for the Protection of National Minorities (Council of Europe 1995), the first legally binding multilateral instrument devoted to the protection of national minorities in general. All new EU countries and candidates have signed, ratified, and entered into force the convention, with the exception of Latvia and Turkey. Six EU member states have not ratified the framework: Belgium, Finland, France, Luxembourg, the Netherlands, and Portugal (Goldston and Guglielmo 2001).

In Central and Eastern Europe, some have complained of a gap between this broad political agreement and effective action, including legal enforcement by the European Court of Human Rights.[11] Existing domestic institutions addressing minority issues also may lack the resources, or the mandate, to coordinate and enforce policy implementation (OSI 2001). Still, minority rights as a distinct approach to Roma issues has been gaining ground in Central and Eastern Europe (Pogany 1999).

Tensions among Policy Approaches

Current policy toward Roma in Europe is shaped by the tensions among various policy approaches, as well as the legacies of past policies. Legacies of exclusion, for instance, live on and conflict with newer policies of integration—as seen in disputes about banning Roma from public establishments or about ways to reduce skinhead violence. Roma communities are also divided between those who advocate more integration with majority societies in Europe and traditionalists who want to maintain a distinct identity. Such divisions may be reflected in debates over whether to emphasize teaching Roma language and culture in schools, in an effort to preserve and promote Roma culture, or to emphasize early education programs that train Roma students in the majority language and culture.

The Roma leaders Nicholae Gheorghe and Andrej Mirga hold that there is no fundamental contradiction

> between integration and maintaining a Romani identity. It is rather a question of a conscious attempt to modernize the Romani identity without necessarily implying its abandonment. Thus, integration or even partial assimilation, which would lead to an undifferentiated incorporation of the Roma into mainstream society, can be regarded as a worthy ideology by Romani elites. The fear of losing their identity, strongly endorsed by the traditionalists, should be overcome by a serious reassertion and redefinition of the Romani identity (PER 1997a).

However, a movement to create a modern Roma identity more compatible with modern economic development and integration into European societies would have to come from the Roma community itself. And one unique aspect of Roma culture in Europe is that such a movement has not taken hold.

A combination of long-standing resistance to integration and a lack of nation-state identity or territorial claims make Roma a unique minority in Europe. One possible parallel is with the Jewish minority in Europe before the Second World War. However, Jews in Europe have been far more integrated into dominant societies and indeed made territorial claims after the war to protect their interests. Another parallel may be with African Americans and Native Americans in the United States, long-standing minorities with difficulties integrating into dominant societies because of racial, ethnic, and cultural differences and legacies of discrimination. Such minorities may be the focus of a variety of different policy regimes over time, or even at the same time, by different actors in the economy, society, and politics.

Today in Europe, the dominant approaches towards Roma policy are rights based. However, a lesson of the transition period is that rights-based policies alone are not enough to improve Roma social conditions. What is needed are economic and social development policies designed to expand Roma opportunities and address the roots of Roma poverty and exclusion. Roma need not just formal rights but real economic opportunities. Creating these opportunities goes beyond the usual legal protections that rights-based approaches normally encompass. Only a few of the constraints faced by Roma can be addressed through legislative measures. The final chapter of this book proposes addressing Roma poverty through inclusive policies that complement rights-based measures and tackling the economic and social issues facing Roma.

CONCLUSIONS

After a difficult transition to market economies and democratic political regimes, the Central and Eastern European countries face serious challenges in addressing poverty and social exclusion. Nowhere are these problems more acute than for Roma. Transition has had a worse impact on Roma than on other groups for a variety of interconnected reasons: legacies of past policies, low skill levels and educational attainment of Roma, a tendency toward cultural separation, a history of poor relations with the mainstream societies and states of Europe, poor policy responses, and a reduction in social spending caused in large part by macroeconomic decline.

Addressing Roma poverty requires, first of all, understanding it. Therefore, the following chapters will set the stage for a deeper policy discussion by asking, What distinguishes Roma poverty from that of other groups in the region? Chapter 2 presents the results of surveys that seek to answer this question, while country chapters on Slovakia, Romania, and Hungary provide a more in-depth look at Roma poverty in selected communities, using interviews with Roma. Country chapters also explore the question, How have the transition countries of Central and Eastern Europe addressed the Roma issue to date? In particular, the Hungary chapter reviews a number of Roma programs and policies and the chapter on Spain provides an example of how Western European countries have addressed Roma issues. Finally, the book concludes with the lessons of this experience and new strategies for the future.

Chapter 2
An Overview of Roma Poverty and Welfare

Poverty is a multidimensional phenomenon that goes well beyond low income or lack of material consumption. According to the World Bank's 2000–2001 World Development Report *Attacking Poverty*, poverty encompasses such things as the psychological pain of being poor, a sense of vulnerability to external events, and powerlessness toward the institutions of state and society (World Bank 2001a). The Council of Europe (1995) has defined poverty as affecting those "persons, families or groups of persons whose resources (material, cultural and social) are limited to the extent that they exclude them from the minimally accepted lifestyle of the countries where they live."

In the case of Roma, poverty is particularly multifaceted. Many Roma are deprived of the resources necessary for adequate living conditions, as well as access to opportunities and channels for participation. These problems are often interconnected. This chapter synthesizes evidence to illustrate the interrelated challenges facing Roma in social welfare, housing, education, and health status. This sets the stage for further analysis of poverty and welfare in the following country chapters on Slovakia and Romania, which look further at geographic and social exclusion and the diversity of living conditions among Roma communities.

The chapter begins with a discussion of some of the particular issues that arise in analyzing data regarding Roma and identifies the caveats that should be considered in interpreting the information. While the gaps and limitations of the information base on Roma are real, this does not invalidate the entire body of analysis. Throughout this book, information from multiple sources and perspectives are presented to assemble a comprehensive view of Roma welfare and living conditions.

MEASUREMENT CHALLENGES

Social welfare data in Central and Eastern Europe are often plagued with problems due to weak and sometimes biased statistical systems that were inherited from the socialist era and the use of definitions and methodologies that are often outdated, inconsistent with international standards, or not comparable across countries. These issues, however, pale in comparison with the challenge of measuring Roma socioeconomic conditions. Seemingly straightforward questions, such as how many Roma live in a particular country, prove extremely challenging.

Different approaches among surveys frequently yield contrasting results and impede data comparability. For example, some household surveys ask respondents to identify their ethnicity, while others ask the interviewer to indicate the respondent's ethnicity or to determine ethnicity by asking about the respondent's native language. The latter approach may underestimate the number of Roma, many of whom do

25

not speak Roma dialects. Other obstacles exist in the analysis of administrative data, such as education and labor market statistics. Several countries have stopped collecting data by ethnicity because of privacy legislation. Czechoslovakia stopped collecting data on students by ethnicity in 1990, and Hungary followed suit in 1993 (ERRC [European Roma Rights Center] 1999; Radó 1997). Government officials are also frequently reluctant to inquire about ethnicity in surveys, for fear of raising ethnic tensions.

More fundamental questions about ethnicity and identity complicate the assessment of welfare. Some Roma do not consider themselves to be Roma or they may affiliate with a different ethnic group. An ethnic Roma living in Hungary may feel more Hungarian than Roma or vice versa. For the purpose of analysis in this book, Roma are defined broadly to include both those who identify themselves as Roma and those identified by others as Roma. This stems both from the data sources used and from the policy focus of this analysis. After all, if policies affect ethnic minorities, they will do so regardless of how people identify themselves.

Another unique challenge of research on Roma is the legacy of biased research. Early studies on Roma in the late nineteenth century in Western Europe sought to confirm theories about genetic inferiority (Fraser 1995). Recent works reviewed in the Czech and Slovak Republics were found to have a social Darwinist slant (ECOHOST [European Centre on Health of Societies in Transition] 2000). More recent scholarship on Roma may suffer from political biases. Roma leaders and activists have an interest in portraying the situation as worse than it may actually be, while government reports may gloss over failings to present a more favorable picture (Bárány 2000).

A further caveat is warranted. The diversity of Roma impedes generalizations at the regional and country level. In addition to notable ethnic differences, there is significant diversity among Roma settlements—rural and urban, assimilated and non-assimilated, homogenous and heterogeneous—as well as in religious affiliation. Some groups speak variations of the Roma language, while others do not. For analytical purposes, this study assumes some commonalities across countries and groups, but its conclusions are necessarily tentative. The qualitative case studies presented in subsequent chapters illuminate some of these differences.

HOW IS POVERTY MEASURED?

Measuring poverty is an inherently subjective task fraught with methodological complexities.[12] There is no correct or scientific method. Empirical analyses of poverty generally focus on measuring income poverty and therefore provide only a partial picture. In this chapter, quantitative measures of poverty are complemented with other data sources, for example on education and health status, to fill in some of poverty's non-income dimensions. The following chapters use qualitative analysis to identify some non-measurable aspects of welfare and exclusion.

Poverty is usually measured using a nationally representative household survey that assesses the welfare of the population. Welfare indicators, including poverty rates, are constructed by using either consumption—measured by household expenditures on food and non-food items—or household income. Consumption data are generally considered more reliable; there are substantial problems with measuring income, including the difficulty of capturing in-kind income. Individuals may also be reluctant to report income from informal activities for fear of having to pay taxes. The disincentives to reporting consumption are less problematic, but methodological questions also remain here, including what to include as consumption and the difficulties that respondents have in recalling household expenditures.

Once the welfare measure is constructed, poverty rates are usually defined as that share of the population living below a designated poverty line. There are many possible poverty lines. The most commonly used lines for analysis are absolute lines, related to basic nutritional and social needs, or relative poverty lines, which are related to prevailing income levels, such as one-half or two-thirds of mean income per capita (per person). Relative lines are useful for measuring poverty at the country level and for international comparisons of the characteristics of the most deprived individuals in a country. Many international comparisons of poverty rates are based on relative lines.[13]

In addition to these measures, the World Bank uses two absolute poverty lines to compare poverty across countries: US$2.15 purchasing power parity (PPP) per capita per day and US$4.30 PPP per capita per day.[14] The adjustment to PPP accounts for differences in price levels across countries. These standard poverty lines allow comparisons of real values between countries. This chapter uses quantitative, income-based poverty definitions and shows how these connect with other dimensions of social exclusion in housing, labor markets, education, and health services.

AN ANALYSIS OF ROMA POVERTY IN THREE COUNTRIES

The following section looks at Roma poverty in three countries: Bulgaria, Hungary, and Romania. Together, these three countries comprise a significant share of the Roma population in the region. It relies on the household survey mentioned in box 2.1; the Center for Comparative

BOX 2.1 WHO ARE THE ROMA?

Estimating the number of Roma in a country is both difficult and controversial. Household surveys and census data rarely include questions on ethnicity beyond asking individuals to report their ethnicity. A household survey conducted by a team of Yale University researchers in 2000 experimented with different approaches when asking about ethnicity. The results provide lessons for future survey design. The dataset takes a multifaceted approach, including questions on self-identification (asking the interviewee to report their ethnicity), interviewer identification (asking the interviewer to identify the ethnicity of the interviewee), language, parents' language, appearance, and family name. This approach allows for analysis based upon differing definitions of ethnicity.

The Roma population can be estimated in different ways using the survey data (see table 2.1). After identification by the interviewer, self-identification yields the largest populations. Very few individuals who report being Roma were not identified by the interviewer as Roma—there were two in the case of Bulgaria and none in Hungary or Romania. On the other hand, the interviewers identified many people as Roma who did not identify themselves as Roma. In Romania, 61 percent of those that the interviewer identified as Roma did not self-identify. The corresponding shares for the other two countries are 38 percent in Hungary and 24 percent in Bulgaria. It is difficult to know how to interpret these results. It may be that Roma in Romania are more integrated and feel more Romanian than Roma. Conversely, Roma in Romania could be more afraid of identifying as Roma than Roma in the other countries.

It could also be that only certain groups of Roma self-identify as Roma. The share of the population who self-identify as Roma is relatively close to the share of the population who report speaking the Roma language at home. For example, in Hungary, only the Wallach Roma speak the Roma language. The other two main groups of Roma in the country—the Beash and Rumungro Roma—generally speak Romanian and Hungarian, respectively. This could mean that self-identification is more likely to capture the Wallach, while other Roma are less likely to consider themselves Roma. The data also suggest that ethnic identity may be weakening over time. In Bulgaria and Hungary, the share of respondents who identify their parents as Roma is higher than the share who identify themselves as Roma.

Research in the Sociology Department of Yale University conducted the survey in 2000.[15] The survey was the first of its kind to address the ethnic dimension of poverty across countries and allows for a comparative quantitative assessment of the living conditions of Roma in the region. In each of the three countries, Roma were oversampled to allow for a more statistically robust picture of their living conditions.

TABLE 2.1 ROMA POPULATION SIZES BY TYPE OF IDENTIFICATION, 2000

(Percent of random sample)

	Bulgaria	*Hungary*	*Romania*
Self-Identification	6.6	3.1	1.2
Language	6.2	1.7	1.6
Mother's ethnicity	7.2	3.1	1.1
Father's ethnicity	6.9	3.5	1.2
Spouse's ethnicity	6.6	1.1	0.8
Interviewer identification	8.7	5.0	3.1

Source: Yale dataset.

Annual household expenditures are used as the main measure of household welfare. Because poverty measures are very sensitive to household composition, the two sets of results were calculated based on (i) per capita expenditure (obtained by dividing total household expenditure by the number of household members); and (ii) per equivalent adult expenditures (where expenditures are adjusted for both the size and composition of the household). In general, this adjustment for household size (per capita or equivalent adult) tends to yield much larger differences in poverty risks between Roma and non-Roma than using unadjusted (per capita) household expenditures, because Roma households tend to be much larger.

Poverty rates for Roma in all three countries are strikingly high—in all cases several times higher than among non-Roma.[16] Table 2.2 summarizes the poverty rates for all three countries under the three

TABLE 2.2 POVERTY RATES AMONG ROMA AND NON-ROMA HOUSEHOLDS, 2000

	50 percent of median		*$2.15 PPP*	*$4.30 PPP*
Country	*Per equivalent adult*	*Per capita*	*Per capita*	*Per capita*
Bulgaria				
Roma	36.1	37.2	41.4	80.1
Non-Roma	3.8	3.4	4.1	36.8
Hungary				
Roma	24.5	26.3	6.6	40.3
Non-Roma	4.5	3.6	0.5	6.9
Romania				
Roma	39.5	43.1	37.6	68.8
Non-Roma	10.9	11.1	7.3	29.5

Sources: Yale dataset; Revenga et al. 2002.

different poverty lines—a relative line amounting to half of median per capita and per equivalent adult expenditures, and then the two international poverty lines, $2.15 and $4.30 per person, per day, adjusted for purchasing power parity.

The highest absolute poverty level among Roma households lies in Bulgaria, followed closely by Romania. Even at the lower line, 41 percent of all Roma households in Bulgaria and 38 percent in Romania are found to be poor—a strikingly high proportion. At the higher line of $4.30 PPP per capita, 80 percent of Roma households in Bulgaria and almost 70 percent of those in Romania are poor. Poverty among non-Roma households at the $4.30 line in both of these countries is also high, but less than half the levels among Roma. Although absolute poverty among Roma households is lower in Hungary, the difference between the situation of Roma and non-Roma households is equally stark. About 7 percent of Roma households in Hungary are poor based on the $2.15 line, as compared to only 0.5 percent of non-Roma households. At the higher $4.30 absolute poverty line— arguably a more appropriate one for prosperous Hungary—as much as 40 percent of Roma households are poor, compared to 6.9 percent of non-Roma households.

There are also very large differences in poverty rates between Roma and non-Roma when using the relative poverty line. On an equivalent adult basis, Bulgaria and Hungary look fairly similar: relative poverty among non-Roma households oscillates around 4 percent, while among Roma households, it is close to 25 percent in Hungary and about 37 percent in Bulgaria. In Romania, the differences between relative poverty rates for Roma and non-Roma are equally large, but poverty among the non-Roma is noticeably higher than in Bulgaria or Hungary, indicating a more skewed distribution of expenditure for all households.

As expected, poverty looks worse among Roma households when using the per capita line, which basically reflects the fact that Roma households have a large number of children. The per capita figures treat every household member as having the same consumption needs, whereas the figures based on per equivalent adult measures assume children have lesser consumption needs.

CORRELATES OF POVERTY

Why are poverty rates so different between Roma and non-Roma households? In large part, this is due to differences in the underlying correlates of poverty, especially educational achievement, employment status, and household size. The main correlates of poverty for Roma and non-Roma alike are the employment status of the head of

TABLE 2.3 MAIN POVERTY CORRELATES, 2000
(Poverty rate, in percent)

	Bulgaria		Hungary		Romania	
	Roma	Non-Roma	Roma	Non-Roma	Roma	Non-Roma
Education						
No school	31.2	N/A	39.6`	47.4	84.3	16.5
Primary	39.8	5.3	27.2	5.07	42.6	16.0
Secondary	31.3	2.9	6.2	1.47	31.8	7.5
Higher	0	0.8	0	0	0	0.6
Employment status of household head						
Employed	20.5	3.3	15.3	2.5	15.6	8.5
Unemployed	48.5	9.1	34.5	15.1	45.3	26.1
Out of labor force	46.7	2.2	50.3	6.9	69.4	20.5
Retired/disabled	17.4	1.2	19.8	2.7	32.9	7.1
Number of children						
Zero	25.2	2.5	14.2	2.8	27.3	7.3
One	34.7	6.1	23.3	3.7	38.8	13.5
Two	49.1	5.6	29.0	9.9	52.7	26.4
Three	59.2	15.8	42.0	11.2	73.4	50.3
Four	65.5	N/A	82.8	44.2	59.9	64.9
National Poverty Rate	37.2	3.4	26.3	3.6	43.1	11.1

Sources: Yale dataset; Revenga et al. 2002.
Note: The poverty line is equal to 50 percent of median of per capita expenditure.

the household, educational achievement of the household head, and the number of children, although the nature of the relationship varies significantly across countries and between Roma and non-Roma families (see table 2.3).

The poverty risk is highest among families where the household head has little education or is unemployed, as well as among families with three or more children. But the association between poverty and these correlates appears stronger for non-Roma families than for Roma. For example, among non-Roma families where the household head has no education at all, the poverty rate is several times that of families where the head has secondary education. Among Roma families, poverty tends to be relatively high irrespective of educational attainment (with the possible exception of Hungary). Similar results occur with respect to employment status: among non-Roma families, the risk of poverty in households where the head is unemployed is many times that of households where the head is employed, but among Roma families headed by an employed person, the risk of poverty remains high. Taken together, the evidence suggests a strong association between Roma poverty and education, employment, and household size. However, for Roma, the probability of being poor is higher than that for non-Roma, irrespective of educational achievement and employment status.

Although these poverty correlates—education, employment status, and number of children—are associated with a high risk of poverty, households with these characteristics do not necessarily constitute the bulk of the poor. In fact, the composition of the poor largely reflects the weight of each demographic group in the overall population. Among non-Roma families, a sizeable fraction of the poor are the so-called working poor—in other words, the head of household is employed. Among Roma, the fraction of household heads who are working is much lower, and their weight in the composition of the poor is correspondingly lower. In the large majority of poor Roma families, the head of the household is unemployed.

Similar differences exist by educational attainment. While among non-Roma a sizeable fraction of poor heads of households has primary or secondary education, the majority of Roma household heads have primary or less than primary education.

MULTIVARIATE ANALYSIS OF ROMA POVERTY

The previous discussion focused on a one-dimensional analysis of poverty, examining how poverty rates differ across households based on a single characteristic, such as education or employment status. But many household characteristics are often correlated among themselves. For example, where the head of a household has a low education level, these households are more likely to be poor; household heads with low education may also face a higher probability of being unemployed, and being unemployed is also correlated with a higher probability of being poor. Does low education increase the risk of poverty directly? Or does it increase poverty through its impact on employment status? Or both? To answer these questions, multivariate regression analysis is used to control for the differential influences of diverse factors. The following highlights these findings.

The results underscore the strong negative association between Roma ethnicity and welfare, even when controlling for other characteristics. In other words, if the other household characteristics are held constant, per adult equivalent expenditure of Roma households is between 20 and 40 percent lower in the three countries than that of non-Roma households—a striking difference. Other household characteristics also affect welfare. The number of children, for example, is strongly negatively associated with per adult equivalent consumption in all three countries. Employment is positively associated with welfare in all cases, while unemployment shows a negative association (although not always a strongly significant one). The relationship between education of the household head and household welfare is positive, as expected, but there are noticeable differences in the returns to education across countries. Returns to higher education—in terms of higher household consumption—are high in all three countries, but highest in Romania.

Additional analysis looked at factors influencing welfare for Roma only. There is no reason why returns to education or other characteristics should be the same for both Roma and non-Roma. If Roma families live in different areas, engage in different activities, or make different decisions regarding household investment and consumption, then the returns to household characteristics may be quite different, in terms of welfare.[17] While beneficial in the short run, such differential behaviors can reduce long-term prospects for escaping poverty. For this reason, additional analysis was undertaken for the Roma households only, including variables in the analysis that are of little relevance to the majority population, but important to Roma welfare.

Location is one factor shown elsewhere to influence behavioral patterns. Residential differentiation or segregation can lower returns to productive endowments for minority groups relative to the returns on the same endowments for the overall population (van der Walle and Gunewardena 2001; Nord 1998). For Roma, location's effect is probably best captured by the difference between those living in a Roma settlement versus those living in a more integrated neighborhood. Another factor that may be important is whether the individual or the interviewer identifies himself or herself as Roma. Households that self-identify as Roma are likely to be from less integrated and more traditional Roma communities and hence may be poorer than other Roma.[18]

The Roma-only analysis does yield some different results, suggesting that using the same model for Roma and non-Roma samples may be inappropriate. Most strikingly, adult equivalent expenditures are lower for Roma households living in Roma-only settlements than for those living in other locations, suggesting a connection between living in a geographically segregated area and welfare. Additional analysis found that much of the difference between the welfare of Roma and non-Roma is due to differences in opportunities and characteristics, such as education levels and employment status. But an important component is structural, reflecting differences in the communities. This likely reflects discrimination, exclusion, and cultural factors. While the quantitative data cannot provide more insights into these issues, the qualitative analysis presented in the following chapters examines these unmeasurable dimensions of exclusion more closely.

HOUSING

The multivariate analysis highlighted a link between geographic location and Roma poverty. This is closely related to housing conditions. Because of the diversity of Roma communities and contrasting conditions across countries, it is difficult to draw conclusions about the characteristics of Roma settlements and housing. Many housing issues are similar to those faced by non-Roma populations, particularly for communities and households that have integrated into non-Roma areas. But Roma confront unique problems. The housing policies of successive empires, socialist regimes, and recent governments have often led to regional and geographic isolation and segregation of Roma neighborhoods. This has, in turn, limited access to public services and raised questions about land and property ownership. Compounded by discrimination from some surrounding communities and municipal governments, conditions in many Roma settlements have deteriorated significantly.

Many socialist initiatives to integrate Roma provided housing along with employment. Current Roma neighborhoods in some areas have their roots in these settlements, although it is unclear how many (Macura and Petrovic 1999). Findings from a government housing survey in Hungary indicate that 60,000 Roma—approximately 13 percent of Roma in the country—live in settlement-type environments that are isolated from the majority population (Puporka and Zádori 1999). This was confirmed in another 1994 survey, which found that 14 percent of Roma lived in settlements (Kémeny et al. 1994). This spatial segregation results from such reasons as the historical location of Roma neighborhoods, municipal planning, and housing preferences. Some Roma communities have chosen to live separately; others that hoped to move hit barriers of discrimination.

In the countries of southeastern Europe that were formerly part of the Ottoman Empire, Roma neighborhoods, or *mahalas*, are common in cities (see box 2.2). Towns under the Ottomans were organized into administrative units based on the ethnicity and religion of the inhabitants. While these divisions—themselves known as mahalas, giving rise to the name—have largely disappeared, Roma settlements based on them still exist. In the countries of the former Yugoslavia, Roma mahalas range from several hundred to several thousand inhabitants; in Bulgaria, some are as large as 15,000–20,000. In some cases, Roma mahalas were originally built on the outskirts of towns, but as urbanization has proceeded and the towns have grown, these settlements may now lie close to the center of some cities.

Another common type of settlement that is rooted in the socialist era is neighborhoods near state-owned enterprises, often in one-company towns. As part of their integration or assimilation campaigns, socialist governments provided housing for Roma along with employment. Rents were either free to employees or heavily subsidized. In the transition period, as many state enterprises were closed or restructured and collective farms broken up, the inhabitants lost their jobs. Many of these areas have become impoverished.

Roma in cities are highly segregated. Research in Hungary traced the growth of these areas to the migration of Roma from the countryside during the economic crisis at the end of the 1980s. Faced with growing unemployment, many Roma moved to Budapest in search of better opportunities. Over time, due to declining living conditions and poor access to municipal services, conditions in these neighborhoods severely deteriorated. Common side effects associated with slums appeared, including drug addiction and rising crime (Ládanyi 1993). While there has been no further research in this area since the transition, the continuing deterioration of living conditions and employment opportunities has probably led to continued rural-urban migration.

The transition process has created problems with the legal status of Roma housing, in part because property rights were often not clearly defined under communism. Some Roma were evicted from state-owned apartments when housing subsidies were withdrawn, properties

---

Box 2.2 Spatial Segregation within Roma
            Settlements

There are common patterns to the internal geography of some urban mahala neighborhoods. The Nikola Kochev district in Sliven, Bulgaria, provides a typical example. Approximately 4,000 to 6,000 Bulgarian Roma live in Nikola Kochev, a settlement traced to the fifteenth century. Most inhabitants are textile workers who are descendants of some of the first workers in a textile industry that dates back to the mid-1800s.

The district's organization reflects the class distinctions within Roma society. The best-off members of the Roma community live in direct contact with Bulgarians on the periphery of the settlement, a large share of the adults are employed, and most of their children attend school regularly and continue on through secondary school. There is a large share of elderly inhabitants in this part of the settlement, as many of the young people have moved to apartments in more ethnically mixed parts of town.

Poverty increases further into the settlement, in an area nicknamed "the Jungle." The inhabitants here are poorer, less educated, and less integrated. Most are unemployed. Conditions in the Jungle are extremely bleak, with houses often constructed from scavenged materials and lacking water and electricity.

Source: Tomova 2000.

privatized, or returned to prior owners. Many Roma now find themselves living illegally in dwellings, either because they had no choice but to squat or because the property rights on their building were transferred following the transition (OSCE 2000). In other cases, poor Roma have intentionally become squatters. These developments have seriously limited access to social services, as residency and ID papers are frequently required for social assistance benefits, health care, and education. In addition, many Roma communities have tapped into public services illegally to channel water or electricity into their settlements.

Housing options for Roma have also been limited by discrimination by municipal officials and landlords. In some cases, local governments have attempted to reduce illegal tenancy by moving settlements to the outskirts of towns.[19] In other cases, municipal officials have overtly banned Roma—as was the case in 1997, when two Slovak villages prohibited Roma from entering and settling. The European Court of Human Rights challenged these bans, and they were lifted. Other municipal governments have reportedly bought land and apartments to ensure that Roma will not be able to settle in them (OSCE 2000).

Questions about the legality of property ownership have arisen with land as well. The post-communist process of land restitution has had a varied impact on Roma. Because Roma were not traditionally landowners, few were eligible to file claims. In some cases, Roma who worked on collective farms were entitled to receive land after the cooperatives dissolved.

Roma neighborhoods are frequently extremely overcrowded and destitute. Some Roma slums have evocative nicknames; for example, "Abyssinia" and "Cambodia" are extremely impoverished areas within Bulgaria's Roma ghettos. The household survey data show that Roma living quarters are smaller than others, have larger households, and are consequently more crowded (see figure 2.1). According to the Yale dataset, Roma households are nearly twice the size of non-Roma households. In Romania, based on a 1998 household survey, Roma dwellings were 20 percent smaller, on average, than those for Romanians, although their household size was significantly larger.[20]

Lack of water, gas, electricity, and public services, such as waste collection, bedevil many Roma neighborhoods. According to the Yale survey data, Roma are less likely to have access to water and sewage than other groups. Access to utilities, including electricity, heating, and water, is significantly lower for Roma households (see table 2.4). Only 9 percent of Roma houses in Bulgaria and 10 percent in Romania had hot water. Access to bathroom facilities and indoor toilets is similarly low. Few Roma households have telephones: only 12 percent in Bulgaria,

FIGURE 2.1 HOUSEHOLD SIZE IN BULGARIA, HUNGARY, AND
    ROMANIA, 2000

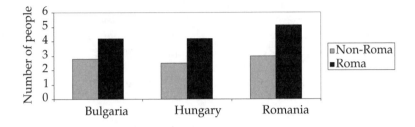

Sources: Yale dataset; Revenga et al. 2002.

41 percent in Hungary, and 26 percent in Romania (in contrast with
between 58 and 81 percent for non-Roma households). Over half of
Roma households in Bulgaria reported wet walls and leaky roofs, significantly more than in the other countries.[21]

Cultural preferences of Roma communities also affect conditions
within Roma settlements, although it is difficult to generalize. Non-
Roma across countries sometimes complain that Roma do not take care
of their surroundings and that they destroy property and public

TABLE 2.4 HOUSING CHARACTERISTICS BY ETHNICITY, 2000
(Percent of households)

Households with:	Bulgaria		Hungary		Romania	
	Non-Roma	Roma	Non-Roma	Roma	Non-Roma	Roma
Electricity	99.6	94.5	99.0	98.1	99.1	94.5
Central or gas heating	16.1	4.1	78.6	35.3	51.2	25.6
Cold running water	96.8	67.6	92.0	65.3	67.4	41.4
Hot running water	39.1	9.4	83.2	45.1	35.3	10.7
Sewer or cesspool	90.3	52.3	58.3	33.4	53.6	30.0
Telephone	80.6	12.1	76.0	41.4	58.2	26.4
Bathroom/shower	82.5	23.5	88.8	50.2	54.3	18.9
Indoor toilet	65.2	15.0	86.4	49.9	52.6	18.3
Wet walls	20.6	50.4	16.6	40.1	21.0	44.9
Leaky roofs	19.2	54.2	9.6	33.0	14.8	40.2
Earthen floor used for sleeping	7.4	36.7	5.8	13.2	19.3	39.0

Source: Yale dataset; Revenga et al. 2002.

spaces. Some of these perceptions may stem from cultural differences. For example, some Roma groups have taboos against adjoining kitchen and toilet facilities. As public housing initiatives did not incorporate the views and culture of Roma into their design, inhabitants have had little interest in the maintenance and upkeep of the buildings. Above all, poverty makes it difficult for households to maintain their housing conditions. In effect, some of these complaints reflect a dual prejudice: exclusion leads to Roma poverty and then fellow citizens castigate Roma for living in squalid conditions—as if anyone chooses to be poor.

LABOR MARKET STATUS

Following the post-socialism transition, perhaps the most dramatic changes for Roma took place in the labor market. In Central and Eastern Europe, employment levels fell significantly during the transition's early years, as restructuring began and subsidies for large state-owned enterprises were slashed.[22] Because of their low skill levels, as well as discrimination in the labor market, Roma were frequently among the first to be laid off; this has directly influenced Roma welfare. Roma have limited opportunities to reenter the workforce, so unemployment rates, and particularly long-term unemployment, for Roma are often exceptionally high. Reports of unemployment rates of up to 100 percent in Roma settlements are not uncommon (see box 2.3).

Roma have historically had connections to traditional occupations. Indeed, many of the names of Roma subgroups derive from associations with particular crafts dating back to the Middle Ages. But few of these connections still exist. Roma were traditionally not landowners and had scant involvement in agriculture. In the early twentieth century, many of the traditional occupations declined with industrialization. Crafts such as metal and woodworking faced competition from manufactured goods, and Roma began to shift into other areas of economic activity.

With socialism, Roma were compelled to move from self-employment and informal sector activity into full-time public sector jobs. Full employment and job security were defining characteristics of the socialist regimes. Employment was encouraged through guaranteed jobs, low wages, and a wide range of associated benefits and services, including housing subsidies, childcare, and health services. Unemployment was considered illegal in some countries, and sanctions could be imposed for part-time work, self-employment, or not working. For example, the right and obligation to work was enshrined in the Czechoslovak Constitution (Ministry of Labor 1997). In 1970, the Romanian government decreed that "social parasitism" and other "deviant behaviors" were punishable with prison and forced labor (Rughinis 2000).

In this context, Roma employment was actively promoted through recruitment and assimilation campaigns. Along with the rest of the population, Roma were brought to work through the industrialization process and collectivization of agriculture. Because of their low education levels, Roma were most frequently employed in low-skilled manufacturing industries. During the socialist period, Roma employment rates in some countries did not differ greatly from those of non-Roma. In the Slovak Republic in the 1980s, for example, 70 percent of working-age Roma were employed (Ministry of Labor 1997).[23] A survey of Roma in Hungary in 1971 found that employment levels of working-age Roma men were slightly higher than those of non-Roma, with employment rates of 88 and 85 percent, respectively (Kertesi 1994).

BOX 2.3 MEASURING UNEMPLOYMENT

Reports of exceptionally high unemployment rates for Roma settlements—between 70 and 100 percent—are common, but difficult to fathom, particularly in countries with active informal sectors. In these cases, it is important to note how unemployment is measured and defined.

In general, there are two main instruments to measure unemployment. First are registration statistics based on the administrative records of the labor offices. But registration data capture only those individuals who report to labor offices and do not reflect any kind of informal labor market activity. These data may significantly underestimate the long-term unemployed. Many countries limit the duration of their unemployment benefits, and once these have expired, people have no incentive to report to the labor offices. Registration data also generally do not capture ethnicity.

Labor force and household surveys are the second important source for measuring unemployment. These surveys ask about economic activity in general and can reflect both informal and formal employment. However, as discussed in chapter 1 of this report, survey data are limited in their ability to differentiate by ethnicity.

Data included in this report are mainly from household surveys and other targeted surveys of the Roma population. Unless otherwise indicated, employment includes the share of the working-age population (defined differently depending on the country and source) that has worked for in-cash or in-kind payment during a set period (either the previous week or month). In this case, informal employment is included. In contrast, unemployment refers to the share of the working-age population that has not worked for payment.

DEVELOPMENTS IN TRANSITION

Large-scale restructuring in the early years of the transition period had an immediate impact on the labor market status of Roma. By 1993, Roma employment levels in Hungary had fallen to 26 percent of the labor force and 63 percent for the population at large (Kémeny et al. 1994). These trends have worsened during the transition period, as Roma have found it difficult to reenter the labor force, and the gap in unemployment between Roma and non-Roma has widened. In the Czech Republic, government estimates for 1999 suggested that 70 percent of the Roma were unemployed, in contrast with 10 percent of the total population (OSCE 2000).

Because Roma were among the first laid off in the early 1990s, the duration of their unemployment has been exceptionally high (see figure 2.2). The gap is particularly bad in Bulgaria, where the duration of unemployment lasted 27 months on average, but soared to 51 months for Roma. Long-term unemployment has been consistently high in Bulgaria during the transition period, indicating the persistence of a stagnant pool of long-term unemployed who are unable to reenter the labor market. Among them is a sizeable fraction of Roma. On the other hand, in Romania, the difference in the duration of unemployment for Roma and non-Roma is not significant.

High unemployment rates among Roma only tell part of the labor market story. Informal sector activity is also an important source of income. The types of activities vary widely, from lucrative trade and work in neighboring countries to more marginal subsistence occupations ranging from seasonal farming to gathering herbs and recycling used materials. Some Roma may prefer more flexible and entrepreneurial informal sector activities and self-employment

FIGURE 2.2 UNEMPLOYMENT DURATION, 2000

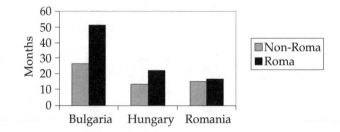

Sources: Yale dataset; Revenga et al. 2002.

to wage labor. This phenomenon is described further in the following country chapters.

Popular stereotypes characterize Roma as lazy. However, survey data indicate that Roma actively seek employment. In Bulgaria in 1997, 46 percent of unemployed Roma reported that they were looking for a job, compared to 19 percent of the total unemployed population. In Romania, 35 percent of unemployed Roma had looked for employment during the previous week, in comparison with 15 percent of the total population. Similar results were found for Hungary (Kertesi 1994). However, more information on Roma values and attitudes toward work is required to understand the data fully. For example, as Roma are more frequently engaged in short-term informal sector activities and may have more than one job, they may inevitably spend more time looking for work.

EDUCATION STATUS

Across Europe, the education status of Roma has historically been low. While significant gains were made in enrolling Roma children in school during the socialist era, the gap in the educational attainment of Roma and the rest of the population was not bridged in any of the countries for which data are available. The evidence suggests that access has eroded during the transition period, and Roma children of basic school age are increasingly not starting or finishing school. These trends are consistent with national developments in enrollments, although data suggest that the decline in access for Roma has been deeper than for the rest of the population.

Gaps in access to education for Roma are not new. Not until the socialist regimes came to power in Central and Eastern Europe following World War II were large numbers of Roma compelled to participate in public education. Education was a key element of socialist assimilation campaigns. It was viewed as an instrument of political and economic socialization that would facilitate the inclusion of Roma into full employment and society. Despite the achievements in reducing literacy and increasing school participation, the efforts undertaken during the socialist era laid the foundation for inequities in education quality, as many Roma were channeled into separate or segregated schools outside the mainstream system.

Education in the Transition Period

Gaps in education persist in the transition period and are most evident in an analysis of the educational levels of the population. Comparable surveys conducted in Hungary in 1971 and 1993 illustrate the trends. In 1971, about 26 percent of Hungarian Roma aged 20–29 had finished 8 years of primary school. This had increased to more than 77 percent by 1993 (Kémeny et al. 1994). Despite these achievements, the educational attainment of Roma lagged significantly behind the non-Roma population, with Roma much less likely to continue on to secondary and post-secondary education.

The Yale dataset also illustrates lower educational attainment for Roma. Most Roma have primary education or less, while most non-Roma in the three countries have some secondary, post-secondary, or university education (see table 2.5). Bulgaria provides the most dramatic example; 89 percent of Roma had primary education or less, while only 10 percent had some secondary education. Less than 1 percent of Roma in all countries continued past secondary school. In contrast, 33 percent of non-Roma had primary education or less, while 54 percent of the population continued on to secondary school and 14 percent to tertiary school. Results are similar for Hungary and Romania.

It is not surprising that education levels vary notably within countries, between urban and rural areas, and across different types of Roma communities. In Hungary, for example, the 1993 survey mentioned

TABLE 2.5 EDUCATIONAL ATTAINMENT BY ETHNICITY, 2000

	Bulgaria		Hungary		Romania	
	Non-Roma	Roma	Non-Roma	Roma	Non-Roma	Roma
Primary or below	**32.7**	**89.6**	**35.0**	**76.4**	**33.1**	**66.5**
No education	1.3	15.0	0.3	4.3	1.9	13.4
Incomplete primary	9.4	39.6	10.7	22.1	15.0	27.0
Complete primary	22.0	35.0	24	49.9	16.2	25.2
Some secondary	**53.8**	**9.6**	**53.0**	**23.4**	**56.3**	**32.4**
Completed primary and apprenticeship	2.2	1.8	25.5	19.0	18.9	13.1
Incomplete general secondary	2.3	1.6	6.1	1.5	6.6	9.0
Completed general secondary	19.4	3.0	17.5	2.7	23.9	8.9
Secondary and vocational	29.8	3.2	3.8	0.2	6.9	1.3
Higher education						
(complete and incomplete)						
Including post-secondary and university	**13.5**	**0.5**	**12.0**	**0.2**	**10.4**	**0.3**
No answer	0	0.4	0.1	0.1	0.1	0.8

Sources: Yale dataset; Revenga et al. 2002.

above found that the share of Roma who had not completed primary education was 16 percent in Budapest, 24 percent in towns, and 27 percent in villages, reflecting different constraints to access (Puporka and Zádori 1999).

Differences between types of Roma are also important. For example, the same survey found that the share of Roma with less than basic education was 23 percent for the Romungro Roma (whose native language is Hungarian), 42 percent for the Bayash (native language is Romanian), and 48 percent for the Wallach Roma (native language is Roma) (Puporka and Zádori 1999). Similar findings were noted in Bulgaria.

Enrollments and Attendance

Disparities in enrollments between Roma and non-Roma suggest that the gaps in educational attainment will persist into the next generation. In Bulgaria and Romania, the Yale data show a significant difference in enrollment levels for children of basic school age. In Bulgaria, Roma enrollment rates were 33 percent lower, while in Romania, the difference is 20 percent (see figure 2.3). In Hungary, the gap in enrollments was not significant, at less than 2 percentage points.

Enrollment rates tell only part of the story. In some cases, students may enroll at the beginning of the year but will not actually attend school. Qualitative studies show this often happens in poor Roma communities where the costs of education for families are high (see box 2.4). It is also important to note that enrollment rates calculated from the Yale survey data indicate only whether children are enrolled

FIGURE 2.3 ENROLLMENTS IN EDUCATION, 2000
(Percent of children aged 6-14)

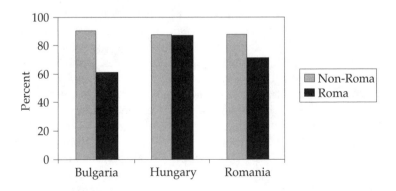

Sources: Yale dataset; Revenga et al. 2002.

Box 2.4 School Dropouts: The Case of the Missing Children

National administrative data in Bulgaria paint a rosy picture of access to education. Gross enrollment rates are nearly universal, and very few children are identified as being out of school. But a qualitative survey found that the reality is much more grim. In fact many children fall through the cracks, never attend school, and do not show up in the official administrative data. These children are frequently those from the poorest households. In the Nadezhda district, a Roma neighborhood in Sliven, the researchers found 273 children who had never been to school. Why is this the case? The study identified several reasons:

- There are no records of children from households that lack residence requirements. This is a serious issue for poor households, particularly Roma families who live in unregistered settlements or in properties with illegal status.
- Monitoring of children has weakened. Children are no longer required to enroll in the school in the district in which they live. There is no coordination between district schools to ensure that all children are enrolled and no system to monitor whether children who have left one school enroll in another.
- There are no mechanisms for following up on children who have been expelled to find out what happens to them and whether they reenroll in school. Similarly, there is no follow up for children who leave school voluntarily and are not officially considered dropouts.
- School and local officials face incentives not to report dropouts to maintain class sizes to avoid school closure.

Source: Kabachieva and Iliev 2002.

in school, not whether they are enrolled in the appropriate level. In contrast with conventional enrollment rates, the rates presented above indicate whether children between 6 and 14 were enrolled at all, which may be misleading, as many children are repeating grades.

Pre-primary attendance may have been most damaged during the transition period. In general, preschool and kindergarten enrollment rates have fallen across the region, as school subsidies connected to state enterprises were withdrawn and fees were introduced (UNICEF 1998). Growing costs have discouraged parents from sending children to school. In the Slovak Republic in 1990, 80 percent of Roma children aged 3–6 attended preschool. This dropped by 60 percent in the 1991 school year, and by 1997, less than 20 percent of Roma children were thought to attend (Ministry of Labor 1997). In Hungary, where preschool is compulsory for all children at age 5, 11 percent of Roma did not attend school in 1997 (Radó 1997). This is a serious development; children who do not start preschool are less likely to attend primary school and may have more difficulty remaining in school. For Roma children, these issues are compounded by the fact that many do not speak the national language at home and thus begin primary school at a disadvantage.

As illustrated in the breakdown of the educational status of the population, the gulf between education levels is wider for Roma than non-Roma, indicating the challenges of moving from one education level to the next. Limited evidence suggests that dropout rates have risen during the transition period—disproportionately so for Roma children (UNICEF 1998). Informal estimates for Bulgaria suggest that 45,000 students drop out of school each year, most of them Roma.

Education Quality

Access to education is also directly affected by the quality of schooling, as students may be deterred from attending school if the quality is low. Uneven quality of education also affects equity of education. There is evidence that the quality of education for Roma students is lower than for the rest of the population. The following section discusses aspects of education systems in the region that influence quality, including the prevalence of "special schools," the segregation of Roma students within the mainstream system, and inadequate teacher training and curricula.

One of the most damaging legacies of the socialist era is the tendency to channel children into special schools for the mentally and physically handicapped. This policy had its roots in the socialist legacy of "defectology," which assumed that differences among students were due to disability rather than environmental conditions, and as a result, should be addressed as medical problems in institutions separated from the rest of society (Ainscow and Memmenasha 1998). The legacy has been the persistence of a parallel system of schools that provide lower quality education and fewer opportunities in post-basic education and the labor market than mainstream schools.

There is widespread evidence of this practice. Data for the Czech Republic are striking (see box 2.5). Estimates for 1997 indicate that 64 percent of Roma children in primary school are in special schools, in comparison with 4 percent for the total population. In other words, Roma are 15 times more likely to end up in special schools than the national average (ERRC 1999). Similarly, in Hungary Roma constitute about half the number of students enrolled in special schools (Radó 1997; 2001).

Regardless of the quality of teaching in special schools, students enrolled in these institutions are at a disadvantage. The curriculum is less rigorous, and expectations are lower. A detailed report on the

Czech schools notes that students in special schools receive fewer Czech language lessons per week and are not expected to read for comprehension until fourth grade, while the expectation for students in mainstream schools is first grade (ERRC 1999).

Opportunities for graduates of special schools are also limited. Even if children are able to overcome low expectations, they are not allowed equal access to school-leaving exams. In the Czech Republic, graduates from special schools are only allowed to enter technical secondary schools, which offer limited training in narrowly defined fields. Students are then dually challenged on the labor market, as employers look unfavorably upon graduates of special schools, and technical training fails to adequately prepare young people for the labor market.

There is growing recognition that the existence of special schools adversely affects the integration and educational development of Roma children. However, the obstacles to change are notable. Not only does resistance to integration come from non-Roma parents and education officials who fear that increasing the share of Roma children in a classroom will lower the quality of education for non-Roma students, but opposition comes from Roma parents as well. Special schools can be attractive to poor Roma families for economic reasons, in that school meals and—for residential institutions, housing—are provided. Some parents also view special schools as safe havens that are free from the discrimination that is more pervasive in mainstream schools.

Even where Roma children are kept within the mainstream school system, they are often segregated into separate classes, or schools. This is frequently related to geography if Roma families live together in a neighborhood. However, there is also evidence of further separation of Roma. In Bulgaria, "Roma schools" are schools in which the share of Roma is over 50 percent. The overrepresentation of Roma in these schools is due to geographic concentration, and attempts by some municipal and education officials to place Roma students together into separate schools.

A recent survey that the Open Society Institute in Sofia conducted found more than 60 elementary, 350 primary, and 9 secondary schools in Bulgaria, where Roma comprised between 50 and 100 percent of the student body. In general, quality and conditions in Roma schools are poorer than in mainstream schools, infrastructure has deteriorated, and materials are lacking (Denkov et al. 2001). There are also serious problems with attendance in Roma schools. Teachers from Haskovo noted that some Roma students had not attended class for an entire year. Similarly, fieldwork in Romania found situations where non-Roma parents would request that their children be taught in classes without Roma students, and teachers would divide up classes to keep Roma separate (World Bank 2000d).

Box 2.5 Entrance to Remedial Special Schools
in the Czech Republic

Roma children end up in special schools for many reasons. A study in
the Czech Republic found that because of discrimination and the highly
discretionary nature of the process, many more Roma children end up
in special schools than the regulations should allow.

Children can be enrolled directly into special schools or transferred
from a mainstream basic school. By law, placement is based upon the
recommendation of the school director in consultation with the parent
and an educational psychologist. In some cases parental consent is not
obtained or is abused. Parents may not realize that they are authoriz-
ing their children to be shifted into a special school.

"My daughter is in the second year of basic school. She is doing
alright. One day in November 1997 her teacher came to see me saying,
'We want to move her to another class which will be better for her.' He
gave me a piece of paper to sign. I should have read it but it was long
and I didn't think a teacher would try to cheat us, so I just signed it. . . .
The next day I got a letter saying that my daughter had been moved to
a remedial special school," a Roma parent in Prague stated.

Educational psychologists play a pivotal role in determining whether
children will be sent to special schools, as they recommend students for
examination and administer the exams. These procedures were found
to be highly discretionary. In some cases children were even transferred
without the required psychological exam. The tests themselves are problematic because psychologists may use a number of different instruments, many of which are culturally biased.

Because of the widespread abuses that have been documented, parents of 18 Roma children from the Czech town of Ostrava initiated legal
proceedings against the government in 1998. The Czech Constitutional
Court ruled in favor of the government. An appeals process opened in
April 2000 in front of the European Court of Human Rights in Strasbourg.

Source: ERRC 1999.

Discrimination against Roma by non-Roma parents, children, and
teachers contributes to low attendance and can both discourage
children from attending school and affect the quality of education in
the classroom. Stereotypes about Roma and their attitudes toward
education lower teachers' expectations about the potential of their students. Discrimination can be both explicit—as in the case of schools
creating separate classes—or more subtle if parents discourage their
children from interacting with Roma classmates. A Czech system
study documented cases where education staff had abused Roma children. One parent from Prague noted, "The teachers who teach Gypsy

children are fine, but the others are terrible. They chase our children out of the dining room and insult them" (ERRC 1999).

HEALTH STATUS

Data on the health status of Roma is scarce and fragmented. However, the information that does exist paints a bleak picture, pointing to significant gaps in health status between Roma and non-Roma populations. Because of the absence of data, it is difficult to discuss health trends during the transition period. On aggregate, Roma are estimated to live about 10 years less than the majority populations in Central and Eastern Europe (Braham 1993). Because of substandard living conditions, Roma communities are particularly susceptible to communicable diseases, including hepatitis and tuberculosis. Very little is known about the incidence of non-communicable diseases among Roma. There are increasing indications that Roma have a higher incidence of health problems associated with unhealthy life styles, including drug and alcohol addiction and HIV/AIDS.

Life expectancy and mortality data for Roma indicate significantly worse health conditions than for the rest of the population. Estimates derived from Czechoslovak census data for the 1990s found that life expectancy for the total population was 67 years for men and 74 for women, while for Roma, the figures were 55 and 60, respectively (ECOHOST 2000). In Hungary the life expectancy gap is estimated at 10 to 15 years. A study conducted in Pest County documented that Roma men lived 13 years less and Roma women 12 years less than non-Roma inhabitants. Estimates of infant mortality rates show a similar gulf. In the Czech and Slovak Republics infant mortality for Roma was double that of non-Roma. However, in Hungary, infant mortality for Roma has declined faster than that of the total population, and the gap between Roma and non-Roma has narrowed. While infant mortality was 38 per 1,000 births for the total population and nearly 118 for Roma in 1970, this decreased to 17 for the whole population and 21 for Roma by 1990 (Puporka and Zádori 1999).

Demographic Trends

Roma have historically had significantly higher population growth than other groups. This has been and continues to be a sensitive political issue because across the region the size of the Roma population is growing much faster than the non-Roma population. In 1958, the Czechoslovak government issued a decree stating that Roma were not of a distinct ethnicity, but rather were a people "maintaining a markedly different demographic structure" (Fraser 1995). Roma women marry at a younger age and begin having children earlier than other groups. This has serious consequences for women's reproductive health. The precise roots of high fertility for Roma are unknown, but likely result from socioeconomic factors, including poverty, low education levels, and cultural preferences.

Because of higher birthrates, the Roma community is significantly younger than other groups. Data from two representative surveys of Roma conducted in Hungary illustrate this phenomenon (Puporka and Zádori 1999).[24] In 1993, 39 percent of the Roma population was under 14 years old, while only 19 percent of the total population fell into this age group. In contrast, 19 percent of the total population was over 60, while only 5 percent of Roma fell into this category. Birth rates for Roma are much higher than those of other groups. Age pyramids from the 1991 Czechoslovak census illustrate a similar phenomenon (see figure 2.4). There is mixed evidence on demographic trends for Roma during the transition period. While overall fertility has declined significantly in Central and Eastern Europe, it is not clear whether this also holds true for Roma. Fertility has dropped in some Hungarian Roma communities (Puporka and Zádori 1999), while a study in Bulgaria found that birth rates were increasing among the poorer subgroups of Roma (Tomova 2000). Regardless of these contrasting messages, the available data suggest that Roma families remain larger than those of other ethnic groups.

FIGURE 2.4 AGE STRUCTURE OF ROMA AND THE TOTAL
POPULATION IN THE CZECH REPUBLIC, 1991

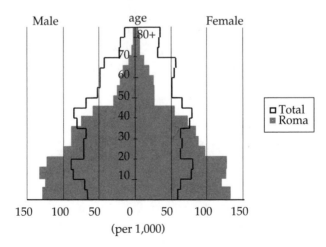

(per 1,000)

Source: Census data from ECOHOST 2000.

Reproductive Health

High infant mortality and perinatal death rates for Roma are linked to women's reproductive health. Due to inadequate access to care, unhealthy lifestyles, including poor living conditions and nutrition, as well as high birth and abortion rates, Roma women are at a higher risk of complications during pregnancy than non-Roma women. A study conducted in Szablocs-Szatmar County in Hungary in the 1980s found that Roma women were twice as likely to have difficulties during pregnancy, as well as premature births and low-birth-weight babies, than non-Roma women (Puporka and Zádori 1999). Similarly, a study conducted in a district in the Slovak Republic from 1995 to 1997 found low birth weights for Roma to be more than double that of non-Roma (ECOHOST 2000).

Maternal health is a serious issue. Because of low awareness levels about health issues and impoverishment among many communities, Roma women face other health challenges that are also common in the general population, including inadequate nutrition and high levels of smoking during pregnancy (OSCE 2000). The Hungarian survey mentioned above found that 63 percent of pregnant women were smokers (Puporka and Zádori 1999).

Contraceptive awareness varies across Roma communities. The qualitative study for Romania found that better-off Roma women were more likely to use contraception (Rughinis 2000). Another study in Romania by Médecins Sans Frontières indicated that many Roma women preferred intrauterine devices because they gave them more independence (OSCE 2000). As is the case throughout the former socialist countries, abortion is much more common than in the West and is used as a contraceptive method. In 1997, abortion rates ranged from 63 abortions per 100 live births in the Czech Republic, to 135 in Bulgaria and 147 in Romania (UNICEF 1999). Small-scale studies in the Slovak Republic and Bulgaria suggest that abortion rates are higher for Roma than non-Roma women (ECOHOST 2000; Tomova 1998).

Communicable Diseases

Poor living conditions, such as overcrowding and lack of adequate sanitation facilities, make Roma communities more susceptible to infectious diseases than other groups. Reports of epidemics of hepatitis, tuberculosis, and parasitic diseases were common during and after the socialist period. Skin diseases, such as eczema, are also common. The last reported cases of poliomyelitis in Bulgaria, FYR Macedonia, and Romania were all in Roma communities (OSCE 2000). In Bulgaria in 1992, 90 Roma children in the regions of Sliven and Sotirya caught poliomyelitis. There were no cases among ethnic Bulgarians. In 1993, a diphtheria outbreak occurred in the same areas (Tomova 2000).

In the 1990s, a number of hepatitis outbreaks were documented in Roma settlements in the Czech Republic and Hungary. In 1990, an outbreak was recorded in Brno, in the Czech Republic, and in 1999, 40 children in a Roma settlement in central Moravia were hospitalized with the disease (ECOHOST 2000). Hepatitis B, a more dangerous form of hepatitis, has been found to have an even higher incidence in Hungary among Roma. Among pregnant women routinely screened for hepatitis B in Hungary, approximately half tested positive and the majority were Roma (Puporka and Zádori 1999).

Tuberculosis is on the rise throughout the region. Hungary recorded a 20 percent increase between 1990 and 1995. Tuberculosis is associated with poor living conditions, putting some Roma communities at higher risk. In the 1960s, a study in the western part of the Slovak Republic found that the prevalence of tuberculosis among Roma was higher than for the majority population (ECOHOST 2000). However, there are no indications currently that incidence is higher among Roma. Reports from physicians working in one of the main tuberculosis hospitals in Hungary found that Roma women were more susceptible to tuberculosis than men (Puporka and Zádori 1999).

Another worrying trend has been outbreaks of measles among Roma in Hungary and the Slovak Republic that may have been due to lapses in immunization coverage. Aggregate immunization rates throughout the region are high, reaching nearly full coverage. However, immunization gaps in Roma communities have been documented. In the Bulgaria case studies, 11 percent of households reported that their children had not been vaccinated, with the rate nearly 20 percent in the poorest sites (Tomova 2000).

Congenital Disorders

Research on congenital disorders among Roma is sparse and frequently problematic. A review of literature on health among Roma in the Czech and the Slovak Republics noted that some research was tainted by concepts of contagion and "social Darwinist" motivations. The studies focused on identifying race-based inferiorities among the Roma and had a greater concern for the health needs of the majority populations than for the Roma (ECOHOST 2000). Nevertheless, the prevalence of genetic diseases among Roma is a valid concern, particularly since some groups of Roma have remained relatively isolated from the majority populations, and a high degree of intermarriage has been documented in some communities, but the extent is not known.[25]

Non-communicable Diseases

Very little information is available on non-communicable diseases among Roma. Across Central and Eastern Europe, mortality from non-communicable diseases is high, particularly for conditions associated with unhealthy lifestyles, such as poor nutrition, smoking, and alcoholism (Staines 1999). Some Roma communities may be particularly susceptible to these conditions because of lifestyles. Prevalence of smoking, alcoholism, and poor diets are reported to be higher among some Roma communities. Another study in Hungary found that smoking was exceptionally high for Roma, and particularly among Roma women. Another survey of students in a Roma school in Hungary found that 85 percent of students between 15 and 22 had tried cigarettes, and 45 percent smoked an average of a package of cigarettes per day (Puporka and Zádori 1999).

Although little information is available, occupational injuries and environmental conditions are also likely sources of ill health among Roma. As the lowest skilled jobs were also most likely to be the most hazardous, many Roma were employed in dangerous professions during the socialist period, including mining and other aspects of heavy industry, such as working with toxic substances. The incidence of disability from workplace injuries is thought to be disproportionately high among Roma. Similarly, exposure to hazardous materials and highly polluted regions is also an issue for Roma, as many live or work in the area of dump sites, mines, and abandoned factories. A recent report described conditions in the eastern Slovak town of Rudnaný, where 500 Roma are living in an abandoned iron and mercury mine. The area is known to be highly contaminated (Erlanger 2000). Many Roma engage in recycling activities, including trading in scrap materials. In a highly publicized case in Hungary, Roma supported themselves by melting down batteries. This created serious pollution, which was blamed for a child's death from lead poisoning (Puporka and Zádori 1999).

Nutrition

Unhealthy diets are an important contributor to poor health status across Central and Eastern Europe (Galloway et al. 2000). Because of low socioeconomic status, Roma are more susceptible to unhealthy dietary habits associated with poverty and low public health awareness. A 1997 nutrition study among children in the Czech Republic found that the nutritional intake of Roma was worse than that of Czech children. Roma had inadequate consumption of vegetables, dairy products, grains, and meats. On the other hand, Roma children were found to consume four and a half times the recommended daily allowance of snack foods containing fat and sugar (ECOHOST 2000). Improper nutrition for children can adversely affect growth and future development. Some evidence of stunting among Roma has already been documented. A study of the growth of children in the eastern part of the Slovak Republic found that Roma children developed more slowly than Slovak children of the same age (ECOHOST 2000).

Sexually Transmitted Diseases and Drug Abuse

There is very little information on the prevalence of sexually transmitted diseases (STDs) and drug abuse among Roma communities. Prostitution and trafficking of women with Western Europe have been on the rise during the transition in Central and Eastern Europe (UNICEF 1999). Women have resorted to employment in the sex industry as a result of the dearth of employment opportunities elsewhere. Estimates reported for the Czech Republic suggested that out of the nearly 40,000 prostitutes in the country, some 25,000 are Roma women (ECOHOST 2000). Prostitution increases the risk of STDs, including HIV/AIDS, for the Roma community at large. However, to date there is no information on disease incidence. A study of Roma in Miskolc, Hungary, found that Roma were uninformed about the risk of AIDS and prevention options (Puporka and Zádori 1999).

Drug abuse is on the rise among some Roma groups. Although the number of addicts is thought to be high, information is scarce because Roma are generally less likely to seek help at testing and counseling clinics and are not counted in surveys (ECOHOST 2000). The head of the Drug Prevention Center in Budapest estimates that 20 percent of patients treated in his clinic are Roma. He categorizes Roma drug users into two groups: young children between 9 and 12, who are addicted to sniffing glue, and older addicts, usually over age 19, who use "hard drugs," including heroin, cocaine, speed, and LSD (Puporka and Zádori 1999). Drug usage and trade may be most prevalent among communities in border areas, as is the case in the Black Sea region of Bulgaria (see box 2.6).

CONCLUSIONS

The evidence suggests that the roots of pervasive Roma poverty are closely linked to low education levels, limited employment opportunities, and unfavorable health status. The unfavorable starting point of Roma at the outset of the transition period—with low education levels and overrepresentation among low-skilled jobs—has led to disadvantages on the labor market. With their situation compounded by discrimination and low expectations of employers, Roma have had

BOX 2.6 HEROIN ADDICTION IN VARNA, BULGARIA

The Black Sea port city of Varna is the third largest city in Bulgaria. According to the 1992 census, 1.3 percent of the population identified as Roma, but the actual number is thought to be significantly higher. Because of its location on the Black Sea, informal trading opportunities with neighboring countries are rife, and recent evidence from the Maksouda Quarter, a Roma mahala on the western outskirts of the city, indicates a flourishing drug trade, particularly in heroin.

The Maksouda Quarter dates back at least a century, to Ottoman times. Formerly a camp for nomadic Roma, the quarter grew rapidly with the establishment of a textile factory at the turn of the century, and additional employment opportunities provided by the Varna shipyards during the socialist period. The population reached 15,000 by the 1970s. Informal sector activity was prevalent even under the socialist regime, because the large numbers of foreign tourists in Varna were attracted by popular beach resorts and opportunities for travel to other Black Sea border states. Among other ventures, currency trading, "trader-tourism" in clothing and other goods, and prostitution are common.

According to estimates by the police and doctors at the Varna Medical University, there were approximately 750 Roma heroin users in Maksouda in 1999. The users were predominately young, between 13 and 35 years old, with two-thirds between 15 and 25. While a few began using heroin before 1989, serious heroin trade and usage took off after the transition, with the increase in travel opportunities. Drugs, including heroin, marijuana, and cocaine, are either bought abroad or brought in by traders from countries.

"There wasn't such a thing before. But when this democracy came, it began all of a sudden. It is mainly [people] from poor families that became addicts. There are also some from rich families, but not so many," said Milko, 40 years old.

More recently, addicts have shifted from smoking and inhaling heroin to intravenous injections. While no HIV cases have been reported yet, there have been hepatitis outbreaks among users. The Varna university hospital has a substance abuse clinic, and many users interviewed identified it as an important source of help and hope for breaking the cycle of addiction.

Source: Konstantinov 1999.

more difficulty rentering the job market than other groups and consequently have become caught in a vicious cycle of impoverishment.

The next two chapters examine these issues further, at the country level through case studies. Persistent disadvantages in education, including low school attendance and overrepresentation in special schools, which limit future opportunities, create a high probability that without policy interventions, the next generation of Roma will remain in poverty.

Chapter 3
Poverty and Exclusion: Roma Settlements in the Slovak Republic

The situation of Roma in the Slovak Republic is unique in a number of respects. More Roma in Slovakia live in settlements on the outskirts of villages and towns than is the case in other countries in the region. Many of these settlements are rooted in exclusionary policies adopted during the Second World War and early socialist period that curbed the rights of Slovak Roma in many ways, including housing. Regulations allowed Roma to enter towns and villages only on certain days and at specific times and ordered them to move their homes a minimum distance of two kilometers from all public roads. This policy formed the basis for the establishment of many Roma settlements, which still exist in Slovakia today.

The geographic and ethnic characteristics of settlements vary significantly. An estimated one-quarter of Roma in Slovakia live in settlements, many of which are in the poorer, eastern regions of the country. The actual number is difficult to gauge, because of the difficulties in measuring the Roma population and defining a "settlement." Living conditions for Roma in settlements are generally worse than for the rest of the Roma population. In this chapter, a settlement refers to a group of people living together in a distinct geographic area, either within or outside of a town or village.

As highlighted in the previous chapter, Roma poverty is multidimensional, encompassing many aspects beyond low income. This chapter explores interrelated aspects of Roma poverty and vulnerability further, including the material dimensions of poverty—nutrition, clothing, and housing—and access to opportunities in the labor market, and social services. It discusses the particular nature of exclusion that Roma experience in settlements in Slovakia.

The chapter aims to address information gaps by bringing together findings from qualitative case studies of Roma settlements with existing surveys. Sociological fieldwork was undertaken to supplement the incomplete picture given by the quantitative data (see box 3.1). Indeed, there is currently no quantitative survey that allows for an assessment of Roma living conditions in Slovakia. This is the first of the chapters in this volume that draws on country-level qualitative analysis. The chapter first provides historical background and current data on the population of Roma in Slovakia. It then describes the nature of poverty in Roma settlements, Roma labor market status, and coping strategies. Finally, the chapter addresses access to public services, including education and social assistance.

ROMA IN SLOVAKIA

Historical Background

The oldest references to Roma living in the territory of the Slovak Republic date back to 1322. Roma came to the area as settlers and

BOX 3.1 THE STUDY OF ROMA SETTLEMENTS IN SLOVAKIA

This chapter is based on a qualitative study of conditions in Roma settlements in three contrasting districts in Slovakia. In each district, Slovak sociologists conducted in-depth interviews with individuals, households, and local public figures, including teachers, doctors, social assistance workers, religious leaders, and local government officials. The research was conducted during December 2000 and January 2001.

The study examined the characteristics and correlates of poverty, conditions in the settlements, and the experience of Roma in these areas. Although the survey is not representative and is subject to the limitations of qualitative research, such as the biases of individual field researchers, the results provide a snapshot of the conditions of Roma in geographically and socioeconomically diverse locations. Where available, quantitative evidence complements the analysis. Three districts were ranked based on unemployment levels and the share of the population receiving social assistance.

- *Malacky* is a better-off district with below-average unemployment (13.5 percent in 1999) and share of population receiving social assistance benefits. Malacky is in the Bratislava region near the capital city. There are very few segregated settlements in Malacky.
- *Stará Lúbovna* is an average region in terms of unemployment, social assistance beneficiaries, and composition of Roma settlements. The district is located in eastern Slovakia in the Prešov region, where the concentration of Roma is high.
- *Rimavská Sobota* is a relatively poor district in the Banská Bystrica region, with a high unemployment level (35 percent in 1999) and a high share of the population receiving social assistance.

The study looks at poverty, including the lack of access to education and employment, income insecurity, social exclusion, and the lack of opportunities for participation in civil society. Poverty is defined in different ways, based on self-assessment of Roma and the interviewers' assessment of material conditions, including housing conditions, nutrition, health care, and access to public services. These measures are inherently subjective and the interviewers' assessments of poverty did not always coincide with those of the households being interviewed.

nomadic groups with travel permits issued by the Holy Roman emperor and the pope. Roma who settled in Slovakia worked as castle musicians and metalworkers and served in the Hungarian royal armies. Anti-Roma policies began to emerge in the fifteenth century in Europe and intensified in the Hungarian Kingdom in the sixteenth century, after the Turkish occupation of central Hungary, when Roma were thought to be Turkish spies. As a result, Roma settlers were restricted to living on the outskirts of towns and villages, and metal-workers were allowed to sell only a limited quantity of goods.[26]

Restrictive policies continued during the early Austro-Hungarian Empire in the eighteenth century. Leopold I declared Roma to be out-laws and ordered all Roma men to be hanged. Policies changed under Empress Maria Theresa and Joseph II, her son and successor. Both sought to assimilate Roma as citizens within the empire. Legislative measures required Roma to settle, pay taxes, and provide compulsory service to local landowners. Other edicts included mandated school and church attendance and improvement of housing infrastructure.

These policies were the first step toward settling the Roma, a fea-ture that still distinguishes Roma in Central and Eastern Europe from those living in Western Europe. Although these policies aimed at assimilation, sometimes aggressively, they also represented the first time that Roma were treated as state citizens. Austro-Hungarian meas-ures were used as models for other European countries, which aimed to assimilate Roma in the nineteenth and the twentieth centuries.

World War II

The Czechoslovak Republic (1918–38) passed legislation that limited the mobility and civil rights of Roma, particularly of nomadic and homeless groups. Laws mandated identification cards and fingerprinting. Condi-tions deteriorated substantially during World War II. Like the Jews, Roma throughout Europe were targeted with discriminatory legislation and subsequently extermination under the "Final Solution." During the course of the "Devouring," as Roma call the Holocaust, approximately one-half million Roma from across Europe were killed.

Roma experience in the Czech and Slovak Republics during the Holocaust differed significantly. The majority of Czech Roma were killed in concentration camps.[27] In contrast, fewer Roma from Slova-kia were deported to camps, although many were sent to forced labor camps. In 1941, several labor camps were established specifically for Roma, where workers lived under extremely poor conditions.

After the German army invaded Slovakia in September 1944, the sit-uation for Slovak Roma became increasingly dire. Mass executions were conducted in several towns and villages, and Roma living in the south and southeastern parts of Slovakia, which were annexed to Hungary during the war, were transported to the Dachau concentration camp.

After World War II, large numbers of Roma migrated from Slova-kia into Czech lands in search of better living conditions and employment. In many cases, migration was driven by state policies, which forced Roma out of certain areas. Over several years, more than 15,000 Roma migrated westward. As a result, the majority of Roma living in the Czech Republic today are originally from Slovakia.

The Socialist Period

The Czechoslovak socialist regime, which came to power after the war, adopted policies aimed at assimilating Roma and eliminating ethnic differences. These measures left behind a legacy that has affected Roma socioeconomic status into the transition period. The government refused to officially recognize Roma as an ethnic minority, but rather identified them as "citizens of a gypsy origin." Without the rank of ethnic minority, Roma lacked certain legal and cultural rights. Among other constraints, this implied that Roma cultural activities were banned. Roma were not allowed to establish their own music ensembles or youth or sports clubs. Roma folk songs could not be sung at schools, and Roma books and magazines were banned.

There were stringent and aggressive assimilation policies in the areas of housing, employment, and school attendance. In 1959, the government embarked upon a violent campaign against nomadism and drew up plans for a "dispersal and transfer" scheme, which aimed to resettle Roma from areas in eastern Slovakia to Czech lands. This program was never fully implemented, although many Roma families were transported to the Czech Republic against their will. A Commission for the Problems of the Gypsy Population in Slovakia coordinated the program; the commission was established in 1966 under the auspices of the Presidium of the Slovak National Council. In 1967 alone, 3,178 Roma were resettled from Slovakia. Of that number, a total of 1,034 Roma returned to Slovakia within the same year.

To combat nomadism, state officials broke up caravans, sometimes slaughtering horses in the middle of the night (Fraser 1995). Policies relaxed somewhat during the period of the Prague Spring reforms in 1968. Roma began to form official organizations for the first time, and approximately 200 Roma musical groups and 30 football clubs were established.[28] Forced migration and resettlement policies resumed following the Soviet crackdown in 1969. Between 1972 and 1980, 4,000 Roma dwellings were destroyed and 4,850 Roma were resettled.

Efforts to improve school attendance were similarly forced. Regulations were issued to implement compulsory schooling. Since the objectives were not communicated to parents, they viewed school attendance as an externally imposed obligation. School attendance did increase dramatically. In 1971, only 17 percent of Roma finished compulsory education; by 1980, this number increased to 26 percent. However, many were enrolled in "special schools" intended for the mentally and physically disabled. These practices have persisted, and large numbers of Roma children in both the Czech and Slovak Republics still study in special schools.

Roma in Slovakia after 1989

With the Velvet Revolution in November 1989 came new opportunities for minorities to express their ethnic identity and participate in civil society. In January 1991, the new Declaration of Basic Human Rights and Freedoms, which the Czechoslovak Federal Assembly adopted, allowed for the free determination of ethnic identity. Subsequently, in April, the government of the Slovak Republic adopted "The Principles of Government Policy Regarding Roma." For the first time in history, Roma were recognized as an independent ethnic minority, with equal status to that of other minorities living in the Slovak Republic.

The first Roma political party, the Romany Civic Initiative, was established after the transition in November 1989. Other parties and cultural associations soon followed. In the 1990 parliamentary elections, Roma were elected to parliamentary posts for the first time, and other Roma representatives were appointed to positions within the Office of the Government, the Ministry of Culture, and the Ministry of Education.

Government activity related to Roma issues accelerated in the late 1990s, with increased local and international attention. In November 1997, the Slovak cabinet adopted the "Conceptual Intents of the Slovak Republic for the Solution of the Problems of Romany Population under Current Social and Economic Conditions." The document outlined the issues facing Roma and institutional responsibilities to address them.

One of the most significant developments was the establishment of the Office of the Plenipotentiary for Roma Communities after the 1998 elections. The office falls under the jurisdiction of the deputy prime minister for human rights, minorities, and regional development and has been headed by a Roma since 1999. The office is charged with implementing government policy regarding Roma.

In 1999, the new government adopted "Strategy of the Slovak Government to Solve Problems of the Romany Ethnic Minority and the Set of Implementation Measures." The document formulated a more detailed action plan for policy measures related to Roma issues. A second phase of this strategy was adopted in May 2000, which further detailed measures to be undertaken. The document charged ministers and heads of regional public administration offices with specific responsibilities. The focus areas within the strategy were human rights, education, unemployment, housing, social security, and health. The strategy was limited in that it failed to specify financing levels and sources for the activities.

Population

The Slovak Republic has one of the largest population shares of Roma in Europe. According to the 2001 census, Roma represent 9.7 percent of the population, making them the second largest minority in the country after Hungarians. As many likely do not report their ethnicity in the census, the actual size of the population is thought to be between 10 and 11 percent of the population, or between 420,000 and

500,000 people. The share of Roma in the population is likely to rise in coming years because of high birth rates. Demographic projections have indicated that Roma could become a majority of the population in Slovakia by 2060 (*Economist* 2001).

A survey of district officials estimated that there were 591 Roma settlements in Slovakia in 1998, in comparison with 278 in 1988.[29] The total number of people living in settlements also has grown dramatically. In 1988 there were approximately 14,988 people living in settlements, and by 1997, this figure had grown to 123,034. During the past decade, some Roma have returned to settlements because of a lack of affordable housing. This, in addition to the high birth rate among Roma living in settlements, largely explains the increase.[30]

The demographic profile of Roma in Slovakia is considerably different from that of the total population. The Roma population is significantly younger and has been growing more rapidly than other ethnic groups. The national birthrate for Slovakia has declined steadily during the transition period from 15.2 live births per 1,000 people in 1990 to 10.7 in 1998 (UNICEF 2000). In contrast, birthrates among Roma have been increasing, especially in the most isolated, segregated settlements. Roma life expectancy is considerably lower than the national average, although recent data are not available. Estimates derived from the 1970 and 1980 censuses put life expectancy for Roma at 55 years for men and 59 years for women, in comparison with 67 for men in the total population and 74 for women (ECOHOST 2000).

POVERTY IN ROMA SETTLEMENTS

In general, there are three types of settlements based on living arrangements between Roma and non-Roma. The first are completely integrated towns and villages. This is the case of Nová Lúbovňa in the Stará Lúbovňa district, a district of average development in the east of the country. The second are separated areas, where Roma live together within a town or village, either on the outskirts or within a particular street or neighborhood, as in Studienka in Malacky. The third type are segregated settlements that are situated outside of the village or town, such as Kyjatice in the Rimavská Sobota district, a settlement 3 kilometers from the nearest town. These definitions are subjective and are used to document general patterns. In particular, the distinction between separated and segregated settlements is frequently blurred.

This study found that poverty has different characteristics in the Roma and non-Roma populations in Slovakia. Poverty among Roma is closely linked to four main factors: (i) regional economic conditions; (ii) the size and concentration of the Roma population in a settlement;

(iii) the share of Roma in a settlement; and (iv) and the degree of geographic integration or segregation of the settlement and its proximity to a neighboring village or town.

The situation of Roma in more economically developed regions is generally more favorable than that of Roma in poorer areas. For example, in 1999, the living conditions of Roma in Malacky, a district with a lower unemployment rate (14 percent) than the national average (17 percent) and close to Bratislava (less than 50 kilometers), were better than conditions in Rimavská Sobota, a district with 35 percent unemployment. Roma houses in segregated settlements in Malacky resembled those of the majority population. They were generally made of solid materials, such as bricks, and had access to electricity. In contrast, housing conditions in settlements in Rimavská Sobota were poorer. Roma there lacked access to basic services, and their health and education status was worse.

Within regions, the poverty level in a Roma settlement appears to be closely connected to its geographic location, the level of ethnic integration, and segregation. Conditions in settlements, which consisted only of Roma, were significantly worse than in more integrated communities. This leads to a vicious cycle: the more isolated and segregated the settlement, the more severe and deep the poverty, the fewer opportunities residents have to leave and work outside of the settlement, and consequently, the higher the chances are that Roma will continue to live in isolated settlements and remain in poverty.

This level of spatial separation is positively correlated to the poverty level. The social status of Roma living in segregated settlements is considerably lower than that of those who are integrated among the majority population. Roma living in segregated settlements in marginalized regions are significantly worse off than those who live in segregated settlements in more developed and economically better-off regions.

The concentration of Roma also matters. The poverty level in areas with a higher share of Roma in the population is higher than in areas where the population density of Roma is lower. Poverty among Roma in districts where at least 5 percent of the population was "officially" classified as Roma—which likely underestimates the true population—was consistently worse than those for the region as a whole.

With the exception of Roma in completely integrated areas and some in separated settlements in better-off regions, high unemployment and dependence on social assistance were common in Roma settlements. While the national unemployment rate was 18 percent in 2000, in the qualitative sample for Roma it was approximately 85 percent. This was due to the inclusion in the sample of segregated settlements where unemployment often reaches almost 100 percent.

The contrasts between Roma living in segregated and integrated areas cut through this chapter. In general, Roma in integrated areas are less poor than Roma living in settlements, and they have greater access to opportunities in the labor market and education. Conversely, Roma living in isolated and marginalized settlements have limited chances for upward mobility and interactions with the rest of society. As conditions within settlements appear to be worsening over time, and the population living in settlements is growing, some observers have noted the emergence of an "underclass" of Roma in Slovakia who are being left behind in the processes of economic and political transition. The following sections explore the extent of poverty among Roma, its roots, and correlates.

Perceptions of Poverty

Roma in urban and rural areas define poverty in both relative and concrete terms (see box 3.2). For most Roma, poverty is a recent phenomenon, and they describe their living conditions mainly in relation to the past. Although none of those interviewed described themselves as prosperous before 1989, most felt that they had lived well relative to prevailing living standards. A minority said that they had always been "poor." The most salient comparison with communism for older Roma was that they all had jobs.

Roma associate the socialist regime with an abundance of job opportunities and benefits, including subsidized consumer goods, utilities, and animals for breeding. Roma also recall having more housing options and better relationships between citizens. A Roma respondent reflected, "People are not as willing to help each other as they used to be because everyone has troubles today." Another noted, "During communism we were better off because everyone had to work, even if it was pointless or unskilled work."

Many Roma also related their descriptions of poverty to their current circumstances. Roma living in segregated areas, as well as many in separated areas, explained that the worst aspects of their present situation were poor housing conditions, overcrowding (e.g., number of people per bed), lack of infrastructure, poor health, lack of adequate food and clothing, lack of a reliable social network, unemployment, and social exclusion. A Roma respondent from a separated settlement explained: "We are poor because we don't have a proper house, we don't have any money and no one to borrow from."

It was common for households living in poor, segregated settlements to identify food insecurity as a main element of their poverty. One woman explained that it was difficult for her to feed her children properly all the time: "We have no cash most of the month to buy food on a regular basis and nobody will give us anything. Here we all have the same condition." Generally, Roma from segregated settlements in marginalized regions associated poverty with material insecurity, while Roma in more developed and integrated regions perceived poverty in relation to secondary needs, such as employment, quality education, and a more inclusive society.

Many Roma also compared their situations to those of fellow citizens. Unemployed Roma living close to non-Roma felt much worse off in comparison with others. Many Roma living in villages or towns with non-Roma believed that it was more difficult for them to find work than their non-Roma neighbors. As one said, "Nowadays all the work is for *gadje*."[31] In contrast, Roma in segregated settlements were less likely to compare themselves to non-Roma.

Insecurity and Shame

Poverty has important social and psychological components. Respondents living in segregated settlements describe poverty as associated with feelings of defenselessness and exclusion from the larger community. Poverty for many is also associated with shame. Even those respondents who appeared extremely poor to the interviewers often preferred to define themselves as "close to" but not completely "poor." For the very poorest, however, "not completely poor" means little more than "not dying of hunger." These responses have their roots in communism, which stigmatized poverty as a consequence of personal failure and laziness.

Many Roma feel that existing institutions are hostile, or at best indifferent, to their predicament. In particular, they lack trust in local governments and related institutions, mainly social assistance offices, and to a lesser extent schools and health care centers. The majority of Roma living in segregated and separated settlements describe a loss of hope for the future and a pervasive sense of uncertainty and insecurity.

Generational and Gender Differences

Although young Roma are less likely to compare their situation to the past than their parents, the experience and interpretation of "poverty" does not vary much across generations. Most young people identify the same problems and constraints in their lives as their parents: lack of jobs, inadequate education, and a sense of exclusion.

For young married couples, poverty means the inability to live independently from their parents, to start life on their own, and to enjoy privacy and independence. In many settlements, young couples live with their parents or their in-laws in a one- or two-room dwelling with three or four of their siblings. Due to the low availability of housing and high costs, many young Slovaks live with their parents; however, circumstances are especially difficult for Roma in poor areas where the size and quality of housing is extremely low.

Perceived poverty among young Roma also has a gender dimension. Some young girls noted that they were worse off than the young men in their communities and had access to fewer opportunities in employment and education. They felt that their only option was to start having children at an early age. A number of young women said that they could not even get unskilled work, while young men in their community at least had the possibility of participating in public works or unskilled jobs. These patterns likely reflect barriers to employment for young women, as well as traditional gender roles for women in closed communities.

The poorest respondents identified common elements of poverty, including inadequate nutrition, (e.g., insufficient food and nutritional composition), poor housing, and ill health. The ability to provide a good education for their children and lead a better life—for example, having opportunities to travel—were also identified by some Roma as important, but this took second place to the more immediate issues of hunger and shelter.

BOX 3.2 TYPOLOGY OF PERCEPTIONS OF SOCIAL STATUS

Roma can be categorized into four groups based on their perceptions of their social status:

1. **Non-Poor:** These Roma do not consider themselves poor, but rather view themselves as average Slovaks. They believe that there are many people who are worse off and that the transition has not led to dramatic changes in their lives: "The only difference between Christmas today and Christmas during the communist period is that today there are fewer presents." In their view, the problems are national, including inflation, unemployment, and subsequent constraints on living standards. This group constitutes a small share of the respondents living in integrated areas (e.g., approximately 25 percent in Malacky) who are either employed or engaged in the informal economy.

2. **Subjectively poor:** This statement characterizes this group: "We are not rich but we are able to support ourselves." This is typical of integrated Roma who believe that the demographic groups hit most severely by poverty include elderly people, young families, and Roma from eastern Slovakia. Their views about more segregated Roma are similar to non-Roma views of Roma: "People there are worse off than dogs, but they are to blame. They should take better care of themselves. When they don't have a job, they should at least keep themselves and their house clean." The majority of people expressing these views had a better starting

(continued)

Box 3.2 (*continued*)

point after 1989; they lived in integrated localities in better-off regions, and most owned their homes.

3. **Relatively poor**: These Roma perceive themselves to be poor and are generally unemployed and living on social benefits: "It is bad without a job, we live from one day to another." Most lived in integrated and partially separated types of settlements and face difficulties in reentering the labor market because of low education levels: "I have no clue what could help us out. If we could turn back time, we would get a proper vocational training or move to another country. People on TV say that everybody is doing better there and that everybody has a job."

4. **Absolutely poor**: This group of poor live mostly in segregated settlements in marginalized regions. They express a strong sense of apathy and helplessness and feel totally excluded from mainstream society: "We have nothing here, no roads, no electricity, no running water, no job. Nobody helps us either, not the mayor, or even the priest in the village." Some receive social assistance benefits, however, in certain cases some have lost eligibility because of lack of documentation and unofficial residency status.

Material Dimensions of Poverty

Hunger and Nutrition

Prior to 1989, very few households had difficulty obtaining basic foodstuffs, because of near-full employment and subsidized consumer goods. Today, the circumstances have changed. Roma households in the poorest settlements reported difficulties in affording sufficient food and maintaining adequate nutrition. Child malnutrition, in particular, was observed to be a frequent problem. Researchers observed evidence of stunting among some children. Some teachers reported that Roma children do not receive school lunches because their parents are unable to pay. A school director in Stará Lúbovňa noted that "in the entire primary school, only one child goes to lunch at school."

Some elderly Roma also reported problems in maintaining adequate food intake and explained that they were unable to afford necessary foods because of the low levels of welfare benefits. An elderly Roma man from the village of Rimavská Píla related that he had to maintain a high protein diet for medical reasons, but could not afford it.

Roma in integrated and segregated communities have contrasting strategies for ensuring adequate nutrition. Roma in integrated, as well as many in separated areas, prefer to plan ahead and economize to secure enough food for the rest of the month, regardless of their employment status. Those who live in rural areas and own land are able to grow vegetables during the summer months, and some do so. The wife of an unemployed Roma man in a community in Stará Lúbovňa reported that they tend to buy things, which last, such as potatoes and beans in bulk. As much as possible, she makes sure that her children have sufficient food, despite the fact that her husband is unemployed and they live mainly on social assistance, "Sometimes I buy on credit, but usually I make sure that we have enough to feed our family during the month."

In contrast, Roma in segregated settlements focus more on their immediate survival and are less able to plan ahead. Consumption tends to increase after social assistance payments are made. A Lipovec resident in the Rimavská Sobota district noted, "Why not eat now that we have money? It doesn't matter what comes tomorrow." In the town of Podolínec in Stará Lúbovňa, a doctor who sees patients from a number of nearby settlements reported that she sometimes sees dehydrated babies. Mothers explain that they have no money for milk after their social assistance benefits run out. Many Roma from marginalized settlements, including some poorer integrated settlements, admitted that during the week before social assistance benefits were paid their family often had one simple meal for the entire week. Many also said that they had to buy cheap food items to make it through the month. A woman explained, "We have to buy the cheapest food and prepare it so that the whole family will not feel hungry. I use fatty meat and potatoes to feed my family."

Very few residents in segregated settlements had access to land to grow food for their own consumption. Some pick mushrooms or berries from the forests. Non-Roma living in nearby villages reported that Roma steal potatoes and other food items from their fields.

Housing Policies

Most Roma in segregated settlements do not own their homes or land. In some settlements, property ownership is unclear. This prevents the improvement of housing conditions—since individuals and local governments are unable to maintain or invest in buildings or local infrastructure. Roma were more likely than non-Roma to have been left out of the property and land privatization processes that took place during the early 1990s. During the communist period, houses were mostly privately held, while the land belonged to the state. The "tenants" would rent their house or flat for 99 years from the state. After 1989, the government privatized land or gave it to municipal governments. The land was then given to the tenants for free if the house had a valid building permit, or appropriate legal status, and if the property was registered with the land-registry office and there were no pending applications for restitution. If these conditions were met, the tenant could apply for the transfer of property to his or her name.

Public communication regarding the process was limited, and many people were unaware of their options and the steps needed to initiate the transfer of land. In theory, the mayor was responsible for informing residents of their rights. However, in practice, few mayors did so. With the exception of one mayor in Stará Lúbovňa, no other mayors in the settlements included in this study provided information to their constituents without being explicitly asked. Roma in integrated areas were more likely to learn about the process from their neighbors, while Roma in segregated areas had more limited access to information. As a result, a larger share of integrated Roma were able to secure property ownership. Those who do not own their land are limited in their ability to make needed improvements to their homes. A man from Kyjov, a segregated Roma settlement in Stará Lúbovňa, explained: "We built our house with a building permit, but there are still problems with the site, although it was officially given to us during socialism. But today the land is not ours, therefore we cannot install any water, gas, or sewage pipes."

Roma in segregated areas face substantial challenges with legalizing their homes. The vast majority of houses in segregated settlements were built illegally, mostly on land with unclear ownership. In some of these settlements, such as the village of Jabloňové in Malacky, Roma moved into the village in the early 1990s and began to build houses on municipal land at the edge of the village. As a result, they do not have legal access to electricity and water. To access electricity, they tap into homes of neighbors who have legal connections and pay them directly.

Houses are often constructed with makeshift materials, do not comply with basic construction standards, and were built without the required permits. Some Roma explained that the only way that they could afford to build a shelter for themselves was to use materials that they found around their settlements, in forests, or in garbage dumps. One explained, "We can never have legalized housing and obtain a permit, so why ask." This creates a vicious circle in which buildings do not have legal status and, as a result, municipalities cannot provide funds for investment in infrastructure, such as roads and public services.

Roma are also poorly positioned to borrow money because of their economic status and lack of access to information on processes and procedures. Loan criteria have become more demanding since 1989, and the process for obtaining a building permit has become extremely complex. Current requirements include 32 individual permits and approvals from different government bodies. The research team encountered many unfinished homes that consisted of one or two rooms and a kitchen. Many of the occupants began building before 1989 and were unable to finish construction because of lack of financial resources and building permits. A Roma in Stará Lúbovňa explained, "I started to build this house before 1989, but could not finish it because I have no chance to put together enough money and cannot get a loan."

Housing Conditions

Housing conditions vary substantially between integrated and segregated areas. Conditions are the poorest in the most isolated and segregated settlements (see box 3.3). The homes of Roma living in more integrated areas and those separated within a village are similar, and it is frequently not possible to identify the owner's ethnicity from the outside of the house.

In segregated settlements, with the exception of Malacky, Roma houses are typically made of wood or scrap metal, plaster, tin, and tree branches. However, the construction type varies within regions depending on the kind of building materials available in the area. In Kolačkov village in Stará Lúbovňa, there is only one stone house, while the others are constructed from wood and clay. In the same district, in Kyjov village, houses and shacks are made of a mixture of stone and other materials, while in Šarišské Jastrabie stone houses are the norm. In Lomnička, a settlement of 1,200 people with only 100 houses, the majority (over 90 percent) of the houses are built from stones and bricks.

The extent of overcrowding within Roma houses is closely related to the degree of segregation and geographic isolation of the community. In general, in both Roma and non-Roma houses in integrated areas, the qualitative study found approximately one and a half people per room, while in segregated settlements, there was an average of three to four people per room.[32] Estimates by district officials put the number of people per dwelling in Roma settlements at nine in 1997.

Box 3.3 Housing Conditions in a Village in Stará Lúbovňa

Kolačkov is a segregated settlement of 220 inhabitants in the Stará Lúbovňa district. None of the houses in the settlement are legally registered. Unemployment is nearly 100 percent. In the village, a family of seven people (the parents, their oldest daughter of 17 who is a newlywed and pregnant, her husband, and three other children) lives in a two-room shack constructed from wood and tin. The house lacks access to water and sewage, and there is no garbage collection in the settlement. The family has a wood-burning stove, which they use for heating and cooking.

Access to Utilities and Public Services

Access to utilities and public services is non-existent or limited in most marginalized settlements. The most serious problems include lack of access to electricity, water, sewage, and garbage collection. Integrated settlements and separated settlements within a town or village were more likely to be connected to services. In the better-off district of Malacky, all settlements, with one exception, had access to electricity and roads. In the other districts, more isolated settlements did not have access to utilities.

Water. Many settlements lack access to running water. Five of the seven segregated settlements in the study and four out of 10 separated settlements had no access to running water. In some areas, residents linked poor health conditions to the inadequacy of the water supply. Residents of Rimavská Píla in Rimavská Sobota complained that their drinking water was contaminated and caused diarrhea, parasites, and trachoma among children. In other areas, parents blamed epidemics of scabies and lice on the lack of running and hot water for washing.

Electricity. In some of the most isolated settlements, electricity was unavailable. In Stará Lúbovňa, two settlements lacked coverage, and in four settlements, households were receiving electricity through illegal connections. The situation was similar in Rimavská Sobota, where seven of the 13 settlements either lacked electricity or relied on illegal sources. Residents of Rimavská Sobota explained that the lack of electricity was particularly problematic in the winter, as it is difficult for them to afford candles or fuel.

Waste Collection. Lack of garbage collection also seriously affects living conditions and creates health problems for residents. In the majority of segregated settlements, garbage collection was either non-existent or sporadic because residents were unable to afford the service. Even in three segregated settlements in Malacky—Lozorno, Malé Leváre, and Plavecký Štvrtok—where nearly all homes had access to electricity, residents complained about the lack of garbage collection. They noted that waste dumps were located near to their settlements, but there were not enough waste bins, and collection was irregular.

The situation was even worse in the poorer districts of Stará Lúbovňa and Rimavská Sobota. In most settlements in these districts, even if garbage collection facilities did exist, residents often complained that the municipalities only collected the garbage a couple of times a year (e.g., twice a year in Jakubany, or once in Lúbotín in Stará Lúbovňa). As a result, some residents throw their garbage into a nearby stream or in the area around the containers.

Roma also complained that garbage dumps were too close to their settlements, leading to the contamination of land and water, and in some cases, attracting rats and stray dogs and cats. Many local authorities blamed residents for not paying local fees for garbage collections. Mayors explained that some non-Roma communities purchased their own waste bins, while this was not the case in Roma settlements. Some mayors provided settlements with containers free of charge, but were unwilling to pay for waste removal. This was despite the fact that there is only a nominal charge for garbage collection.[33]

Lack of garbage collection perpetuates negative stereotypes about poor hygiene among Roma. Some non-Roma blame Roma for the situation of poor waste collection in settlements. An educated non-Roma commented:

> Gypsies are themselves responsible for the terrible situation around their communities. I know of a situation where there is a garbage bin close to a building occupied by gypsies, but since it is 20 meters from the building and they are too lazy to walk there, they just throw their garbage out of their windows.

Heating. Most Roma households rely on wood, the cheapest form of fuel, for heating. Gas was available to some households in integrated areas. In Stará Lúbovňa, households in three integrated settlements used gas. In one of the segregated settlements, only one household had access to gas. In Malacky, a few households in three settlements used gas, while the rest relied on wood. Roma generally expressed little interest in having gas pipes installed because of the significantly higher costs. In the majority of houses in rural areas, wood-burning fireplaces were used for both heating and cooking. Residents argued that they could not afford gas since it was extremely expensive to install a service pipe.[34]

Sewage. Only households in integrated areas have access to standardized plumbing. Most segregated and separated communities used septic tanks or nothing at all. A few households in each district have toilets, but the majority use latrines. In Stará Lúbovňa and Rimavská Sobota, toilets were available in three settlements included in the studies. In Malacky, with the exception of Plavecký Štvrtok, all settlements had access to toilets.

Household Assets

Ownership of cars was quite unusual. A few Roma in integrated and separated areas had cars. Only a limited number of households had telephones. In segregated settlements only a few residents owned cellular phones and cars, in many cases these were local moneylenders.

ECONOMIC ACTIVITIES AND COPING STRATEGIES

The emergence of unemployment has been one of the most serious social problems of economic transition in Slovakia. By 2000, unemployment had reached nearly 19 percent of the labor force—the highest rate in the Organisation for Economic Co-operation and Development (OECD). Unemployment is closely linked with poverty. Households headed by an unemployed member are more than six times more likely to be poor than households headed by an employed individual.[35] Roma were more immediately affected than other groups by enterprise downsizing at the outset of transition and now comprise a disproportionate share of the unemployed.

Education levels are closely related to labor market status in Slovakia. Unemployment rates for workers with basic education or less were close to 40 percent in 2000 (Sanchez-Paramo 2001). Workers with vocational and apprenticeship education have higher unemployment rates than workers who have completed general secondary education. Changes in labor market demand have favored workers with more flexible academic backgrounds, rather than narrow technical training. As discussed further below, very few Roma complete secondary education, and those that do are more likely to have participated in vocational and apprenticeship schools than academic secondary schools. The composition of registered unemployment by ethnicity reflects the education status of Roma (see figure 3.1).

Unemployment

The labor market status of Roma has changed dramatically during the transition period. Under socialism, many Roma held formal public sector jobs, most commonly in agricultural cooperatives, factories, public construction, and mines. Many of these enterprises closed or were substantially restructured over the last decade. A 1997 survey by the Ministry of Labor, Social Affairs and Family estimated that Roma comprised between 17 to 18 percent of the total unemployed in 1996, with this figure as high as 40 to 42 percent in eastern districts with large Roma populations (e.g., Košice, Spišská Nová Ves). Similarly, the National Labor Office registries, which contained ethnicity information until 1997, suggest that, for the country as a whole, Roma represented as much as one-quarter of all the registered unemployed in the Slovak Republic through 1999.[36] Furthermore, the share of Roma receiving unemployment benefits was lower than the share among the

FIGURE 3.1 REGISTERED UNEMPLOYMENT BY ETHNICITY, 1999

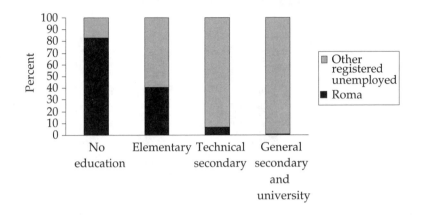

Source: Ministry of Labor, Social Affairs and Family, Slovak Republic.

total population. This was mostly due to the long duration of unemployment for Roma.

The majority of unemployed Roma have been out of work for over one year. According to Ministry of Labor, Social Affairs and Family data for the first half of 1999, 92 percent of Roma registered as unemployed had been out of work for over one year, in comparison with 63 percent of the total population, and 17 percent of Roma had been unemployed for over four years (see figure 3.2). Most of the Roma interviewed for the qualitative study had been out of work for over two years.

Even though unemployment is a problem faced by Roma across Slovakia, to a large degree its extent is linked to regional economic conditions. In Malacky, where the overall district unemployment rate was 13.5 percent in 1999, unemployment among Roma ranged from 60 percent in integrated settlements, to nearly 100 percent in the most segregated settlements included in the survey. In Stará Lúbovňa and Rimavská Sobota, where total unemployment rates were higher, unemployment among Roma was between 80 to 100 percent.

Many Roma identified ongoing unemployment and insecurity as the most demoralizing aspects of their lives. A resident of Klenovec in Rimavská Sobota who had found employment explained, "We were happy that we found a meaningful way of spending a day. In two or three years a man gets used to doing nothing and then it gets really tough." Another respondent noted, "When I had a job, it had a positive impact on the family because everybody felt more secure." Roma also expressed discouragement with the lack of employment opportunities. Roma in segregated settlements are particularly disadvantaged,

FIGURE 3.2 UNEMPLOYMENT BY DURATION, JUNE 30, 1999
(PERCENT OF TOTAL UNEMPLOYED)

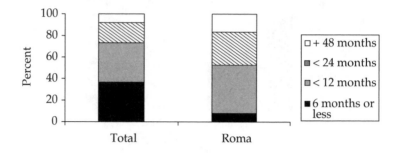

Source: Ministry of Labor, Social Affairs and Family, Slovak Republic.

as job prospects are generally limited to seasonal employment in neighboring towns and villages. A 35-year-old father of five in a marginalized settlement in Stará Lúbovňa explained: "Who is going to give me a job? I have no education, no skills, and am Roma. Even in my neighboring village nobody wants to give us any work."

Unemployment is high among young people, especially women. Most young Roma interviewed from the settlements who were under the age of 25 had never been formally employed. Young women generally do not enter the labor force because of early pregnancies. Many get married and begin having children soon after completing primary school. Nearly all of the girls over 18 interviewed for this study, with the exception of those from more integrated villages in Malacky, or those in completely integrated areas in other districts, were already married with children or pregnant. Women in more integrated areas were more likely to be employed in traditionally female jobs as teachers, cleaning ladies, or public administrators.

Employment

The employment status of Roma included in the survey differed according to the degree of segregation. The majority of Roma from highly integrated settlements had finished secondary vocational education and had regular jobs, regardless of gender. In contrast, of Roma who were employed in the settlements, most were engaged in unskilled labor, frequently in seasonal agricultural work, or construction. In many settlements, public works are the only source of employment. A few Roma were employed in more skilled labor, including construction and stone masonry, some with vocational training. However, not all Roma with vocational education had jobs.

Labor Mobility and Migration

Labor mobility is low among Roma and non-Roma in Slovakia. Of those Roma in the study areas who were employed, most worked in the immediate surroundings of their settlements, because of transportation costs. Very few Roma sought employment in neighboring districts or countries, such as the Czech Republic and Hungary. Those that did commute to the Czech Republic complained that their wages were too low to make it worthwhile and that employers were often late in paying wages or did not pay at all. Roma were more likely to work abroad if someone else in their family or settlement had gone first and had had a successful experience. Roma from Malacky and Stará Lúbovňa were working in the Czech cities of Hradec Králové and Ostrava. However, Roma noted that commuting had been more common during the socialist period: "Hardly anyone from our village goes to the Czech Republic these days, as it was in the past."

Other Roma work in construction or seasonal agriculture in nearby towns or villages, where transport expenses are lower. Moving permanently—or for extended periods of time—to other districts or towns was not an option for most Roma. Roma from segregated communities are too poor to afford to move, and those from separated communities are also discouraged from migration because of high costs and insecurity about finding work. It is more common for Roma families to move from towns and villages to settlements, rather than the other way around.

Discrimination

Many Roma cited ethnic discrimination as a significant barrier to employment, and as a rationale for not seeking work outside of their communities and villages. Although Slovakia has adopted anti-discrimination legislation, consistent with International Labor Organization conventions, Roma still described experiences of discrimination. A number of Roma related anecdotes about friends or relatives who had applied for a job and, although they were accepted over the phone, were subsequently rejected as soon as the employer realized that they were Roma. While none of the Roma in the study had experienced this directly, it undoubtedly had an effect on their readiness to apply for jobs.

A school director explained that a Roma had applied for a teaching position in his school. He had a difficult time deciding whether to hire her, since he suspected that non-Roma parents might protest his decision. In the end she was not hired. A director of a vocational school in Podolínec for cooks and waiters reported that he had difficulty finding restaurants, which would accept his Roma students for practical training.

Roma also explained that they were denied employment because of low education levels: "Even trained people have no chance to find a job, so how could I find one?" Women noted this problem even more than men: "Men are allowed to take jobs for which they are not trained, but from a woman, they always require that she be trained." Labor market discrimination was a source of stress for many Roma, and in many cases led people to give up their job search. A young Roma in Rimavská Sobota expressed a common sentiment: "No one will employ a Gypsy anyway. Why try?"

Public Works Programs

Many Roma participate in public works programs run by the Ministry of Labor, Social Affairs and Family through local municipalities. This program was initiated in 2000. Jobs generally last three months and most commonly involve unskilled work, such as cleaning streets and parks and garbage collection. Jobs do not include training or preparation for future employment. A significant share of Roma, especially those in separated settlements in all of the three districts, participated in these projects. However, these programs may not always reach Roma. In two localities, Roma explained that they were denied participation in the local public works program because the mayor preferred to hire a non-Roma applicant.

Some Roma respondents complained about the quality of work in the public works program and observed that, in some cases, work was focused almost exclusively on cleaning around non-Roma houses and ignored Roma neighborhoods and settlements. On the other hand, many Roma interviewed explained that public works were a better alternative to unemployment: "When a man has a job, it is easier to live, he is healthier, he has more energy and life is more fun."

Coping Strategies

Informal Sector Employment

Due to limited formal employment opportunities, many Roma work in the informal sector. Because of the absence of taxes and official and unofficial fees, informal employment is frequently more attractive than formal jobs for both employers and employees. Common activities include salvaging and selling scrap metal, petty trade, and part-time work in agriculture and construction.

One of most widespread informal economic activities for Roma in the study settlements was working as musicians. This was particularly the case for Roma in Jesenské, Hodejov, and the urban ghetto on Dúžavská Cesta in Rimavská Sobota. A few Roma had small workshops where they produce tools for construction workers, such as in Kaloša in Rimavská Sobota. Another common activity, mainly among those from segregated localities, was to salvage scrap material for resale. Other occasional and informal employment, especially for men, included helping non-Roma with minor construction tasks. Some men painted houses, and women worked as cleaning ladies.

Roma in geographically isolated and segregated areas have fewer opportunities for informal employment because their communities are closed off from broader society; moreover, they have limited connections outside of the settlement to help them find work. A number of Roma admitted to resorting to theft as a coping strategy, including stealing potatoes, firewood, and construction materials.

Access to Credit

Roma lack opportunities to borrow money and therefore have limited capacity to establish small businesses. Credit is scarce and costly for all small borrowers in the Slovak Republic, but Roma may face additional hurdles. In many cases Roma lack collateral to borrow because of unclear property ownership. Access to loans from commercial institutions is virtually zero. Some Roma do borrow small sums from neighbors, friends, and relatives, as well as through local Roma usurers. In some communities the Roma leader, or *vajda*, lends money, however, interest rates were reported to be extortionate—at 40 percent or higher, while the interest rate for consumer credit was around 14 percent.

Subsistence Farming

Growing food was not reported to be an important coping strategy for the majority of Roma, including those who actually own land. Many Slovaks cultivate land, including small plots and gardens, to support their consumption. This practice was common during the socialist period, although never for Roma. Nearly all Roma households in integrated settlements and some living on the margin of villages own at least a small amount of land. Most household plots are small, ranging from 8–10 × 3–4 meter plots in back of their houses, but may be larger if not adjacent to the house. Some more affluent households did cultivate land. Crops vary according to region and include potatoes, wheat, grapes, and vegetables.

The majority of Roma in segregated settlements do not own land. In two settlements in Stará Lúbovňa, families owned their homes and land and have been involved in agricultural activities for three generations. In Studienka and Malé Leváre in Malacky, all of the households owned land, but only half grew crops. Roma explained that they did not make use of land for a number of reasons. In some cases the plot was too small to be viable, in other cases the soil was poor, there was no convenient source of water, or the household could not afford the necessary inputs. Others explained that cultivation of land was not traditionally a Roma occupation.

Very few families raised animals. Some families in the settlements, including those without land, kept chickens and, in some cases, pigs. However, raising livestock for household or commercial use was not reported. This was mainly due to the lack of land. Only five families included in the study cultivated land and raised animals. Some non-Roma explained that the breeding of animals for home use had declined during the transition period. Prior to 1989, it was common for agricultural cooperatives to give employees animals for domestic use, but now "[Roma] do not breed them since no one hands out small pigs for free anymore."

ACCESS TO SOCIAL SERVICES

Roma in settlements are more likely to be geographically isolated and out of the range of coverage of health services and education— particularly preschool. Communication problems between non-Roma service providers and Roma also affect access and quality of services. Some Roma who are not fully proficient in the Slovak language are unable to communicate effectively with teachers, doctors, social workers, and other service providers. Social isolation and mistrust between Roma and non-Roma also influence relationships and access to services.

Education

According to the 1991 census, 77 percent of Roma had completed primary education, 8 percent had completed vocational training, and less than 2 percent had completed academic secondary or university education.[37] An earlier survey from 1990 found that 56 percent of Roma men and 59 percent of Roma women had not completed primary education (Vašečka 2000a). Education patterns of Roma in the settlements were consistent with this pattern. The majority of adults interviewed in the settlements had some primary education, although not all of them had completed all grades.

Almost all Roma from segregated areas, as well as some from separated areas, had not completed secondary school. In many cases, students dropped out after completing 10 years of compulsory education. Secondary education in Slovakia includes three main types of schools: *gymnasia* (or grammar schools); vocational schools; and specialized secondary schools. Gymnasia provide general academic training and prepare students to continue on to university. In 1998, 21 percent of Slovak secondary students were enrolled in gymnasia. None of the Roma interviewed for the study were enrolled in or had attended gymnasia.

Vocational schools include apprentice schools, which prepare students for specific occupations through two-year programs, secondary vocational schools, which offer two- to three-year programs, and secondary specialized schools, which prepare students for the labor market in specialized fields through professional programs. Most secondary school students are enrolled in vocational and apprentice schools—46 percent in 1998—and 33 percent in secondary specialized schools. Graduates from secondary vocational schools are not eligible to enter higher education institutions unless they complete an additional two years of education and pass an examination, while graduates from secondary specialized schools may continue on to university. The majority of Roma who had continued on to secondary school were enrolled in apprentice schools or secondary vocational schools. Roma from integrated areas and some better-off Roma from separated areas were more likely to attend secondary specialized schools. Most of the respondents who had graduated from these schools had jobs.

Many Roma do not see a direct relationship between education and employment, partly because of widespread unemployment. The majority of Roma in separated and segregated communities have only primary or unfinished secondary education. In general, unskilled workers have found it increasingly difficult to participate in the labor market. This may reflect in part the lack of demand for labor with low skills; it may also be due to high payroll taxes and other non-wage costs, which—given differences in productivity—make unskilled labor relatively costly compared to hiring workers with higher skills.

School Attendance

Teachers and school directors in the study districts reported that the attendance of Roma children had been declining since 1989. Particularly in the poorest settlements, many children were observed playing in the streets during the school day. Some doctors reported that Roma children came to them to ask to be excused from school. Very few Roma children in the areas visited for the study continued beyond compulsory education.

Under socialism, penalties for truancy were more stringent and frequently enforced through various mechanisms, including interrogation by the police, placement of children in institutions, and reduction of social benefits. Some examples of these types of penalties were found in the study sites. In Rimavská Sobota, teachers reported absent students to the police and cut welfare benefits to motivate attendance. As a result, many parents understood education more as an obligation to the state than to their children. One parent explained: "They must go to school, this is the law. The teacher was here and told us, if we do not send our children to school, we will lose our financial support."

Children from the most segregated and isolated settlements face the greatest challenges in accessing education. Some settlements are simply too small to be able to have their own school. In Malacky and Stará Lúbovňa, all separated settlements either had primary schools or there was a school close by. In Rimavská Sobota, five settlements included in the sample had fewer than 500 inhabitants and no primary school, so children commuted to neighboring villages. Roma mothers from Kyjov, in Stará Lúbovňa asked school officials not to let their children go on to the fifth grade because they were unable to pay for transportation to the new school.

Poverty and a lack of basic infrastructure are also notable barriers to school attendance. The absence of electricity in isolated settlements makes it difficult for children to study and do homework. Some Roma children need to stay home to help with housework and take care of siblings. As a result, they have difficulty keeping up with the curriculum. In the poorest areas, such as segregated settlements in Stará Lúbovňa and Rimavská Sobota, there were reports that children were unable to attend school because they lacked clothing and shoes.

Preschool Attendance

Few Roma children from segregated settlements attend preschools. Preschool in Slovakia is not compulsory and generally includes children between 3 and 6 years of age (see box 3.4). Most segregated settlements lack preschool facilities. An exception was the settlement in Plavecký Štvrtok in Malacky, where the church had opened a preschool mainly for the children of the settlement. Many parents interviewed did not recognize the value of preschool and felt that mothers could adequately prepare their children. A Roma mother explained, "All of my children are at home, together with me. I am at home, so why send them to kindergarten?" Parents also cited costs related to attending kindergarten, such as fees and clothing, as a deterrent. "Kindergarten is not free of charge. We would need to pay and we cannot afford that." [38]

Because Roma children begin primary school unprepared, they face additional difficulties in adapting to the school environment. These circumstances exacerbate preconceptions of non-Roma students and teachers that Roma are not capable of learning and lead to further exclusion. In many cases, Roma are placed in separate classes or special schools because of their lack of preparation.

Language

Roma in Slovakia also differ linguistically. Over half of Roma in Slovakia are thought to speak some of the Roma language, but it is not known how many speak it at home. Many Roma living in the south of the country speak Hungarian. Roma from isolated and segregated settlements may be introduced to the Slovak language only once they enter primary school.

Teachers are poorly equipped to handle this gap in the children's knowledge and, in some cases, send Roma children to separate class-rooms or special schools if they cannot keep up with the rest of the students. School directors explained:

> Children from segregated [Roma] settlements do not master the Slovak language and do not understand their teachers. The teachers do not speak the Roma language, so they communicate by using gestures.

> In a school where teachers do not speak the Roma language at all or only some, the first grade is not enough for these children to eliminate the gap [with other children].

> It is easier to remove the language barrier in mixed classes, but many Roma kids are in separate classes.

The issue is even more complex in ethnically diverse areas, such as Slovak-Hungarian areas in the south. In Rimavská Sobota, some chil-dren speak Hungarian in addition to the Roma language, but are not proficient in Slovak. Others are neither fully proficient in Slovak nor Hungarian, yet attend Hungarian schools. The situation is similar in some villages in Stará Ľubovňa, where most non-Roma speak Ruthenian.

Demand for Education

Low demand for education among some Roma families discourages children from attending school. This has its roots in chronic unem-ployment, which is common in many Roma settlements due to the lack of job opportunities and the disconnect between education and the labor market. The dismal labor market situation leads parents to undervalue the importance of education. A Roma parent noted, "My daughter completed secondary school, now she is sitting at home without work." Another asked, "Why force our children to study when there aren't jobs for the educated ones?"

In some cases, parents, especially those from integrated and sepa-rated localities where employment opportunities are greater, acknowl-edged the importance of education for their children's future. A grandparent in Malacky explained, "My grandson is a first-grade stu-dent. We sent him to kindergarten and hope in the future he will put more importance on education than we did." A resident of Rimavská

Sobota concurred: "I think that Roma should change. For example we need to make sure that our children go to better schools, because their future depends on that."

A significant share of Roma view education as a system representative of gadje society, which is of limited relevance for them. Parents explained: "From the beginning, since the first grade our children have difficulties understanding what is going on: other children are singing the songs we do not know." And "All poetry, literature, history is not about and from our life."

Parental Involvement

As there is low demand for education among Roma in isolated and segregated communities, Roma parents are less likely to be involved in their children's education. Many Roma students lack effective role models. Roma parents are frequently poorly positioned to help their children with schoolwork at home because of their own limited educational backgrounds. In more integrated areas some parents were involved in schools. A parent in Malacky noted the importance of being involved: "I help my children learn every day, if I miss out on one day of reading with my son, the very next day he has a problem. Therefore I help them study every day." However, most Roma students lack the advantages of other students whose parents assist their children with schoolwork and/or hire private tutors.

Box 3.4 Zero Grade Classes

"Zero grade classes" were first implemented in Slovakia in 1992 to prepare children for basic school through provision of basic social, cultural, and hygiene skills. Children attend zero grade class after preliminary psychological tests at the age of compulsory primary school attendance. These classes are located at primary schools. The zero grade program is designed to prepare children to attend regular compulsory first class after one year. Together with socialization, language preparation is emphasized along with basic skills such as reading and writing.

The zero grade program is mainly targeted to districts with high Roma populations. There are 61 primary schools out of 2,362 across Slovakia that have zero classes. There are 85 zero grade classes in these 61 schools, covering 1,057 children. These classes are free of charge and provided by teachers from regular primary schools.

Source: Ministry of Education, Slovak Republic.

Special Schools and Classes

Roma are at a higher risk of receiving lower quality education because of institutional factors and incentives, which lead to separate education for Roma and non-Roma. Special schools are a legacy from the socialist era and were designed to provide special education for children with mental and physical disabilities. A disproportionate share of Roma are enrolled in special schools. In the Czech Republic, which inherited a similar system, a 1997 survey indicated that 64 percent of Roma children in primary school were in special schools, in comparison with 4 percent of the total population (ERRC 1999). Although data are not available for Slovakia, the situation is likely to be similar. A majority of Roma students from the segregated settlements in the qualitative study attend special schools.[39] Students enrolled in special schools are at a dual disadvantage, first, because the curriculum is less rigorous and expectations of teachers are lower than in mainstream schools, and second, because opportunities for graduates of special schools are limited.

Even when Roma children are educated within the mainstream Slovak school system, they may be placed in separate Roma classes. The majority of primary schools in segregated and separated settlements have separate classes for Roma students. Maximum class sizes are low and provide teachers with a rationale for separating Roma children.[40] According to teachers, non-Roma parents favor this separation by arguing that Roma students slow down the educational process. These dynamics create an environment that can be hostile. A Roma mother in a village in Stará Lúbovňa observed, "Children are not racist. It is their parents that tell them to keep separate, and that is why they tease our kids and call them names."

Some Slovak teachers argued that Roma should attend special schools and classes because they need special care and assistance, which cannot be provided in a regular classroom. Others took an opposite view. A third grade teacher at a primary school in Šarišské Jastrabie in Stará Lúbovňa explained: "It is simplistic to consider these children mentally disturbed—and there should be even more reasons to step up the effort. If you can do it, they catch on."

Despite the disadvantages of special schools and classes, some parents interviewed believed that their children receive more attention at special schools and are not singled out. A Roma mother said, "The youngest son does not go to a kindergarten, since I am at home. My son and daughter go to a special school. At the beginning my son went to a normal primary school, but he was not good in reading, so the teacher suggested he go to a special one. We are satisfied with him, he gets only A's. We put our daughter into a special school ourselves." Most Roma parents expressed a preference for mixed classes, so that their children would be exposed to the Slovak language.

The director of a special school noted, "Approximately 30–40 percent of children attend special primary schools on the basis of their parents' decision. Sometimes, the parents do not want to put their first child here, but as they have more children, they find out that here the children achieve better results than in a 'normal' primary school." Roma parents also indicated that they preferred special schools because there are more Roma children and their children are "protected" from discrimination and hostility from non-Roma students. In some cases, special schools provide housing, making them more financially attractive to parents.

Teachers

Teachers are central to the quality of education and play an important role in motivating student attendance and performance. In many settlements, teachers were poorly prepared to work with Roma children. Many teachers interviewed expressed an interest in training and teaching materials in Roma culture and history, as very few of them had any knowledge of Roma issues. Prejudices and low expectations of Roma students by teachers can adversely affect student performance. This phenomenon manifests itself in different ways. Some parents complained that teachers did not let their students bring textbooks home because they believed Roma children would destroy them. As a result, students lacked the opportunity to do homework and adequately prepare for classes.[41]

The study also found a number of examples in which teachers and school directors took the initiative to reach out to Roma communities and support Roma children at school, but these sporadic examples stemmed from individual initiative. Educational advisors also played an important positive role in some schools. In Šarišské Jastrabie, advisors worked with Roma parents to encourage them to send their children to school and continue on to secondary education. In some communities, such as Jarovnice, Teplý Vrch, and Jabloňové in Malacky and Rimavská Sobota, teachers and school officials maintain close relations with Roma parents and children. They make frequent visits to Roma settlements and work to mitigate conflicts between children.

Some teachers visit Roma settlements on their own initiative to persuade parents to send their children to school. Because Roma from segregated and some from separated settlements often do not have officially registered residences, local and school officials would not know about some Roma children without the assistance of teachers. A teacher explained the challenge of convincing parents to send their children to school: "One boy told me that his father did not want to enroll him in a secondary school. So I invited his father to school and tried to convince him that it was a good idea. I think now [the boy's] chances are about 50-50."

In areas where teachers and school directors were more available and involved in their communities, Roma parents expressed satisfaction with the schools, and children were happy to attend school. Roma mothers explained:

> The teacher visits our settlements on a regular basis. She has bought some books for my children and also organized common afternoons for them.

> We go to school meetings, but that is not the only meeting with the teacher. He comes here, to the settlement, and borrows tapes with Romany music. Children then learn Romany songs with the teacher.

The interviews indicate that such initiatives have increased communication between Roma parents and schools in these communities.

Social Assistance

Social assistance benefits provide an important source of income for many Roma households. Nearly all of the long-term unemployed Roma interviewed for this study, and especially those living in poorer segregated settlements, are dependent upon social assistance benefits for income support. Many noted that these benefits were indispensable, but felt that they were not adequate to secure basic living conditions. For many outsiders, the dependency of Roma on benefits reinforced stereotypes of Roma as social parasites who would rather receive income support than work.

Reintegration of unemployed Roma workers into the labor force may be made more difficult by the distorted incentives arising from the design of the social safety net. Social assistance in Slovakia lacks mechanisms that allow benefits to taper off gradually as workers become employed, building pro-work incentives. Consequently, the system penalizes those who find employment and sets up a dependency trap. The relationship between the safety net design and distorted work incentives is not in any sense unique to Roma families, but the demographic characteristics of the Roma, with relatively low levels of educational attainment among the adults and a large number of children, make them particularly vulnerable to falling into this dependency trap.

Many Roma complained that the reforms to the Act on Social Assistance, which cut benefits for those who had been unemployed for two years or more, made it impossible for them to survive on social assistance. Although this change was intended to promote work incentives, Roma in isolated settlements were particularly disadvantaged because of the absence of job opportunities. Non-Roma social workers and local government officials also felt that the current system of child allowances and the subsistence minimum provided incentives for Roma to have large families. While there is no empirical evidence to confirm this, the importance of these benefits for the survival of many poor Roma families breeds resentment and contributes to the impression among non-Roma that Roma are overly dependent on the state.

Roma relations with social workers were reportedly more contentious than their relations with other public service providers. Roma view social workers as representatives of the state, and they are frequently the only contact Roma have with government authorities. Social workers are responsible for conveying "bad news" on eligibility for benefits and, as a result, are often the target of frustration with decisions that are not necessarily under their control.

Social workers are poorly prepared to work with Roma communities. This lack of preparation is linked to systemic problems within the welfare system itself. Social workers in Slovakia rarely do field visits and are not trained to work directly with clients. Instead, their jobs are largely administrative, focused on disbursing cash benefits. Social workers explained that they had no time left for field visits and complained about the administrative burden of their work: "Every time the law is amended, we have to check and review all files. We often work late in the evening and do not have time for fieldwork." Only two of the social workers interviewed for the study actually visited Roma settlements. The lack of contact between Roma and social workers contributes to poor communication on both sides.

Many Roma complained that social workers were not responsive to their needs. "They come to our settlement only when they want to screen us." It appeared that social workers were not effective at communicating with Roma, as many Roma lacked basic information on social assistance programs and eligibility criteria. Some Roma asked the interviewers for information on various benefits. In other cases, Roma appeared well versed in the eligibility criteria of benefits.

REDUCING POVERTY IN SETTLEMENTS

An important finding of the field work in Slovakia is that the degree of segregation and marginalization of a Roma settlement is correlated with the poverty level in the settlement. While these linkages need to be validated through further research, the basic findings are clear. Roma living in more remote and segregated settlements have fewer opportunities to participate in the mainstream economy, access social services, and tap into social networks and information about economic opportunties such as jobs. In other words, geographic and social exclusion are important correlates of poverty. In contrast, Roma in integrated areas are more likely to interact with non-Roma and are better informed and positioned to identify and take advantage of opportunities.

These results have important policy implications. In the first place, they highlight the diverse nature of Roma in Slovakia and the need for varied approaches to different circumstances. Secondly, they indicate that interventions, which reduce isolation and exclusion of Roma through integration, can facilitate the improvement of living conditions over the longer term. This does not imply that programs and policies should revert to the type of forced assimilation that was prevalent under the socialist period. Rather, policy and project design need to be sensitive to Roma culture and the desire of communities to maintain their cultural identity. This objective can be ensured through participation of Roma. A number of successful projects use Roma mentors as liasons between Roma and non-Roma communities. For example, Roma teacher assistants who work with parents or peer advisors who assist with job placement can facilitate integration, while strengthening the Roma community.

In 2004, the Slovak government set up a Social Development Fund to tackle poverty and exclusion in Roma settlements and other marginalized communities. Social development funds are demand-driven instruments that support local development projects in poor and marginalized communities. While the fund does not explicitly target Roma, its criteria for project selection are designed such that the poorest Roma settlements will be among the beneficiaries. The fund will provide capacity-building support to help communities identify their priorities and to design and implement projects, including small-scale infrastructure and community services, social services, and employment and training initiatives. While the fund is only one instrument for mitigating the severe conditions in Slovakia's settlements, it is promising as a mechanism for identifying the neediest communities, building bridges between Roma and non-Roma communities through joint development initiatives, and capacity building to give communities the tools and resources to improve their own living conditions.

Overcoming divisions between Roma and non-Roma communities is central to addressing poverty and exclusion. Measures in this regard need to involve Roma and non-Roma alike. Multicultural education and inclusion in the curriculum of the history and culture of Roma and other minorities is an important vehicle for overcoming cultural barriers. Training of teachers, local government officials, and other personnel working in social services can be important mechanisms to fight discrimination in public services. Finally, public information campaigns can promote multiculturalism and raise awareness about discrimination. Addressing Roma poverty in Slovakia is a complex challenge, which will take time, patience, and collaboration among many partners, but also greater understanding of the opportunities and challenges ahead.

Chapter 4
Roma Diversity in Romania

Romania has the largest Roma population in Central and Eastern Europe, and one of the most diverse. This variety reflects historical, religious, linguistic, and occupational characteristics, which are often overlapping. Roma communities are also varied in terms of regional settlement patterns, integration levels, and economic and social development. However, Roma in Romania face common issues related to access to education, health care, social assistance, and housing that underpin widespread poverty. This chapter looks at these common challenges, drawing from case studies that provide a more detailed understanding of the interlocking mechanisms of Roma poverty.

Poverty in Romania, and that of Roma in particular, is related to interconnected factors, including inherited policies from past regimes, fiscal constraints associated with the transition process, policy design, and aspects of exclusion within society. Romania faces these issues within an international environment concerned with human rights and minority protection, particularly in the context of Romania's candidacy for EU accession. This chapter examines the situation of Roma in Romania at the nexus of these converging factors. After an initial discussion of the historical setting, the second section explores the diversity of nine Roma communities analyzed as case studies. The third section examines access to social services for Roma, and the final section discusses social and ethnic relations between Roma and others in Romania.

FROM SLAVERY TO CEAUȘESCU

The history of Roma in Romania is particularly dark and difficult, characterized by enslavement until 1856, repression and extermination during the Holocaust, and forced assimilation under the socialist Ceaușescu regime. The legacies of these different regimes have had important implications for the overall status of Roma in Romania. While the socialist period brought some improvements to Roma in social and economic terms (see chapter 2 for a general discussion), the assimilationist policies of this era were accompanied by considerable political repression and created a gulf of mistrust between Roma and the state that continues to this day.

By most accounts, Roma first arrived in Romania's historical provinces of Wallachia and Moldavia toward the end of the eleventh century (Crowe 1991). Initially free to pursue their crafts and trades, by the fifteenth century Roma slavery was institutionalized in the Romanian provinces and lasted well into the nineteenth century (Panaitescu 1941; Gheorghe 1983; Beck 1989; and Crowe 1991 and 1994). Romanian rulers brought large numbers of Roma slaves back from various military campaigns.[42] At the turn of the sixteenth century, the Romanian provinces fell under the Ottoman Empire. During this period, the conditions of both the slaves and the Romanian peasantry deteriorated further. Because Roma had unique skills as artisans, craftsmen, and metallurgists, laws were enacted to ensure that they would remain slaves.[43] Slaves were generally treated poorly, and cases of torture and death were not uncommon (CEDIMSE-SE [Center for Documentation and Information on Minorities in Eastern Europe—Southeast Europe] 2001).

Throughout Europe, the Enlightenment of the nineteenth century brought about a change in attitude toward Roma and minorities in general. By the middle of the century, a number of prominent owners had freed their slaves. Slavery was finally abolished in the 1850s and 1860s. However, the situation of Roma did not improve appreciably after the abolition of slavery, and many fled. This exodus was initially stimulated by fears of reenslavement and subsequently continued due to deteriorating socioeconomic conditions (Crowe 1994). Of those Roma who stayed, few were given land, and those who did receive land often lacked the skills to cultivate it effectively. During these times, Roma were engaged in occupations ranging from metalworking and carpeting to bottle collecting, divination, and begging (Zamfir and Zamfir 1993b). Others, unable to find any other means of survival, offered themselves for resale to their old masters (Hancock 1997).

The redrawing of boundaries following World War I brought a large new, mostly Hungarian, minority population to Romania. The share of minorities in Romania's total population increased from 8 percent to nearly 30 percent after the war, significantly altering the state's ethnic composition (Livezeanu 1995). Of this number, less than 1 percent were estimated to be Roma (Crowe 1991). Although agreements signed by Romania following the war included measures for the protection of minority rights, these were not implemented, largely because of the assimilation policies of the new government. The Depression of 1929 was followed by an increasingly nationalist and oppressive period, characterized by increased prejudice against Roma.

As for Roma elsewhere in Europe, conditions for Roma in Romania deteriorated significantly with the rise of fascism and the onset of World War II. Between 1941 and 1942, under the fascist Antonescu regime, an estimated 25,000 to 36,000 Roma were expelled and transported to camps in Transdneister (seized from Ukraine). At least half died of cold, starvation, and disease (Crowe 1991).[44] From 1944 to 1947, under the increasing influence of the Soviet Union, many minorities were promised improved rights as a part of Stalin's efforts to use "the national minorities as a means for undermining anti-communism in Romania" (Crowe 1991). Initially, many Roma and members of other minorities joined the Romanian Communist Party to gain positions in the local and regional administrations and general upward mobility.

Policies toward Roma during the socialist era were largely assimilationist. Many Roma farmers and nomadic Roma were forced into employment in agricultural collectives and heavy industry. These efforts continued through the 1970s. Traditional Roma occupations were declared illegal (Gilberg 1974; Beck 1985); many Roma were relocated;[45] and cultural expression was suppressed through bans on folk music and the use of the Roma language (CEDIME-SE 2001). Roma were also often subject to persecution by police and local officials (Zang and Levy 1991). While policies aimed at settling Roma by providing them with housing, education, and jobs did lead to overall improvements in their living standards, deteriorating economic conditions during the final years of the communist regime led to the emergence of widespread unemployment and poverty. On the margins of a rapidly changing society, some Roma began to turn to illegal means for survival, perpetuating societal stereotypes and hostility (Zamfir and Zamfir 1993b).

THE TRANSITION PERIOD AND BEYOND

For Romania's minorities, the overthrow of the Ceauşescu regime in 1989 brought the potential for new economic and political opportunities. Over the past decade, however, very few Roma have been able to take advantage of them. The particularly acute economic decline in Romania led to rapidly falling living standards for the entire population. Roma have been disproportionately affected by trends of rising unemployment, growing poverty, shrinking social assistance, as well as limited access to housing, education, and health care. As discussed in chapter 2, the share of Roma who are poor is more than twice as high as that of non-Roma.[46] The deterioration of Roma living conditions has been exacerbated by entrenched patterns of discrimination, prejudice, and incidences of ethnic violence (Cartner 1994; ERRC 1996; OSI 2001).[47]

The situation of Roma in Romania has attracted particular attention in part because they constitute the largest absolute population in Europe. According to the 1992 census, less than one-half million Roma live in Romania. Unofficial estimates are much higher. For example, Zamfir and Zamfir estimated that in 1993, the Roma population was just over 1 million (or 4.6 percent of the total population), a figure subsequently revised to 1.5 million in 1999 (Bárány 2002).

THE DIVERSITY OF ROMA SETTLEMENTS

A qualitative study of nine case studies of contrasting Roma communities was undertaken to document the diversity of Roma social and economic conditions in Romania (see box 4.1). The sites were selected for their diversity along a number of dimensions, including urban and rural locations, ethnic and religious composition, income sources and economic opportunities, socioeconomic status, and political participation levels (see table 4.1). The sites are located in six different counties, or *judets,* in Romania: Bucharest, Tulcea, Vaslui, Covasna, Hunedoara, and Timis. Field research in these communities was undertaken in 1999.

As highlighted in the discussion of Slovakia in the previous chapter, the physical locations of the Roma communities in rural

---

BOX 4.1 A QUALITATIVE STUDY OF ROMA COMMUNITIES IN ROMANIA

In 1999, qualitative fieldwork was conducted in nine sites in six districts across Romania to get a more complete picture of living conditions and access to social services. The sites are Zabrauti (a neighborhood within Bucharest), Babadag, Iana, Saint (Sf.) Gheorghe, Valcele, Ciopeia (a village within the Santamaria Orela commune), Timisoara, and Nadrag. Table 4.1 provides the summary. As with the Slovakia study, caution should be used in drawing general conclusions from the qualitative case studies. Where possible, national level data is included to provide context.

In an attempt to reflect the diversity in Roma settlements in Romania, the selection of the case study communities was based on considerations that included geographic diversity; historical factors; variety of Roma subgroups; income sources and living standards; the degree of integration of Roma in their respective communities; family and social structures; and degrees of political participation and access to information channels in their respective communities.

Study information was gathered from more than 65 in-depth interviews between June and November 1999. Key informants included educational personnel, such as teachers, administrators, and staff; medical staff, including doctors, nurses, and clinic and hospital administrators; local government authorities; NGO representatives; and religious officials. More than 165 interviews were also conducted with individuals (155) and groups (10) of Roma in these localities. In addition to extensive interviews and site visits, additional primary and secondary materials were collected and analyzed.

Table 4.1 Main Features of the Case Study Sites, 1999

Case Study Community	County/ Judet	Rural/ Urban	Type of Roma Subgroups	Community Origins
Zabrauti	Bucharest	Urban	Mixed (including Sporitori, Ursari, Turkish Roma, and Vatrasi)	Squatters occupied seven abandoned apartment buildings after 1989. The majority are Roma.
Babadag	Tulcea	Urban	Muslim "Turkish" Roma	In the 1950s, Roma families were settled in Babadag as part of the housing policies of the socialist government.
Sf. Gheorghe (Örko quarter)	Covasna	Urban	Hungarian-speaking Roma	Roma settled in Örko after the Second World War.
Timisoara	Timis	Urban	Mixed community of Rudari and Caldarari	Roma settled in this neighborhood in the 1950s from neighboring villages, but also from more distant regions.
Aninoasa (Iscroni quarter)	Hunedoara	Urban	Lingurari and Rudari Roma	Most Roma migrated to the Jiu Valley during the socialist era and found employment in the mining industry.
Iana	Vaslui	Rural	Lingurari and Rudari Roma	Roma first came to Iana as freed slaves following the 1864 rural reforms and later as veterans of the First World War.
Valcele (villages of Araci, Ariusd, Hetea, and Valcele)	Covasna	Rural	Lingurari and Rudari Roma	Unknown origins
Ciopeia	Hunedoara	Rural	Caldarari Roma, relatively wealthy	Unknown origins
Nadrag	Timis	Rural	Small community of Hungarian-speaking Roma	Roma arrived in Nadrag in the late 1970s from the northern town of Satu-Mare, following a powerful earthquake.

and urban areas reflect different degrees of geographic exclusion, which, in turn, are related to other types of exclusion within society. Urban localities in the study include the Zabrauti neighborhood in the capital city of Bucharest and a Roma community in Timisoara, one of the largest cities in Romania. The Roma communities of Babadag and the Örko quarter of Saint (Sf.) Gheorghe, are located in smaller, provincial towns, while the Iscroni quarter in the small town of Aninoasa is located in the industrialized Jiu Valley, a mining area in southwestern Romania, which was hard hit by restructuring in the 1990s. The four villages within the Valcele *commune*, a rural municipality, Ciopeia, and the Iana and Nadrag communes are all located in rural areas.

Particularly in the rural locales, geographic exclusion contributes to economic exclusion through limited economic opportunities and transportation to urban areas. Rural Roma communities frequently lack basic infrastructure and utilities, such as paved roads, running water, electricity, and telephone lines. In urban areas, communities are frequently ghetto-like, located in distinct neighborhoods, and often situated on the periphery of cities or towns. In Sf. Gheorghe, Roma live in small houses scattered on hillsides on the outskirts of towns. Other Roma in the area live in two dilapidated blocks of flats, which are separated from the other houses by a concrete wall, nicknamed the "Berlin Wall."

Each of these communities reflects different combinations of Roma subgroups. Some localities are quite heterogeneous, such as the Zabrauti community, which contains multiple ethnic groups. These groups range from quite traditional, speaking primarily the Romani language Sporitori, to more integrated, speaking primarily or only Romanian. The Babadag community has three main Roma groups, the largest of which are Muslim Roma. In Iana, the majority of Roma actively participate in the Orthodox Church. Nadrag and Sf. Gheorghe are more homogenous communities, which consist primarily of Hungarian-speaking Roma. Primarily relatively well-off Caldarari Roma populate the Ciopeia village in Hunedoara.

The communities vary significantly in their origins and histories. The most recent, Zabrauti, emerged after 1989, when Roma occupied deserted apartment buildings in Bucharest as squatters, due to housing shortages and deteriorating economic conditions. In contrast, the Roma village in Iana has existed in Vaslui since 1864, when Roma slaves were freed and were granted land under rural land reforms. Roma in Babadag arrived at the end of the Second World War, while Roma settled in Nadrag and Iscroni during the socialist period, when low-skilled labor was in demand for the mining industry.

The nine communities differ substantially in size, and there is considerable disagreement between the official and unofficial population figures. According to official data, there are no Roma in Iana. However, 1999 estimates made by local authorities and service providers suggest that between 1,200 and 1,500 Roma live in the commune. Similarly, 1992 census data for Babadag report that Roma account for nearly 10 percent of the population, while unofficial estimates put the figure closer to 16 percent. Local officials in Valcele believe that Roma

TABLE 4.2 ROMA POPULATION IN THE CASE STUDY COMMUNITIES

Case Study Community	Total Population	Roma Population (1992 Census)		Roma Population (1999 Unofficial Estimates)	
		Number of Roma	Share of Overall Population (percent)	Number of Roma	Share of Overall Population (percent)
Zabrauti	[ ]	1,000	[ ]	800	[ ]
Babadag	10,435	969	9.3	1,700	16.3
Iana	3,850	0	0	1,200–1,500	30–40
Sf. Gheorghe (Örko quarter)	68,359	886	1.3	2,500–5,000	3.6–7.3
Valcele (villages of Araci, Ariusd, Hetea, and Valcele)	3,500	300	8.6	2,018	57.7
Ciopeia	4,000	289	7.3	290	7.25
Aninoasa (Iscroni quarter)	5,985	29	0.5	500	8.4
Timisoara	334,115	2,668	0.8	[ ]	[ ]
Nadrag	3,250	0	0	65–70	2.1

Sources: National Commission of Statistics for the Census; estimates of local officials and service providers.

make up nearly 60 percent of the population, while the 1992 data indicate only 9 percent. According to local sources, Sf. Gheorghe has the largest Roma community, between 2,500 and 5,000 Roma, while Nadrag has the smallest, at 70 people (see table 4.2).

INCOME SOURCES AND ECONOMIC OPPORTUNITIES

Prior to the socialist period, many Roma worked in traditional trades. During the socialist period, and particularly under the Ceauşescu regime, many Roma were forced to abandon these trades for work in state-run agricultural cooperatives, forestry, and industries, such as construction, manufacturing, and food processing. Although the production and trade of traditional goods were considered illegal economic activity under the socialist regime, some Roma continued to work in these trades, either full-time or part-time, to supplement their income from official employment.

While income sources in the Roma communities vary widely, there are some common features. In a 1993 study, Zamfir and Zamfir found that income derived from formal wage employment constituted a significantly lower proportion of average income for Roma than for the majority population. Roma still employed in traditional trades tended to have income levels that were higher than the national average.[48] A substantial percentage of Roma income was derived from a combination of part-time, casual, and self-employed work, much of which was conducted in the informal economy and at times on the margins of legality. High levels of Roma unemployment in the formal sector reflected low qualifications for jobs. The 1993 study found that 60 percent of employed Roma were unskilled, and only 2 percent reported having middle or higher-level qualifications. Exclusion and discrimination also limit labor market opportunities. Roma report that they are generally the last hired and first fired. More recent survey findings suggest relatively low Roma unemployment rates in Romania (24 percent) compared to those in Bulgaria, the Czech Republic, Hungary, and Slovakia (UNDP 2003). According to the same survey, the lower rates are due in large part to high levels of Romanian Roma participation in the informal sector. Around 16 percent of Roma are estimated to be predominantly reliant on state support for their survival.

The situation of Roma in the village of Ciopeia illustrates typical employment patterns—shifting from traditional trades to formal sector employment during the socialist period and subsequently to informal employment during the 1990s. Ciopea is located in Hunedoara judet, a former center of heavy industry and mining. Ciopean Roma are largely Caldarari, a traditional subgroup that speaks the Romani language. Relative to other Roma and Romanian communities in the municipality, Roma in Ciopea have been well-off. Prior to the socialist regime, Ciopean Roma were engaged in traditional occupations, including manufacturing bricks and buckets and selling handmade soap. During the Ceaușescu regime, many became employed in a large metallurgical factory in the area or at the local butcher's shop. Although it was illegal, some workers continued their traditional roles, and others began trading merchandise with nearby Serbia.

Following the revolution in 1989, many Ciopean Roma were laid off when restructuring began at the factory. Since then, involvement in trade, employment abroad, and other informal sector activities has intensified. Many Ciopeans sell and barter secondhand clothing at flea markets in Hateg and Petrosani (towns 40 kilometers away) and with neighboring villages. Still others have emigrated or taken on short-term work in Western Europe, most commonly in Germany.

Although Roma living conditions and economic opportunities depend substantially on regional economic conditions, with few exceptions, nearly all Roma in the case sites were poor and worse-off than non-Roma in the area.[49] Bucharest and Timis are among the most prosperous counties in Romania. Sf. Gheorghe is also a relatively prosperous town. On the other hand, Babadag has been severely affected by the collapse of heavy industry, as has the Jiu Valley, where Hunedoara is located. Consequently, unemployment is high among the Roma communities in Hunedoara, including Ciopeia and Iscroni. The economy of rural Nadrag depended in large part on a local mechanical factory. After successive waves of layoffs, the factory closed in 1998, causing Nadrag's economy to collapse. Valcele, Iana, and Ciopeia are largely agricultural economies. With the exception of those in Iana, Roma generally do not own land and subsist either on day labor or other non-agricultural occupations, such as small trades or work abroad.

For the communities in the more prosperous counties, such as Zabrauti, Babadag, Sf. Gheorghe, and Timisoara, Roma income levels vary from moderate to extremely low (see table 4.3). In other communities, such as Valcele and Nadrag, the interviewers identified nearly all of the families as extremely poor. Overall, urban communities have higher and more mixed income levels, while rural communities, with the exception of Ciopeia, range from low to extremely low. In Ciopeia incomes were higher, and Roma living standards were found to be largely equivalent to non-Roma.

In the study sites, Roma employment was categorized into four main types of occupations: work abroad, day labor, trade, and subsistence occupations. Few Roma in the communities are employed in the formal economy, either as salaried workers or as owners of small businesses or farms. Rather, the most lucrative and steady sources of income come from trade and work abroad, including day labor, such as selling newspapers. Trade in secondhand clothing, itinerant trade in villages, and agricultural day labor also help prevent families from living in extreme poverty.

The poorest families survive on day labor and informal activities, such as recycling waste, used iron, and other scrap metal. Two families interviewed for the study, one in Zabrauti and one in Timisoara, lived exclusively from scrap dealing, and both lived in extreme poverty. This type of employment can have negative long-term consequences. Because of the itinerant nature of the work, older children are needed to help care for younger children while their parents are working, and thus they are unable to attend school. Child labor was also evident in Valcele. Older children, over 14 years old, worked as day laborers with their parents.

TABLE 4.3 INCOME SOURCES AND ECONOMIC STRATIFICATION, 1999

Case Study Community	Rural/ Urban	Income Levels	Primary Income Sources		
			Moderate Income	Low Income	Extremely Low Income
Zabrauti	Urban	Mixed	Employment[a]	Day laborers;[b] small trade[c]	Day laborers; waste recycling; begging
Babadag	Urban	Mixed	Itinerant trade in villages	Itinerant trade in villages	Day laborers
Sf. Gheorghe (Örko quarter)	Urban	Mixed	Work abroad (Hungary)[d]	Work abroad; day laborers	Day laborers; waste recycling
Timisoara	Urban	Mixed	Work abroad (Western Europe); trade	Employment	Recycling (bottles and used iron)
Aninoasa (Iscroni quarter)	Urban	Low to extremely low income		Mining; trade (second-hand clothing)	Recycling (used iron)
Iana	Rural	Low income		Agriculture; day laborers; retirement pensions	
Valcele (villages of Araci, Ariusd, Hetea, and Valcele)	Rural	Extremely low income			Day laborers (local and itinerant); informal manufacturing; gathering and trading[e]
Ciopeia	Rural	Moderate to low income	Work abroad (Western Europe); trade	Trade (second-hand clothing)	
Nadrag	Rural	Extremely Low-Income		Employment; day laborers; gathering and trading (fern leaves)	Day laborers

a *Employment*: wage labor in the formal economy.

b *Day labor*: employment for predominantly low-income Roma as day laborers in agriculture or other sectors, such as construction.

c *Trade*: employment gained through itinerant trade or more formal trade in local and regional markets.

d *Work abroad*: employment sought in Western European or neighboring countries, such as Hungary.

e *Subsistence occupations:* work includes gathering and trading natural commodities, such as fern leaves, forest fruits, or mushrooms or recycling used materials, such as clothing or scrap metal.

ACCESS TO SOCIAL SERVICES

Roma poverty in Romania and other countries of Central and Eastern Europe is intertwined with numerous factors, including relatively low educational attainment and poor access to health care, social assistance, and housing. This section explores access to social services in the case study communities, using surveys and the words of Roma to illustrate general trends and the diversity of situations.

Access to Education

Roma in Romania tend to have higher illiteracy levels and lower levels of educational attainment than the total population. A 1992 study found that compared to the estimated national illiteracy rate of 2 to 4 percent (Ministry of Education 1998), 44 percent of Roma men and 59 percent of Roma women were illiterate in 1992, and an estimated 27 percent of Roma never attended school, or if they had, it was only for a few years (Zamfir and Zamfir 1993a; 1996). There is also evidence of worsening trends in recent years. Data from two nationally representative household surveys found that for Roma, the share of the population that had not completed basic education grew from 36 percent in 1994 to 44 percent in 1998.[50]

Low preschool attendance is a serious issue in Romania that has implications for children's future participation in school. According to the 1992 census, 40 percent of children under 8 years of age did not attend kindergarten or school. A more recent study, from 1998, reported that 17 percent of Roma children between the ages of 3 and 6 participated in preschool, in comparison with 60 percent for the whole population.[51] The share of Roma who continue beyond compulsory basic education is also dramatically lower than for the rest of the population. One study found that only 7 percent of Roma men and 3 percent of Roma women had completed secondary school, compared to 73 percent of men and 63 percent of women in the general population (OSI 2002). This study also reported that there was some evidence that the proportion of Roma completing secondary school has increased over the last two decades.

Considerable variation may exist among Roma groups in terms of participation in education. Zamfir and Zamfir (1993a) found that Roma children are proportionally more likely to regularly attend school if their fathers are employed, if they live in mixed rather than predominantly Roma communities (60 percent compared to 33 percent), and if their mothers have had more than 8 years of schooling (73 percent), compared with mothers with no schooling (21 percent).

TABLE 4.4 SCHOOL ATTENDANCE TRENDS FOR ROMA, 1993

Age (in years)	Number of Students in Sample	Attendance Rate			
		Regularly	Occasionally	Ceased	Never
7	139	48.4	6.6	8.8	36.3
8	348	44.6	14.9	7.0	33.5
9	318	52.4	13.9	10.4	23.4
10	404	51.4	15.5	14.2	18.9
11	318	48.4	15.1	19.6	16.9
12	458	42.4	15.6	20.7	21.3
13	377	43.3	17.2	21.8	17.6
14	402	41.0	13.2	37.6	8.3
15	442	29.4	9.4	41.5	19.6
16	111	30.5	8.5	45.8	15.3

Sources: Zamfir and Zamfir 1993 and 1994.

Further data suggests that the proportion of Roma pupils who drop out of school increases with age (see table 4.4). According to these data, at the age of 7, over half of all Roma children attend school, either regularly (49 percent) or occasionally (7 percent). By the age of 9, school attendance becomes the norm, with over 66 percent of Roma children enrolled full-time or part-time. However, between the ages of 9 and 13, an increasing number of Roma students drop out of school. By age 15, the proportion of children attending regularly decreased by one-third compared to attendance rates at age 14. More than 15 percent of Roma 16 year olds reported that they never attended school.

The case studies confirmed the sharp decline in Roma school attendance after the fourth grade. The number of Roma students repeating the fourth grade was also higher than for other grades. In the schools in Valcele, for example, the proportion of Roma students enrolled in school steadily decreases with age (see table 4.5). In the first grade, Roma students make up 93 percent of all students. By the eighth grade, the percentage of Roma students declines to 53 percent. Many Roma students repeat grades. As a result, they tend to be older than average. The decline in the number of students in fourth grade may be related to the greater exposure to more teachers and subjects and the larger number of academic requirements. The stigma of repeating grades or receiving remedial instruction may also contribute to the high dropout rate among Roma.

TABLE 4.5 SHARE OF ROMA STUDENTS IN VALCELE, 1999

Grade	Total Number of Students	Percent Roma	Roma Students Repeating the Year	Over-aged Roma Students
1st	123	94	61	13
2nd	99	95	30	30
3rd	83	73	11	17
4th	72	82	3	11
5th	58	79	18	20
6th	28	64	4	6
7th	24	54	3	7
8th	15	53	—	—
Total	**502**	**83**	**130**	**104**

The organization of education differed across the study sites. Roma children were educated in separate classrooms in Zabrauti, Sf. Gheorghe, and Timisoara, while schools in Timisoara and Sf. Gheorghe offered some Roma language training. In four of the nine communities, Zabrauti, Babadag, Ciopeia, and Timisoara, at least one staff member was able to speak the Roma language. Basic characteristics of education in the study sites are summarized in table 4.6.

While the educational opportunities for Roma differ throughout Romania, the Romanian Education Law does not stipulate general education to be organized on the basis of ethnic criteria. Schools organized for minority groups, where all classes are conducted in the students' mother tongue, are an exception. More recently, however, the government has implemented a number of special educational initiatives targeted to Roma children (see box 4.2). Areas with majority or relatively large Roma populations may request tailored educational programs for their children. For example, in Zabrauti, special Roma language classes and a daily lunch program were organized for students in cooperation with the Step-by-Step program. While this program is no longer active, it was reportedly well received by Roma in the community. Local conditions and attitudes also account for differences in educational practices.

Economic Constraints

Both Roma and educational personnel cite poverty and economic constraints as significant obstacles to education. Poor parents often cannot afford the necessary school supplies, shoes, clothing, and food. Teachers have observed that many Roma students come to school without proper food and clothing. One student in Iscroni explained that she had to stay

TABLE 4.6 ACCESS TO EDUCATION IN CASE STUDY COMMUNITIES, 1999

Case Study Community	Special Classrooms for Roma	Hours of Roma Language	Roma-speaking Teachers and Staff	Concerns of Teachers and School Administrators	Concerns of Roma Parents and Students
Zabrauti	Within the local school	No[a]	Yes	Low parental support, both material and educational	Discriminatory attitudes from teachers and non-Roma pupils
Babadag	No	No	Yes	Absenteeism; high dropout rates	Limited access to the Step-by-Step educational program due to prohibitive costs and administrative obstacles to enrollment
Iana	No	No	No	None reported	Insufficient capacity (for kindergarten)
Sf. Gheorghe (Örko quarter)	Within a distinct school	Yes	No	Low parental support	Corruption and inefficiency in allocating support to students.
Valcele (villages of Araci, Ariusd, Hetea, and Valcele)	No	No	No	Inadequate curriculum; low parental support; poor attendance; high dropout rates	Discriminatory treatment and violence against Roma children
Ciopeia	No	No	Yes		
Aninoasa (Iscroni quarter)	No	No	No	Low parental support; high dropout rates	High costs of education; limited attention from teachers.
Timisoara	Within a private educational center	Within a private educational center	Yes	Absenteeism; High dropout rates	Corruption and incompetence (in the private educational center).
Nadrag	No	No	No	Poor results; repeating grades	

a One teacher on staff speaks the Roma language, but does not offer Roma language instruction.

Box 4.2 Government Education Initiatives Targeting Roma

The Romanian Ministry of Education and Research has organized a number of initiatives specifically for Roma students. The Second Chance project is an experimental project, which was organized in 1999 in cooperation with the Center for Education 2000+.[a] The program provides the opportunity for young Roma school dropouts (aged 14–24 years) to complete basic primary and secondary school, together with additional vocational training. Graduation certificates are provided to those who successfully complete a 3.5-year program, giving students the possibility to register for the primary school graduation examination and facilitating access to the labor market.

As of 2001, 300 students were enrolled in 11 schools in six counties of Romania. In addition, 120 teachers were trained in remedial education and student counseling, 16 monitors were responsible for monitoring the implementation process, and 10–14 Roma mediators facilitated cooperation between schools and Roma communities. Some of the challenges faced by this project include a relatively high turnover of teachers, the need for more vocational apprenticeship opportunities in the community, and students dropping out due to financial constraints.

As an extension of the project, the ministry, in partnership with the EC's PHARE program, launched the program Access to Education of All Disadvantaged Groups, with a Special Focus on the Roma Communities.[b] The main objectives include increasing access to quality preschool education, reducing the number of Roma children who drop out of school early, and providing dropouts with a second chance to complete basic education. Financing for 2002–04 totals 8.3 million euros, with PHARE providing 7 million euros and the remainder from national co-financing.

In addition, in 2000 the Ministry of Education reserved a limited number of places for Roma in high schools, vocational schools, teacher training colleges, and universities. Finally, to address the economic constraints to education, a new initiative is under way that provides free school supplies and a school snack to specific categories of children in need, including many Roma children.

Notes:

a The Center for Education 2000+ was initiated in 1999 as a partnership between the Open Society Institute-Romania and the Ministry of Education and Research. It aims to provide professional and financial assistance for the elaboration, implementation, and evaluation of educational programs in Romania.

b See http://europa.eu.int/comm/enlargement/pas/phare.

Sources: PHARE 2001; Center for Education 2000+ 2002.

home from school so that she could wash her only set of clothes. While many parents are able to buy clothing second hand, affordable shoes are scarcer. Schools provide free textbooks; however, most students were required to provide their own notebooks and school supplies, as well as lunches. A group of Roma women interviewed in Valcele discussed the costs of sending children to school.

> Now, before it is cold and before the earth freezes, they go more. After the winter comes, we won't send them any more—we don't have clothing and shoes. . . . There is no food also. And the children won't stay. If we take them, they stay one hour and then they come home running, because they are hungry. They see the other children eating, and they aren't.

Another obstacle is the pressure for children to work and support their families. Others in the community may scorn students who continue to attend school and stop working. Young Roma are often expected to work. A mother of seven children in Timisoara explained that older children, particularly girls, are often forced to stay home to care for younger siblings while their parents work.

> I cannot send my children to school because I have nobody else to help me with the bottles. Look, I have small children—now if I go away, wandering on the roads for three months . . . with another baby coming . . . who will take care of them?

This pressure to work is particularly intense in the higher grades. A Roma student from Timisoara with an exceptional talent for math graduated from high school and was admitted to the Architecture Department of Timisoara University. While studying, he also taught math at an educational center for Roma students. Yet in his second year of the university, his father forced him to leave school to support the family. Although at the time of the interviews he was selling newspapers in Italy, his teachers reported that he was determined to continue his studies.

Absenteeism is not limited to poor families. More affluent families who rely on work abroad as their main source of income often require their school-age children to accompany them during their travels, forcing the children to drop out of school. In Timisoara, many of these children have difficulty restarting school upon their return. This is not always the case. In communities such as Iscroni and Babadag, where more well-off families earn most of their income from local business or trade, parents were more inclined to send their children to school and often carefully monitored their performance. For example, in

Iscroni, teachers reported that wealthy Roma families hired private tutors. These parents considered private tutoring necessary for their children to achieve a higher performance level in school.

Demand for Education

The motivation of parents and their attitudes and expectations toward education also have an important influence on school attendance. Many parents resisted sending their children to school, citing reasons such as the need for their children to work, fears of discrimination and maltreatment of their children, and a general skepticism about the utility of education. Roma from Timisoara indicated that the most common occupations for Roma, such as trade and work abroad, did not require education. Others did not see how education would lead to higher employment. A young Roma mother from Iana was skeptical about whether her children's education would improve their chances of becoming anything more than agricultural workers, though she still hoped that they would benefit from education.

> What can my children become? It is now as it was before—when could they ever become something? Never. They can pull the hoe but what else? May they learn well . . . yet they will work the land.

Some teachers blamed the absenteeism of Roma students on parents, either because they were not interested in their children's education or because they felt that parents misused their resources and deprived their children of adequate food and clothing, which kept their children out of school. A number of teachers in Ciopeia and Iscroni noted the lack of support at home for completing homework.

On the other hand, many Roma emphasized the importance of education for their children. Many cited practical reasons for sending their children to school, ranging from literacy, which is a basic qualification for many jobs, to gaining the required number of years in school for a driver's license. Teachers in Zabrauti, Babadag, Iscroni, and Ciopeia noted that many Roma parents demonstrated an interest in their children getting at least a minimal education to improve their employment prospects.

Discrimination and Exclusion

Another category of constraints to Roma education relates to discrimination and exclusion. Many Roma were reluctant to send their children to school because they feared prejudice and that their children would not be accepted in mainstream schools. A father of a Roma student from Zabrauti described the kind of stereotypes his son was exposed to.

The other children look at my children differently: "Look at the Gypsies from Zabrauti!" Others are calling them "Ghetto Boys!" . . . So I sent my boy to the school with special classes, because it is closer and I have heard there is some assistance, some free notebooks. . . . I have money now, but maybe next year I will not have any more, so I thought that a notebook and a pen would do good. . . . But the boy didn't want to go: "I won't go there, Daddy!" "Why?" "Why should they call me 'Ghetto Boy' and mock me? Am I a 'Ghetto Boy'?" So I sent him to the General School in (the neighboring) Sebastian quarter, to the normal school.

Other parents complained of discrimination against Roma and favoritism toward non-Roma students. Discrimination ranged from teachers ignoring Roma students, pejoratively calling them "gypsies," and even treating them violently. In Valcele, some students complained that teachers either disregarded them or physically abused them. Students also cited examples of favoritism toward non-Roma students in which the teacher only offered help to non-Roma students. One young mother from Iscroni complained that her son was held back from the second grade and said that the teachers, rather than the parents, should be blamed.

They didn't allow my child to graduate from the first grade. . . . They wouldn't let him go. They don't take care of him, but they say it is my fault that I don't take care of him at home. . . . But this is why I send him to school, to learn there.

Access to Health Care

Reliable information about the health status of Roma in Romania and their access to care is scarce or non-existent. Yet there are identifiable trends. Roma life expectancy is significantly lower than that of the majority population, while child mortality and fertility rates are higher (Kalibova 2000). Compared with non-Roma, Roma are more likely to suffer from health conditions directly associated with poor nutrition and living conditions. A significant number of Roma have limited or no access to medical care. A recent survey indicates that health insurance coverage rates among Roma are relatively low, with 37 percent of respondents indicating they did not have health insurance (UNDP 2003).

The case study communities have varying access to health care, based on their geographic locations (see table 4.7). Services are necessarily more limited in the more remote, rural areas. This is the case throughout the country, for both Roma and non-Roma. In Valcele, the two Roma communities are situated at the periphery of the commune on communal grazing land and in an isolated village. The nearest medical center, in Araci, is two kilometers away. In Iana, some Roma reported that they travel over a half-hour by cart to get to the nearest medical services. In both cases, the lack of telephones in settlements was a barrier to emergency health services. Roma in rural areas also noted that physicians are not regularly available. One doctor worked in Valcele, and in Iana, a part-time doctor consults only on Saturdays.

Family planning services are often not available in local health clinics, and women sometimes must seek more expensive treatment from gynecologists in the nearest town. These women were reportedly more likely to have unwanted pregnancies, resort to abortions, or rely on informal information as their main source of family planning information.

Economic Constraints

Roma explained that the costs of medical services limited their access to care. These costs generally include payments for medication and costs associated with hospital care. In all cases, except for Nadrag, outpatient visits were officially free of charge. In Nadrag, where the only medical center has been privatized, consultation costs for adults as well as for children were as much as 75,000 lei (US$5). These costs made seeking medical care prohibitively expensive for many Roma families. Despite the absence of official fees, informal charges, particularly for hospital care and specialized services, are widespread. A woman from Sf. Gheorghe recalled that she had gone to the hospital for an emergency appendectomy, but the doctors refused to treat her if she did not pay 50,000 lei (US$3). A mother from Valcele explained the difficulties her daughter faced obtaining an abortion:

> My daughter didn't want to have the baby. . . . She even went to have an abortion, but the doctor refused. She was in the third month, and the doctor could have done it, if he wanted. And I gave her money. . . . I did the impossible almost, and I gave her 160,000 lei (around US$10) but the doctor wouldn't do it. Maybe if I had four or five hundred, a million, maybe he would have done it. She went once and it was in vain. I sent her again. I forced her, she went to another doctor, but this one refused too. What should I have done—should I have killed her? May the child live—if it comes, it comes.

Compounding the prohibitive costs of health care was a general confusion over the rules of the health insurance system, which was introduced in 2000, at the time of the interviews. Under the insurance system, all Romanians need to be registered with a family physician to be eligible for care. For those working in the formal sector, contributions are made through payroll tax deductions, while the self-employed, including farmers, are to make contributions on their own. The uninsured are covered by the state budget, with eligibility determined by registration for social assistance. However, because social assistance covers such a small share of the poor in Romania, many uninsured were not registered and fell through the cracks. The process has confused health care personnel and patients alike, and many Roma have gone uninsured.

In Babadag, a doctor reportedly stopped providing subsidized medications to Roma, because she had received written instructions to provide them only to insured patients. The doctor noted that only one Roma household—a relatively well-off family engaged in cross-border informal trade—had paid their health insurance contribution (approximately US$20 per month). Some Roma have also been left uninsured due to the increasing choice of family physicians to select only low-risk patients. A physician in Tirgu Secuiesc, a town in Covasna County in the Transylvania region, explained:

> I do not register gypsies as a family physician. I do not accept gypsies. . . . They come here and ask for money, ask for medicines. . . . They have a lot of nerve. You have to keep an eye on them when they enter here. I do not think they are poorer than other people. They go to Hungary with business; they probably have more money than we have. They go by car to ask for social aid.

Communication between Patients and Service Providers

One of the key factors influencing access to health care for Roma is the quality of communication between health care personnel and patients. While there are positive examples, this relationship is more often characterized by miscommunication, distrust and, in some cases, discrimination on behalf of the practitioner. The attitudes and perceptions of both patients and medical staff can have a significant impact on how health needs are conceptualized and the quality of service delivery. Roma noted that health personnel treated them poorly. A young mother from Sf. Gheorghe complained:

> I don't know why, but some doctors speak so rudely with the people. . . . [W]hen I went there and I saw this, I felt offended and I left. I went and I bought the medicines myself. . . . They said, "Where are you hurrying? Wait,"and other people went ahead of

me, and they offended me. I felt like crying. . . . I was waiting there for 2 or 3 hours, and afterwards they cursed me. So I went and I bought the medicines myself. . . . It is better to go to the pharmacy. I tell them what hurts me and I ask for the proper medicine.

From their side, medical personnel frequently perceive Roma as irresponsible patients. Some providers felt that Roma parents feed their infants improperly and often give them inappropriate food for an infant. Other doctors noted that children were dressed too warmly in summer and not warmly enough in the winter, leading to pulmonary infections. Some expressed concern about poor hygienic practices that can lead to skin diseases.

Medical staff also complained that Roma patients did not take their advice. Doctors noted that parents do not follow prescribed treatments for their children. A general practitioner in Babadag explained that Roma patients did not heed her advice and took medicines irregularly. This doctor no longer trusts Roma parents to dispense expensive medicines at home, asserting that "It would be a waste." Now she believes that Roma should be given treatments only if they are hospitalized and supervised by medical staff. These doctors indicated that they prefer to dispense medications through injections, so that they can control the treatment.

Medical staff claimed that Roma refuse to immunize their children. In Zabrauti, Roma children were kept out of school because they did not have the appropriate immunization records. According to physicians, Roma parents refuse immunizations because of a general mistrust of formal medicine. Many Roma mothers fear immunizations that induce fever as a side effect. In Valcele, the doctor reported that nurses make repeated home visits to Roma families to immunize children and face refusals for various reasons. Some parents claim that their children are sick, while others say that their husbands would beat them if their child were immunized. In one particular polio vaccination campaign in Araci (a village in Valcele), the nurse recruited the police to accompany her on home visits. After a few days, a rumor spread in the village that the vaccine was really a sterilization device, and the campaign was quickly abandoned.

Some health care officials have resorted to tricking their patients to persuade them to get immunized. A doctor from Babadag explained:

> (Roma) have never been willing to have their children be vaccinated. . . . We have to motivate them with methods adequate to their values. For instance we told them that a vaccine is very expensive, 60,000 lei, and we administer it for free now, later they will have to buy it. We threatened some illiterate

TABLE 4.7 ACCESS TO LOCAL MEDICAL SERVICES IN CASE STUDY COMMUNITIES, 1999

Case Study Communities	Spatial Accessibility of Medical Services[a]	Availability of Medical Personnel	Use of Family Planning[b]	Need Expressed by Medical Personnel	Concerns of Roma Respondents
Zabrauti	High	High	High	Immunizations; infant care; lack of ID papers	
Babadag	High	Low	High	Immunizations; infant care; pulmonary and skin diseases for children	
Iana	Low	Low	Low		
Sf. Gheorghe (Örko quarter)	High	High	Low	Immunizations; childcare; affordable medications	Discriminatory treatment
Valcele (villages of Araci, Hetea, and Valcele)	Low	Low	Low	Immunizations; infant care; scabies	Long distance to health services
Ciopeia	High	High	High	Immunizations; tuberculosis	
Aninoasa (Iscroni quarter)	High	High	Low	Immunizations	
Timisoara	High	High	High		
Nadrag	High	High	Low	High costs (Only private medical care is available.)	

[a] Availability of a health clinic within a reasonable distance (including transportation availability).

[b] Access was considered low when respondents had systematic complaints about reproductive services; the use of family planning was considered high when the researchers encountered cases and/or reports of such practices, especially concerning contraception instead of abortions.

parents with false papers, telling them that they will have to pay penalties if they do not have the children come for vaccination. [She displays the false penalty certificate, smiling.] We put a lot of stamps on it. . . . Sometimes we brought policemen with us in the area to be more convincing. And it worked many times.

A doctor in Iscroni relied on the same method as the nurse in Araci, often sending local police officers with nurses on vaccination campaigns. Some doctors reported that they threatened parents by telling them that they would restrict their eligibility for medicines unless their children were immunized. Until 1993, doctors in Sf. Gheorghe made the distribution of powdered milk for infants dependent on the child being immunized. Some teachers in Örko even admitted locking Roma children in a classroom so that the nurses could immunize them.

It is difficult to gauge the degree to which these problems are related to distrust of the health system by Roma or other factors, including low education levels and economic incentives. A doctor in Zabrauti, for example, claimed that many Roma patients come for free medication. If the medication was not free, she predicted, they would resort to more traditional remedies. Roma resented these assumptions. In Babadag, for example, Roma protested the suggestion that they sought out "old women's advice" rather than modern medical treatments. "We don't go to old women," they remarked, "we know to go to the doctor."

Access to Social Assistance

Social assistance cash benefits are an important source of income for many poor Roma families. Because of the deep fiscal crisis of the transition period, the availability of social assistance benefits has been severely restricted throughout Romania. Alongside the budgetary constraints, the transfer of responsibility for delivering social assistance benefits to local governments has left benefits unpaid in many of the poorest areas. Local governments have become caught in a vicious cycle of impoverishment, as it is the poorest municipalities that have the greatest need for social assistance, but are least able to pay them. In response, local officials have used their own discretion to adopt various coping strategies, such as limiting coverage of benefits by creating additional eligibility criteria, decreasing benefit levels, or ceasing payments altogether (World Bank 2000d).

As a whole, coverage of social assistance has dropped to extremely low levels in Romania.[52] The country's main monthly cash benefit program for the poor reaches very few households. In some of the case study communities, benefits were either paid irregularly or stopped altogether. Benefits were available on a regular basis in

Zabrauti, Iscroni, Timisoara, and Nadrag, and only intermittently in Sf. Gheorghe and Ciopeia. Benefits were discontinued for over three years in Iana, two years in Babadag, and one year in Valcele (see table 4.8).

TABLE 4.8 ACCESS TO SOCIAL ASSISTANCE IN CASE STUDY
    COMMUNITIES, 1999

Case Study Community	Social Problems	Means-Tested Income Support	Eligibility Criteria
Zabrauti	Substandard housing; extreme poverty	Available	None
Babadag	Extreme poverty	Discontinued	For educational grants, recipient must submit a passport as proof they have not traveled abroad.
Iana	Extreme poverty	Discontinued	N/A
Sf. Gheorghe (Örko quarter)	Substandard housing; extreme poverty	Intermittent	None
Valcele (villages of Araci, Ariusd, Hetea, and Valcele)	Substandard housing; extreme poverty	Discontinued	N/A
Ciopeia	-	Intermittent	Social worker discretion
Aninoasa (Iscroni quarter)	Substandard housing; extreme poverty	Available	None
Timisoara		Available	School attendance; proof of land ownership; active job search. For educational grants, proof of unemployment.
Nadrag	Substandard housing; extreme poverty	Available	None

In Babadag, the number of households receiving social assistance dropped dramatically, from 1,207 families in 1995, to 75 in 1998, due to budget constraints. The mayor estimated that approximately 75 percent of those who lost benefits were Roma. Even though the households may have been eligible according to the national legislation, local officials limited eligibility based on additional criteria because they could not afford to finance all eligible beneficiaries. One official believed that many Roma applications were rejected on illegal grounds. "Many of these families have been denied benefits on the grounds that the head of the household is able to work," he remarked, "or because they have a television, or a pig, or because they live with their parents . . . or because somebody has some information that they are involved in trade."

In some cases additional eligibility criteria may create positive incentives for beneficiaries, if for example, they are required to work or send their children to school. In other cases, additional rules may exclude beneficiaries who are unable to work or lack the necessary documentation for receiving benefits. In Timisoara, the city council and mayor restricted access to benefits by adding a mandatory work requirement of five days per month. Children were also required to attend school, and benefits were only paid to those who could prove permanent residence in Timisoara. Additional restrictions included asset tests, which excluded households that owned land and animals. The number of aid recipients dropped from 3,000 in 1995, to 306 in January 1998.

Similar strategies were adopted for the payment of school scholarships for low-income families. These education benefits are paid to poor households to cover school-related expenses. In Babadag, the school director devised a method to exclude some Roma families that had incomes from informal trade. He asked the Roma parents to bring their passports to school to prove that they had no visas and consequently no incomes from trade. The director reported that this reduced the number of Roma applicants substantially. Other Roma children were excluded from receiving benefits because they had not passed certain exams. In one of the Timisoara schools, the principal decided to ask the parents to submit a formal proof of unemployment and other documents to apply for benefits.

Roma expressed dissatisfaction with the reductions in social assistance and particularly with the disparities across localities. In areas where benefits were paid irregularly, Roma were aware that benefits were being paid elsewhere. A Roma woman from Babadag explained: "I received benefits twice. . . . In Cernavoda they pay it every month, why is it that we don't receive this money? In Medgidia they give it every month, why don't we get it?" Her comments also reflect a common perception among Roma of the disparity in the availability and levels of social assistance between municipalities. In Timisoara, a Roma woman explained the difficulty of her situation; she no longer received benefits because she did not send her children to school. However, she could not afford to send her daughter to school due to reductions in her benefits. While she collects bottles to support the family, her older daughter must take care of the younger children and subsequently cannot attend school.

Access to Housing

An increasing number of Romanians, both Roma and non-Roma, risk exclusion from housing as a result of privatization and housing restitution, changes in the legal status of land, and declining incomes. It is difficult to generalize about Roma housing conditions because of the diversity of situations. Many Roma in Romania live in integrated areas, while others live in urban slums, such as Zabrauti in Budapest, or rural settlements, such as Iana and Nadrag. Many urban and rural Roma communities suffer from a lack of infrastructure and services. Poor infrastructure—bad roads, lack of water or sewage systems, and absence of telephone lines—are more pronounced in rural areas. Internal migration from rural to urban communities has contributed to the expansion of urban settlements and to the growth of an informal system of supplementary social security where rents, gas, and electricity bills are unpaid, but evictions and stoppages do not immediately occur (Save the Children 2001a).

Conditions in Roma neighborhoods are frequently poor, with problems of extreme overcrowding and a lack of social services. According to 1998 household data, on average, Roma homes in Romania are 20 percent smaller than those of non-Roma, although Roma households are significantly larger.[53] Lack of access to utilities, such as water, gas, and electricity, and public services, such as waste collection, is a significant problem in many neighborhoods. In 1998, only 24 percent of Roma in Romania had access to public water facilities within their housing units, compared to 46 percent of the total population. Similarly, 34 percent of Roma households had no toilet facilities (indoor or outdoor), in comparison with 28 percent of total households.

The absence of quality and affordable housing was an issue flagged by Roma in almost all of the case site communities. In Zabrauti, Nadrag and Iscroni, where most residents live in public housing owned by the city, people mentioned poor maintenance and the lack of investment in housing. In Nadrag, residents reported that they were unable to pay their rents or electricity costs, and houses are often in extremely poor repair. As one young mother reported:

> The toilets are broken. . . . Yesterday our administrator called us to clean everything, because, he said, an inspector is going to come. . . . He is a very kind man, he helps us. He provided us with a hose to clean here, because it was such a misery, you couldn't count the dirt piles here. . . . Because we have only two toilets, but they are broken, and the misery spills out.

In Aninoasa, the Roma neighborhood consists of dilapidated barracks with outside water taps and non-functioning public toilets. In the Örko neighborhood of Sf. Gheorghe, most people do not own the land on which their houses are built, and the neighborhood has outdoor plumbing that poses a serious health risk. In the rural communities of Valcele and Iana, young couples often build homes illegally, due to the scarcity of affordable land. Illegal housing is also a problem in Zabrauti, where houses often have outside water taps, improvised electrical installation, and no central heating or gas connections.

Because of the legacy of state-provided public housing during the socialist period, expectations among the population are high. Most Roma expect that local governments will address housing shortages and improve the quality of existing houses. Local government responses in the sites have varied. In Valcele, the mayor's office proposed granting land to Roma to build new housing on communal grazing land, but the city council opposed the plan. Roma from Valcele were disappointed that the mayor had broken her electoral promise to provide them with land. In Zabrauti, in cooperation with the local mayor's office, UNDP initiated the legal transformation of four buildings, which residents had occupied illegally as squatters, into official public housing. While the project was legally approved, implementation has proven difficult. In addition to these bureaucratic obstacles, some tenants have had difficulty meeting rental requirements due to the lack of identification papers or criminal records and face evictions.

In Sf. Gheorghe, where the community center functions as a homeless shelter and a temporary housing facility, the mayor proposed a comprehensive urban renewal strategy for the Roma neighborhood. The mayor of Aninoasa intends to move all the inhabitants of the Roma quarter of Iscroni to another quarter situated at the periphery of the town to build a new civic center in a central location. While the move would entail an improvement in housing conditions, Iscroni residents oppose the initiative, most likely because of the undesirable location.

SOCIAL AND ETHNIC RELATIONS

Relations between Roma and the Majority Population

The frequency and quality of contact between Roma and non-Roma varies, depending in part on the geographic location of Roma communities, but also on the socioeconomic status and the age of the settlement. In general, the relationship between Roma and non-Roma has been characterized by miscommunication and mistrust. Equally, aspects of Roma society may contribute to their isolation, as well as to popular stereotypes and myths. Indeed, Roma social exclusion may be traced in part to the nature of their interaction with non-Roma and the mutual construction and negotiation of boundaries between the two.

The strongest evidence of continuing mistrust is the lack of geographic integration of Roma and non-Roma communities. With the exception of Iana, Roma and non-Roma in the study sites generally do not live together. Rather, Roma tend to constitute relatively segregated pockets located next to non-Roma neighborhoods. In Iana, which was first settled in 1864, Roma are more integrated, particularly in comparison to Roma in more recent and heterogeneous communities, such as Zabrauti in Bucharest. Nevertheless, despite the high level of integration between these groups, Roma are still called the pejorative term "gypsy." In Iana, there were a number of mixed marriages, while they were found to be rare elsewhere.

In other communities, relations between Roma and non-Roma are reportedly much more strained and reflect a high degree of social distance based on a lack of contact between ethnic groups. Such isolation starts young. Roma children in Zabrauti are not fully integrated into mainstream classes and are still required to attend "experimental classes," which are not only segregated, but are also relatively isolated within the school building. A teacher reported that Roma students often do not mingle with other children during breaks.

The socioeconomic status of Roma groups also has a bearing on interethnic relations, as well as relations between Roma groups. Wealthier Roma are more integrated, often adopting some of the cultural practices of Romanians. For example, in Babadag, despite the high proportion of Muslim Roma and lingering adherence to traditional dress and customs, most Roma names are Romanian rather than Muslim in origin. Furthermore, most Roma women, particularly wealthier ones, get married in traditional white bride's dresses customary in Romanian wedding ceremonies. Some Roma in Ciopeia are relatively well-off and have two-story houses and more expensive cars. In general, Roma in Ciopeia reported fewer tensions between ethnic groups. However, difficulties remain. As one Romanian respondent remarked, "We have no enemies, but also no friendships with the gypsies." Examples of tensions and discrimination were reported involving access to running water, land distribution, and access to community celebrations.

Relations with Public Officials and NGO Administrators

Relationships between Roma and public officials are mixed, depending largely on individuals and circumstances. In some cases Roma reported encountering sympathetic officials who recognize and attempt to accommodate the particular needs of Roma, but more often they reported being met by indifference, hostility, intolerance, and corruption of officials who are already strained by inadequate resources.

One of the dominant stereotypes about Roma is that they are the "undeserving poor." The pervasiveness of this view was evident in discussions with local officials. In Hetea, a Roma village in Valcele, the Romanian administrator of a Dutch aid program described Roma as "thieves" and "lazy." In Babadag, local officials were reluctant to pay social assistance to Roma, citing similar reasons. The mayor himself claimed that Roma do not work but "stay in the pubs all day long," grow nothing on their land, and are overly reliant on trade. Not everyone ascribes to such beliefs. The social assistance coordinator in Babadag denounced the widely-held concept that "Everything bad that happens is the gypsies' fault," arguing that special programs are needed to improve the situation of the Roma.

Relations with local police were frequently described as strained. In Zabrauti, Roma reported frequent police raids and fines for illegal dwelling. Over time, relations with the police have evolved from what the Roma perceived as arbitrary, punitive, and often violent interventions, to the total absence of a police presence.

Finally, pervasive mistrust and suspicion between program administrators and the community threatened the success of a number of outside development initiatives. This was most evident in Sf. Gheorghe where Roma inhabitants accused a priest and teachers involved in a project of stealing donations. At the same time the program administrators accused Roma of misusing aid and failing to abide by the goals of the programs. The examples of these programs highlight the importance of cooperative relationships between the state and local service providers. For example, in Zabrauti coordination between the assistance program and the local administration was effective and facilitated the project. The mayor of the fifth district of Bucharest, which governs Zabrauti, was a partner in the program and allocated resources. Local officials also managed to secure the doctor's cooperation to improvise medical records to allow Roma children to attend the local kindergarten.

CURRENT POLICY DEVELOPMENTS

Over the last decade, government, political parties, and non-governmental organizations have made significant efforts toward improving the condition of Roma in Romania. While many of these efforts have been improvised and uncoordinated, there is evidence that efforts are beginning to draw on more than a decade of project learning and experience to implement a more coherent, systematic approach. The adoption of a national strategy to improve the condition of Roma in 2001 reflects such efforts.

Since 1989 Romania has ratified the main international documents addressing racial and ethnic discrimination. In November 2000, Romania became the first EU candidate country to enact general anti-discrimination legislation. In April 2001, a public administration law was enacted allowing for the use of minority languages in areas where minorities constitute at least 20 percent of the population.[54] The use of non-Romanian languages in criminal and civil proceedings is also constitutionally guaranteed, although this does not always happen in practice. Specialized institutions dealing with minorities have also been set up. In 1993, the Council for National Minorities was established as a consultative body of the Romanian government. A Department for the Protection of National Minorities was established in 1997 within the Prime Minister's Office, including an Office for Social Integration of Roma.[55] Following the 2000 elections, these offices were relocated to the Ministry of Public Information and renamed the Department of Inter-Ethnic Relations and the National Office for Roma.

At the parliamentary level, there are standing commissions on minorities and human rights, which function both within the Senate and the Chamber of Deputies. After 1989, a number of Roma political parties were established, including the Democratic Roma Union, the Ethnic Federation of the Roma, the Roma Party, and the Roma Union. Despite these improvements, Roma remain underrepresented in local political institutions. While there are currently no Roma senators, during the November 2000 elections, a Roma Party member was elected to the Chamber of Deputies.

Both Roma and non-Roma organizations have played an important role in discussions and agenda setting with respect to Roma affairs, particularly concerning the National Strategy of the Government for Improving the Condition of Roma (Government of Romania 2001). Approximately 150 NGOs in Romania are devoted to promoting

Roma rights and interests and pressing for change in minority policies.[56] However, the small size and marginal resources of many of
these NGOs limit their influence.

The National Strategy for Improving the Condition of Roma

In April 2001, the government adopted the National Strategy of the
Government for Improving the Condition of Roma, which aims at
stimulating Roma participation in the economic, social, educational,
and political life of society through their involvement in sectoral
assistance and community development programs, as well as
through programs for the prevention of institutional and societal discrimination.

The duration of the strategy is intended to be 10 years (2001–10),
with the first four-year action plan focusing on the following areas:
administration and community development, housing, social security,
health, economy, justice and public order, child welfare, education,
culture, communication, and civic involvement. The strategy is organized, coordinated, and implemented through a series of structures,
including the establishment of a Joint Implementation and Monitoring Committee, Ministerial Commissions for Roma, and County
Offices for Roma and local experts for Roma issues.

Progress and Challenges

The adoption of the National Strategy marks a significant milestone
in the official policy approach toward improving the situation of
Roma. One of its greatest strengths is that the strategy was elaborated
with the participation of delegates from ministries as well as Roma
leaders and representatives from a variety of NGOs. The strategy's
priorities are widely seen by Roma and non-Roma leaders as reflecting those of Roma representatives.

The National Strategy for Roma is to be carried out through a
series of institutions established at multiple levels of government,
each of which is intended to include both government and Roma
representatives. This includes a Roma Office within the Ministry of
Public Information with judet-level representation, commissions
within ministries to address sectoral policy, and a government-level
Joint Implementation and Monitoring Committee to oversee organization and implementation of the strategy. While significant
progress has been made in establishing these institutions, there is
considerable variation in the degree to which they are currently able
to achieve the goals laid out in the strategy. The initiation of 40 pilot
projects has provided valuable experience and lessons about the

Box 4.3 THE PARTNERSHIP FUND FOR ROMA:
            PILOT PROJECTS

Between January 2001 and April 2002, the Partnership Fund for the Roma,[a] a grant fund made available by the EC's PHARE program provided 900,000 euros to support 40 pilot projects to improve the situation of Roma communities in Romania. In keeping with the principles and goals of the National Strategy of the Government for Improving the Condition of Roma (2001), the main aims of these projects were to test policy initiatives of the Romanian government and to support partnerships between local authorities and Roma organizations. These projects tested many of the action items included in the National Strategy, such as new schools for Roma children, vocational and preschool educational projects, the renovation of apartment blocks, income generation projects, Roma-managed farms, an environmental project, and health projects. All projects were monitored and evaluated throughout and were offered technical assistance by the local management organization (The Roma Communities Resource Center—the RCRC—in Cluj Napoca) as well as the PHARE team.

A recent evaluation found these pilot projects to be generally successful.[b] Many provide useful examples of positive partnering between a range of public institutions (schools, town halls, regional inspectorates, and prefectures) and Roma organizations (NGOs and local initiative groups). These experiences also provide valuable insights into the specific kinds of challenges and misunderstandings that arise in such collaborative attempts. Some PHARE staff and Roma NGO leaders have raised concerns about the longer-term sustainability of individual projects, as well as the degree to which the lessons learned will be incorporated into policy. The original fund has been amalgamated with the RCRC, and in 2002, they received a new grant fund from PHARE Romania (The Civil Society Development, Improvement of Roma Situation Fund).

Notes:
a The Partnership Fund for the Roma was a component of a larger, PHARE-funded project called The Improvement of the Roma Situation in Romania. The two main aims of the project, developed by leading Roma and government representatives as well as the European Community Delegation, were to provide technical assistance to the Government of Romania for the development and implementation of a strategy to improve the Roma situation and the implementation of the Partnership Fund (Murray 2002).
b Murray 2002.

opportunities for collaborative efforts between local officials and Roma representatives (see box 4.3).

While these steps represent important progress on the National Strategy, much work remains to be done in elaborating and strengthening the institutional framework and implementation. While a number of structures have been put in place, the degree to which they are active varies considerably. There is also a general lack of clarity about the specific roles and responsibilities of representatives at different levels. Further, questions have been raised about the criteria used for appointing county and local representatives. The Roma Party has developed a close relationship with the Social Democratic government elected in 2000. While this has granted the Roma Party greater influence over Roma affairs, it has also prompted criticisms about the politicization of Roma appointments in the public administration. Finally, an ongoing concern is the lack of systematic monitoring, evaluation, and enforcement of the strategy.

CONCLUSIONS

This study of Roma in nine communities in Romania shows that Roma face a number of interlocking challenges. Each of these communities has faced varying degrees of labor market exclusion and limited access to education, healthcare, social assistance, and housing. The case studies demonstrate that the nature and extent of this poverty and exclusion reflect both localized geographic and economic conditions and considerable diversity among Roma populations. These challenges point to the need for integrative policies that can be adapted to local circumstances.

This study has examined the extent of this diversity and its effects on access to social services by looking at Roma social conditions in a variety of towns and villages in urban and rural locations throughout Romania. These cases showed variation in relations between Roma and non-Roma ranging from integration to exclusion. They also suggested a relationship between geographic and economic exclusion. Rural communities lack basic infrastructure and utilities and have more limited economic opportunities and access to education and health care than urban communities. Moreover, while regional economic conditions were found to be influential on Roma living conditions and economic opportunities in general, Roma in all localities tended to be worse-off than their non-Roma counterparts. Few Roma were employed in the formal economy; rather, the majority relied on other sources, including trade and day labor.

Access to social services is hampered by a variety of interrelated factors. For example, persistently low levels of educational attainment reflect difficulties in accessing education due to economic constraints, discrimination by educators, as well as Roma attitudes toward education. Relations between Roma and non-Roma were found to play an important role in perpetuating patterns of exclusion. Miscommunication and distrust on both sides compound other forms of exclusion. Efforts such as the training of Roma mediators to facilitate "back to school" programs represent a positive step toward improving the communication between Roma communities and service providers.

Chapter 5
Project Experience in Hungary

Since 1989, more policy and project activity related to Roma has taken place in Hungary than in any other country in Central and Eastern Europe. Considerable research has been conducted; a wide range of Roma-related NGOs have been set up; and numerous projects and pilot projects have been implemented. Successive governments have played an active role in setting policy. Nevertheless, Roma remain among the most marginalized groups in Hungary. As chapter 3 illustrated, their socioeconomic conditions remain well below the national average. There is still room for improvement in the development of effective policies for Roma and their integration into Hungarian society.

This chapter marks a departure from the country studies of the two previous chapters, focusing on the experience of projects and policies. It explores reasons why Hungary has seen a generally higher level of activity on Roma issues and policies toward minorities than other countries in the region and examines some of the project experiences close up. It concludes with an assessment of some lessons learned from the experiences of selected projects and points to future directions in national policy. Looking to the future is important because of the large and growing share of the Roma population in the country—estimated at between 4 and 6 percent. The significant size of Hungary's Roma population and the marked deterioration of their living standards during the transition are important factors that continue to motivate government attention.

A REGIONAL FRONTRUNNER

There has been a far greater proliferation of Roma policies and programs in Hungary than in other countries. Why? In the first place, Hungary's post-transition development process has been both faster and more successful than most. Hungary was among the leading countries for EU accession in the lead-up to enlargement in May 2004. Second, Hungary has historically had a greater involvement in minority issues than its neighbors because of the large number of Hungarians who live as minorities in other countries. Third, the growth of civil society has been more rapid in Hungary than in other countries.

EU Accession

The EU accession process accelerated the adoption of policies related to minorities in Hungary. While the process influenced developments in neighboring countries, the impact came earlier in Hungary. Integration into the EU had been a key goal of Hungary since 1990. In December 1991, Hungary and Poland were the first countries in Central and Eastern Europe to sign association agreements with the EU. In March 1994, Hungary became the first of the transition countries to submit an official membership application. At the outset Hungary was long considered a frontrunner for accession, given its relatively high level of development. Formal negotiations commenced in 1998 and were concluded in December 2002.[57] Following the EU's decision to offer admission to 10 accession countries, including Hungary, at the Copenhagen summit in December 2002, those countries were formally admitted to the EU in May 2004 and took part in European Parliament elections as members in June 2004.

EU policy relating to ethnic minorities, and Roma in particular, informs the political criteria for accession under the subchapter on "human rights and the protection of minorities" that was adopted at the 1993 Copenhagen European Council. In its 2002 Regular Report on Hungary's progress toward accession, the European Commission concluded that Hungary had adopted most of the major international legislation on human rights. Hungary developed a wide-ranging institutional framework for the protection of minorities and the promotion of cultural and educational autonomy. However, it lacks a unified law against discrimination. Current anti-discrimination provisions are fragmented and are included in laws regulating different fields, such as employment and education (Kádár et al. 2002). Since the 2001 Regular Report, Hungary has continued to make progress on the short-term Accession Partnership priority: implementation of the medium-term program for the integration of Roma. According to the 2002 Regular Report:

> The institutional framework (of the medium-term program) has been further strengthened and a new monitoring system introduced. Still, Roma policy is not well integrated into general social development strategies and exists as a separate and parallel project. Roma continue to suffer discrimination. The Government is currently revising its Roma policy. The envisaged adoption of a comprehensive long-term strategy and comprehensive anti-discrimination legislation would be major steps forward in this regard (Commission on the European Communities 2002).

Over the past decade, the EU provided support to Hungary for Roma projects and programs to meet the objectives of the Copenhagen criteria. Between 1992 and 2001, the PHARE program allocated 1,259 million euros to Hungary and another 120.7 million euros in 2002.[58] PHARE support on Roma issues has been earmarked for projects in education, community development, policy formulation, and monitoring.

Hungarian Minorities and Minority Policies

Hungary's approach toward its ethnic minorities is also influenced by a concern for the rights of Hungarians living as minorities in other countries (Crowe 1991; 1994). The reorganization of Hungarian territory in the wake of World War I led to the relocation of millions of former citizens, mostly Hungarians, to other countries. Following the division of the Austro-Hungarian Empire and the 1920 Treaty of Trianon, Hungary lost nearly 70 percent of its previous territory, and 60 percent of its total population, including 28 percent of the Hungarian speakers and the large bulk of its minorities. Hungarians continue to make up substantial shares of the population in a number of neighboring countries: nearly 11 percent in Slovakia (1996), 7.1 percent in Romania (1992), and roughly 4 percent in Austria and Yugoslavia (1991) (see table 5.1).

Policies toward Hungarian minorities abroad do not necessarily translate into the full realization of domestic minority policies. For example, Roma, who are classified as an "ethnic minority" rather than a "national minority," were not originally covered under early drafts of the Minorities Act (Cahn 2001).

The Growth of Civil Society

Hungary's attention to minority concerns is also a function of the significant level of civil society development in the country. NGO activity has been greater in Hungary than in many other countries of the region, in part because of the less restrictive nature of Hungarian communist rule and earlier adoption of legislation regarding NGOs

TABLE 5.1 HUNGARIAN MINORITIES IN OTHER COUNTRIES

Country	Year	Number	Percent of Total Population
Austria	1991 census (based on language used)	33,459	4.3
Croatia	1991 census	22,355	0.5
Romania	1992 census	1,624,956	7.1
Slovakia[a]	2001 census	520,528	9.7
Yugoslavia	1991 census (taken while still united)	345,376	3.9

a Government of Slovakia (1997); OSI (2001).
Source: Government Office for Hungarian Minorities Abroad, http://www.htmh.hu/english.htm.

(Bárány 2002). While the socialist era was characterized by a state monopoly of all spheres of political, social, and economic life, civil organizations, including Roma organizations, were gradually able to secure more autonomy than those under more totalitarian regimes, which did not even allow the formation of such groups (Bárány 2002).

The 1959 Hungarian Civil Code provided for the establishment of civil society organizations (Jenkins 1999). This code explicitly recognized, although under strict administrative control, "social organizations," including political groups, trade unions, and organizations of women, youth, and other groups. Many of the early organizations formed in the final years of socialism survived the transition in 1989, changing their names and transforming themselves into new legal entities (Jenkins 1999). For example, many informal political associations became political parties. In 1993 a unique type of governmentally supported NGO, the "public foundation," was formed (see box 5.1).

BOX 5.1 PUBLIC FOUNDATIONS IN HUNGARY

There are two main types of NGOs in Hungary: associations and foundations.[a] In 1993, a separate, intermediate category of "public foundations" unique to Hungary was created. The government establishes public foundations to fulfill a specific public policy objective. While supported primarily through government financing, they are independent bodies that are intended to be both "state" and "civic" in character.

The identification, development, and implementation of their goals are overseen by an advisory or trustee board, which can consist of members of government (national, county, or municipal), civil society representatives, business interests, and research and academic communities, as appropriate to the foundation goals. In some cases, a representative from a relevant ministry has a position on the board, and the ministry may provide additional direction and oversight. Public foundations are found in all sectors (e.g., education, health, labor, environment, the arts, and culture) and operate at the national, county, and municipal levels. By 1995, there were 458 public foundations, or 3 percent of all foundations, representing just over 1 percent of the total NGO sector (Jenkins 1999).

The Public Foundation for Hungarian Gypsies

In 1990, NEKH was established to develop and oversee minority policy. In conjunction with this office, two public foundations were set up in 1995 to manage the government funds allocated for improving the situation of Roma. In the same year, the Public Foundation for National and Ethnic Minorities was set up, primarily to promote self-identity and

(*continued*)

Box 5.1 (*continued*)

to preserve the cultures of minority communities. Later in 1995, the Public Foundation for Hungarian Gypsies was established. The foundation's objectives are to promote social integration, mitigate unemployment, increase Roma school attendance, and protect civil rights. While by-laws do not exclude outside funding, to date financing has come almost exclusively from the state budget. Total combined government financing was 350 million forints for 2001 and 2002. The majority of this funding is allocated to a scholarship program, enterprise promotion, and support for income-generation projects.

The foundation also supports a wide variety of programs, including small business development and training Roma officials in public administration. The foundation works closely with government and civil society organizations with similar interests. Funding applications can come from Roma MSGs, communities, foundations, municipalities, and individuals.

The foundation's decision-making authority rests with a 21-member Board of Trustees, which is responsible for the mandate of the foundation and for approving all funding applications. The Public Foundation office consists of 10 employees, over half of whom are Roma. They assist the board, administer the projects and funds, and oversee the completion and processing of the applications. In addition, five independent external monitors help prepare applications and monitor and evaluate projects.

Notes:

a These organizations are defined in the Hungarian Civil Code on Associations (sections 61-64) and Foundations (section 74). Both of these organizational forms existed under communism, subject to tight administrative control. Such controls were relaxed and independence from government supervision was instituted through the Law on Association (Law 1990/II, January 1989) and an amendment to the Civil Code (Law 1990/I, January 1990).

Source: Office for National and Ethnic Minorities.

This legacy has contributed to the remarkable post-transition growth in civil society organizations. The NGO sector grew fivefold between 1989 (with just under 8,800 organizations) and 1995 (with more than 43,000 registered organizations) (Jenkins 1999).[59] At the same time, the number of organizations involved in social policy increased significantly, from virtually no presence in the early 1980s, to between one-fifth and one-quarter of NGO activity in 1995. There are also numerous associations active in the areas of culture, religion, and business.

Many of these organizations have focused on the expansion of services and rights for ethnic minorities in general and for Roma in particular. In the last decade, the greater availability of state and NGO funding for Roma issues has led to a rapid proliferation in Roma organizations and events. By the end of 1991, 96 civic bodies concerned with such issues had officially registered (Kállai and Törzsök 2000).[60] By 1994–95, there were nearly 500 organizations, and by 1998, there were over 1,000 registered Roma organizations, including self-governments (discussed further below) and self-organized groups (Kováts 2001a). Financing mechanisms have enabled the growth of the NGO sector in Hungary. Taxpayers are able to earmark 1 percent of their personal income tax for non-profit organizations and another 1 percent for churches. Both are significant sources of financing for Roma interventions.

Despite this growth in activity, the influence of many groups is limited by inadequate access to financing. Because of legislative, financial, and organizational problems, only a small number have survived for more than a few years (PER 1998). Most NGOs, including those concerned with Roma issues, are small and donor driven, "their existence tied to the implementation of specific projects and their activities defined at least in part by the agendas of the organizations that fund them" (OSI 2001).

GOVERNMENT POLICIES AND APPROACHES

Successive Hungarian governments have played an active role in policymaking and establishing institutions to address minority policies in general and Roma issues in particular. Perhaps most notably, in 1993 Hungary adopted the Minorities Act, which granted considerable cultural, educational, and linguistic rights to Hungary's 13 recognized minorities through a system of national and local minority self-governments (MSGs).[61] This system is unique to Hungary. The country has also established the Office for National and Ethnic Minorities (NEKH) and the independent Minorities Ombudsman to oversee minority rights and protections. Most recently, following the 2002 elections, the government established a new Roma Office under the Office of the Prime Minister, to coordinate Roma policy across the government.[62]

Government funding for minorities is distributed through multiple channels (see table 5.2). Roma populations often benefit from general programs for minorities. For example, the largest budget allocation goes to the education of minorities. In 1999, a total of 4.6 billion forints was allocated for preschools, schools, and dormitories for national and ethnic minorities and for additional subsidies for non-minority bilingual educational institutions (Implementation Report 1999). In the 1999–2000 school year, the Public Foundation for National and Ethnic Minorities provided support for 586 Roma secondary school students

TABLE 5.2 GOVERNMENT BUDGETARY SUPPORT FOR MINORITIES

	1997 *(million ft)*	1998 *(million ft)*	1999 *(million ft)*
National Minority Self-Governments (total)	306.0	398.7	506.0
Roma National Self-Government	96.0	120.0	138.0
Local Minority Self-Governments (total)	300.0	350.0	730.0
Minority civil organizations	70.0	79.1	87.8
Public Foundation for National and Ethnic Minorities	395.0	474.0	530.0
Public Foundation for Hungarian Gypsies	170.0	250.0	280.0
Minority Coordination and Intervention Budget[a]	50.0	55.0	44.0
Ministry of Education, for minority tasks	274.9	290.0	250.0
Gandhi Foundation	325.0	230.0	210.0
Minority theaters	62.0	67.0	74.0
Ministry of National Cultural Heritage (support for cultural programs and minority literature)			100.0

a The Minority Coordination and Intervention Budget is used for solving crisis situations concerning minorities that require urgent resolution.
Source: Implementation Report 1999.

and 111 Roma university students.[63] Budgetary allocations specifically targeted for Roma include those for the Roma national and local minority self-governments, the Public Foundation for Hungarian Gypsies, and the Gandhi Foundation. The Gandhi Foundation has also received a significant proportion of government financing, beginning with 325 million forints in 1997, and falling to 210 million forints in 1999.[64]

Office for National and Ethnic Minorities

NEKH was one of the first new institutions established in 1990. Its mandate has been to assist in the development of government minority policies and to review and monitor the situation of minority communities. Its activities in supporting Roma include financial support to Roma organizations, such as the National Roma Information and Cultural Center, the network of Roma Minority Community Houses, as well as to various Roma magazines and radio and TV programs. Since the mid-1990s, NEKH has taken a leading role in developing and overseeing the implementation of the government's Medium-Term Package for Roma.

While there has been consensus about the necessity of NEKH's activities, concerns have been raised about its ability to effectively perform its mandate, due to a perceived lack of authority and difficulty in coordinating across government agencies. Many of NEKH's responsibilities related to the social integration of Roma and coordination on sectoral policies have been transferred to the new Roma Office following its establishment in 2002. This change is intended to strengthen coordination and monitoring of Roma policies at the interministerial level. Responsibility for Roma culture and minority rights remains with NEKH.

The Medium-Term Package

The first version of the Medium-Term Package was adopted in 1997 and was aimed at furthering the social integration of Roma in Hungary. It outlines measures to be undertaken in education, culture, employment, housing, health, anti-discrimination, and communication. Implementation efforts were to be coordinated by the Council for Gypsy Affairs, a body established in 1995 to harmonize the efforts of government ministries and other bodies in addressing Roma issues. A 1999 review shifted the primary emphasis to education and culture and replaced the Council for Gypsy Affairs with the Inter-Ministerial Committee for Gypsy Affairs.[65] Implementation itself is assigned to different government ministries and other bodies, in cooperation with the Roma National Minority Self-Government (NMSG). In 2000, budgetary resources allocated for the implementation of the Medium-Term Package amounted to around 4.86 billion forints (Kállai and Törzsök 2000).[66]

The adoption of the Medium-Term Package was an important step in addressing Roma concerns in Hungary. However, its effectiveness to date has been limited (OSI 2001). Main critiques revolve around weak coordination across the government and a general lack of competence and authority, both of which significantly hamper implementation. This lack of coordination, combined with a lack of clarity, transparency, and financial resources have limited the package's effectiveness.

The Parliamentary Commissioner for Ethnic and National Minorities

The Parliamentary Commissioner for Ethnic and National Minorities (Minorities Ombudsman) is an independent institution established to monitor the implementation of minority rights, to investigate complaints, and pursue remediation for the infringements of the rights of national and ethnic minorities.[67] According to the ombudsman's office, Roma have lodged the vast majority of complaints. Their concerns are disproportionately related to acts of discrimination (OSI 2001). The ombudsman reports that prejudice and discrimination against the Roma are widespread in areas such as law enforcement, employment, education, housing, and access to public and private institutions (Commission of the European Communities 2000). Further, the ombudsman reported that approximately 48 percent of complaints submitted by Roma in 2000 were filed against local governments (Ombudsman 2000 in OSI 2001).

The Minorities Act and the Role of Minority Self-Governments

The Minorities Act of 1993 expanded minority rights in Hungary and established Hungary's unique MSG system, which allows minorities to form their own elected bodies to work in partnership with both local and national governments. The act guarantees all recognized minorities individual and collective rights. The act explicitly established Roma as one of the 13 recognized national and ethnic minorities in Hungary for the first time. The MSG system was established as part of a general approach toward minority integration, through recognition of the collective rights of minorities, and the introduction of unique mechanisms for resource allocation and political voice.

The National Minority Self-Government system for Roma and other minorities was established in 1995. Representatives and spokespersons of local MSGs vote for the NMSG.[68] The first Roma NMSG was a coalition formed by the Lungo Drom Gypsy Association, which won all 53 seats. The government is required to provide funding for NMSG headquarters, infrastructure, and operating costs.

The scope of authority and duties of the NMSG fall into two general categories: independent decision making in specific areas[69] and consultation and oversight on sectoral policies and administration (Articles 38 and 39) (Walsh 2000). In this latter role, the NMSGs act as mediators between local MSGs and the government and as consultants in the drafting of legislation that affects the minority at all levels of government. They are also expected to take part in the supervision of minority education. Despite these guidelines, the Roma NMSG as well as those of other minorities have been challenged by the lack of precedent and clarity on the nature of the relationships between the NMSGs and local MSGs and their corresponding governmental authorities (Kováts 2001b).[70] While the Roma NMSG had an important role in shaping the Medium-Term Package for improving the condition of Roma and has undertaken a number of high profile initiatives, insufficient finances and the absence of governmental financial guarantees have limited its capacity to fully exercise its rights (Kováts 2001b).

Local MSGs are elected bodies at the local level. They do not have a vote in the majority local governments, but they can veto any local government decision over matters that may affect them, particularly those concerned with education, culture, local media, efforts to sustain cultural traditions, and the use of minority languages (Commission on the European Communities 2000; Doncsev 2000). The first MSG elections were held in 1994–95 and resulted in a total of 738 MSGs, of which 477 were Roma. Following the second round of elections held in 1998, the number of local and Roma MSGs nearly doubled, to 1,367 and 753, respectively (NEKH 2000). By June 30, 2000, there were 738 Roma local MSGs out of a total of 1,339 local MSGs, compared with 271 German, 75 Croatian, and 75 Slovak.[71]

The MSG system has garnered international attention and has raised the profile of Roma issues and the status of Roma communities and their representatives, as well as those of other minority groups in Hungary. However, its effectiveness has been mixed. A national survey of 232 Roma political leaders in 1998 showed that some Roma MSGs had been more active in political and social areas within their communities than others (Schafft and Brown 2000).

Many Roma MSGs have been able to successfully initiate a variety of projects to the benefit of their communities. The same survey identified the frequency with which MSGs engaged in different kinds of development initiatives, as well as which of these were perceived to be most important (see table 5.3) (Schafft and Brown 2000). Over 75 percent indicated that their MSG was involved in the provision of social welfare and just over 60 percent identified cultural

TABLE 5.3 ROMA MSG LOCAL DEVELOPMENT INITIATIVES, 1998

Development Initiatives	Involvement (percent)[a]	Cited among "Most Important" MSG Activities (percent)[b]
Social welfare programs	78.8	21.4
Cultural programs/festivals	61.1	18.1
Education/job training	60.7	30.2
Agricultural support	58.4	32.0
Local media programming	45.5	9.0
Economic enterprises/ business start-up	42.4	12.7

Notes: Based on interviews with 232 Roma leaders. See footnotes, below.
a As reported in close-ended question responses.
b As reported in open-ended question responses.
Sources: Schafft 1999; Schafft and Brown 2000.

and educational/training programs. The provision of local media programming and economic enterprise/business start-up activities were less frequent (46 percent and 42 percent, respectively). Agricultural support was cited as the most important activity, followed by social welfare programs, and education/job training. Least important were opportunities for local media programming.

The survey suggests that some Roma MSGs do function as a valuable resource to their communities. It also found that the more successful MSGs with higher institutional capacity tended to exhibit higher levels of social cohesion among Roma themselves. They successfully built relations between Roma and non-Roma based on norms of trust and cooperation and could create effective institutional linkages outside of the locality (Schafft and Brown 2000).

This study and others have identified a number of factors that limit the effectiveness of MSGs, including their relatively narrow focus on "cultural" issues, financial constraints, limited capacities and influence, and their perceived lack of legitimacy. The following summarizes some of the main challenges to effective minority self-governance.

Dependence on Local Governments for Financing

MSGs receive a small amount of funding annually from the state budget and therefore are required to seek funding from multiple sources, including county and local governments and outside bodies. The Minorities Act does not provide for any explicit financing to MSGs. The amount specified by the Budget Act for MSGs is allocated in equal proportions among municipal governments, irrespective of their size or the size of the minority population in the area. These funding considerations have three important consequences. First, in practice, MSGs are increasingly dependent on local municipal governments for funding, which can compromise their independence. Second, financial constraints in many cases prevent MSGs from implementing even their short-term mandates, let alone meeting the expectations of the electorate (Kállai 2000). Third, funding uncertainties limit medium- and long-term strategic planning.

Lack of Capacity and Influence

In addition to a general lack of financing, some of the most significant problems reported about the MSG system are related to their lack of capacity (Kállai 2000). For example, most MSGs do not have sufficient information about the various legal, tendering, lobbying, and cooperating opportunities, and little of this information is readily available, even from the Roma NMSG. Second, minority representatives tend to lack political experience and professional training. These problems are compounded in the case of Roma MSGs, given the smaller pool of professionally trained, educated, and politically experienced Roma candidates.

Lack of Legitimacy/Representativeness

Roma MSGs are also criticized for being unrepresentative. One reason is that there is no requirement that representatives who are elected to the MSG need to be a member of that minority. While the Minorities Act addresses the difficult question of who is a minority, relying solely on self-identification implies a degree of flexibility that has caused difficulties, particularly in terms of minority representation (Kállai and Törzsök 2000). For example, in the 1998 round of local elections, a number of individuals were elected to MSGs, even though they did not belong to that minority. This happened in the town of Hajdúhadház, where two non-Roma were elected to the Roma MSG. The role of non-Roma in MSGs is controversial. On the one hand, a mix of Roma and non-Roma can facilitate cooperation, particularly with the local government. On the other it can undermine the local Roma community's confidence in the MSG.

Focus on Cultural Issues

As outlined in the 1993 Minorities Act, the most important task of MSGs is to build cultural autonomy for minorities. While this issue in all its forms—educational, linguistic, and maintenance of traditions—is an important aspect of improving the status of Roma, it may not always be the most urgent issue for local Roma communities. More pressing are concerns related to the disproportionately high unemployment rates and the mass impoverishment of much of the Roma population, which are only indirectly addressed via the current MSG systems.

PROJECT EXPERIENCE: AN OVERVIEW

This overview covers a selection of Roma projects initiated in Hungary during the first decade following transition, while the following section draws some general lessons. In spring 2000, the World Bank collaborated with a team of Hungarian researchers to compile a database of Roma projects in Hungary.[72] At that time, no aggregate information was available on the types of projects that had been implemented, their size, coverage, geographic concentration, or sectoral focus. Policymakers, the NGO community, and others involved in the Roma issue had no information on which to base their project development and partnership.

The database aimed to review the landscape of Roma projects that had been implemented in Hungary from 1990 to 1999 and to provide a basis for an assessment of Roma policy in this period. The review focused on selected projects in the areas of employment, education, housing, and health and was designed to create a resource that would be useful for policymakers, NGO officials, Roma leaders, and others involved in Roma projects. The inventory identified 1,396 projects with a total cost of 3.6 billion forints that were implemented and financed by central and local governments, NGOs, and the private sector.

A broad definition of "Roma projects" was used. Some projects included in the inventory had both Roma and non-Roma beneficiaries, such as the social land project discussed later in this chapter. The aggregate data from the inventory illustrate a steady increase in project activity related to Roma during the 1990s, as well as in the amount of resources spent (see table 5.4).

The spike in expenditures in 1993 represents a grant of 215 million forints, which the Soros Foundation provided for the establishment of the Gandhi secondary school for Roma in Pécs in southern Hungary. In 1996, the increase in expenditures represents the government's initiative to establish the Public Foundation for Roma (see box 5.1). Of this amount, approximately 30 percent was allocated to income-generating programs, 20 percent to small business development, and 15 percent to scholarships for students.

A fund established in 1998 by the Roma NMSG and the central government to help local governments co-finance regional development

TABLE 5.4 PROJECT INVENTORY, 1990–99

Year	Number of Projects	Total Expenditures (thousand ft)	Percent of Government Expenditures
1990	1	150	0.00
1991	19	6,218	0.00
1992	29	70,657	0.00
1993[a]	47	413,726	0.02
1994	63	179,486	0.01
1995	116	279,332	0.01
1996	241	569,910	0.02
1997	288	555,877	0.02
1998	253	643,731	0.02
1999	339	922,240	0.02
Total	**1,396**	**3,641,327**	**0.07**

a The 1993 increase in resources reflects the investment of the Soros Foundation in the Gandhi School.

Source: World Bank project database.

programs through grants significantly increased the total resources allocated for Roma projects. The fund started with 100 million forints and finances primarily the upgrading of local infrastructure. The first programs were launched in 1999, but as the flow of information from Regional Development Councils to the relevant government ministries is limited, only some of these projects are included in the project inventory.

Regional Distribution of Projects

The geographic distribution of projects across counties in Hungary reflects the country's ethnic diversity. Table 5.5 illustrates the regional breakdown for all projects that could be mapped to a specific county.[73] The regions with the largest shares of Roma, Northern Hungary, the North Great Plain, and Southern Danubia, have the greatest share of projects. These are also the regions that have consistently had the highest unemployment rates,[74] indicating that project activity may also reflect greater need in those areas.

Per capita expenditures on projects vary significantly across regions, but were the highest in Southern Danubia. This reflects higher spending in two counties—Baranya and Tolna. In Baranya, a significant amount was spent on the Gandhi School in Pécs. In Tolna, 280 million forints were spent on infrastructure for utilities. In Zala County in Western Danubia and Jász-Nagykun-Szolnok County in the North Great Plain region the situation is different, as a large number of Roma organizations have been involved in implementing projects.

TABLE 5.5 PROJECTS BY REGION, 1990–99

County	Percent of Total Projects	Percent of Total Roma[a] (thousand ft)	Total Expenditures	Per Capita Expenditures
Budapest	4.5	8.2	93,590	2,472
Central Region	2.4	6.0	63,403	2,302
Western Danubia	3.5	5.0	111,096	4,803
Northern Danubia	2.1	5.5	22,799	905
Southern Danubia	16.5	14.2	784,492	11,993
Northern Hungary	34.3	27.9	865,739	6,722
North Great Plain	29.0	25.4	817,098	6,965
South Great Plain	7.7	8.0	205,703	5,571
Total	**100.0**	**100.0**	**2,963,920**	**6,413**

a 1992 estimates by G. Kertesi and G. Kézdi.

Source: World Bank project database.

TABLE 5.6 DISTRIBUTION OF PROJECTS BY SECTOR, 1990–99

Sector	Number of Projects	Percent of Total Projects	Total Expenditures (thousand ft)	Percent of Total Expenditures	Average Project Size (thousand ft)
Education	200	14.3	1,024,233	28.1	5,121
Employment	1,121	80.2	2,174,272	59.7	1,940
Health	36	2.6	32,795	0.9	911
Housing	3	0.2	2,700	0.1	900
Community centers	9	0.6	11,877	0.3	1,320
Miscellaneous	29	2.1	395,451	10.9	13,636
Total	**1,398**	**100.0**	**3,641,328**	**100.0**	**23,828**

Source: World Bank project database.

Sectoral Distribution of Projects

There is a wide divergence in the activity level (measured as a percentage of total projects and as a percentage of total expenditures) in each sector examined in the inventory. The highest activity levels took place in education and employment and the lowest levels in health and housing (see table 5.6).[75] In education, 21 percent of the total expenditures represent the investment in the Gandhi School. The Soros Foundation's scholarship program also comprises a significant share of the resources allocated to the sector. During the period covered by the inventory, 3 percent of projects were devoted to health issues and less than 1 percent to housing. Projects categorized as "miscellaneous" are multisectoral, generally addressing housing and employment issues, and are largely financed by the Regional Development Councils. Community development projects in Borsod-Abaúj-Zemplén County (57 million forints) and the installation of gas pipes in Tolna County (280 million forints) comprise a large share of this category.

Funding Sources

Between 1990 and 1999, most projects were implemented with government financing (62 percent), although a significant portion (38 percent) was financed by private foundations (see table 5.7). Government ministries financed 23 percent of all projects, representing the largest percentage of total expenditures (38 percent).[76] Government sponsorship of projects also included public foundations (30 percent of all projects and 10 percent of total expenditures) and the Regional Development Councils (with only 2 percent of all projects accounting for 16 percent of total expenditures). Public foundations supported 31 percent of all projects.

TABLE 5.7 PROJECTS BY DONORS, 1990–99

Donor	Number of Projects	Percent of Total Projects	Total Expenditures (thousand ft)	Percent of Total Expenditures
Private foundations				
Autonómia Foundation	474	34.0	274,409	7.5
Network for Democracy (DemNet)	4	0.3	8,379	0.2
Soros Foundation	52	3.7	824,902	22.7
Government financed				
Public Foundation for Modernizing Public Education	4	0.3	5,500	0.2
Ministries	318	22.8	1,364,313	37.5
National Foundation for Employment (OFA)	12	0.9	117,784	3.233
National Institution for Health Prevention (NEVI)	29	2.1	21,602	0.6
NEKH	37	2.6	63,891	1.8
Public foundations	431	30.9	369,349	10.2
Regional Development Councils	34	2.4	586,615	16.1
Total	**1,395**	**100.0**	**3,636,744**	**100.0**

Source: World Bank project database.

Two private non-profit foundations, Autonómia and Soros, accounted for 30 percent of the total expenditures for this period. The Autonómia Foundation undertook the greatest number of projects (34 percent of the total), accounting for 8 percent of total expenditures. The Soros Foundation was responsible for 23 percent of all expenditures.

PROJECT CASE STUDIES

In addition to the project inventory, the Hungarian research team undertook more in-depth case studies on a select set of projects, based on interviews with project administrators and beneficiaries. As noted throughout this book, there has been limited evaluation of Roma projects. While these assessments do not substitute for rigorous project evaluation mechanisms built in ex ante, they provide insight into issues and lessons. The case studies were designed to validate the information collected during the inventory and to see if projects included in the database were actually implemented on the ground. Based on that experience, general lessons can be drawn to inform future projects.

Case Study # 1: Segregated Education in Hajdúhadház[77]

The case of the education of Roma children in Hajdúhadház illustrates how poorly designed incentives can undermine policy objectives. In Hajdúhadház, as is the case throughout Hungary, local governments receive subsidies to support the education of Roma children. However, as illustrated in this case, the subsidies work to reinforce segregation and compromise the quality of education for Roma students.

Hajdúhadház is a town of 13,000 in eastern Hungary. It is situated 12 miles from Debrecen, the second largest city in the country. Approximately 2,400 residents are thought to be Roma, and the share of the Roma population in the town is growing rapidly. According to local estimates, about half of the children who registered for school during the past few years are Roma. The local economy has deteriorated since 1989. In 2000, the unemployment rate was estimated at 40 percent for the whole population and 95 percent for Roma. According to local leaders, the large majority of educated residents leave the area for opportunities elsewhere. Local relations between Roma and non-Roma are generally characterized by segregation, hostility, and tension.

There is a high degree of segregation within the Hajdúhadház schools. The majority of Roma children attend separate remedial classes in the two primary schools in the town, the Földi János and Bocskai Schools. They study separately from non-Roma children, with different teachers, textbooks, poorer conditions, and fewer resources than their peers. A 1999 report by the Debrecen public health service "strongly objected" to conditions in the Roma section of the Bocskai School. The classroom walls were rotting, the floor was unstable, toilets broken, and lighting insufficient. Since there was no gymnasium, physical education classes were held in the hallways and classrooms.

Bridging Classes

Both schools receive state subsidies for the education of Roma children. According to law, these resources are intended for remedial "bridging" classes and courses on Roma culture and education. Bridging classes are intended to overcome the educational disadvantages of Roma children—many of whom do not attend preschool—and to integrate them into the mainstream education system. In practice, these programs tend to perpetuate segregated education and are constrained by the lack of qualified staff and resources. In 1998, 67 percent of the Roma students in the Földi János School studied in segregated Roma classes.

Students in the bridging programs learn the same material as those in mainstream classes, but go through less material at a slower rate. As a result, while the aim may be to bring Roma students up to standard levels, their chances of returning to mainstream classes are reduced each year that they stay in the bridging classes. In addition to the bridging classes, an estimated one-fourth of Roma students in Hajdúhadház study in special classes for the mentally disabled that the Bocskai School runs. In 2000, 132 out of 156 students in the special education classes were Roma. It is very rare for children who attend these classes to continue their education on to secondary school.[78]

In Hajdúhadház, students are placed in the bridging classes based on the evaluation of teachers and whether they have attended preschool. While preschool in Hungary lasts three years, only the final year is compulsory. As a result, Roma students are frequently placed in bridging classes, because they generally attend only one year of preschool. The Földi János School principal explained, "The only selection criteria [for bridging classes] is preschool education. To place someone in the normal class without complete preschool education would be similar to a race between a Trabant and a Mercedes."

The educational subsidies are also earmarked to support the inclusion of Roma culture and history in the curriculum. While the intentions of this policy are positive, the schools and teachers were unprepared to provide this type of instruction. While more than half of the 160 teachers in Hajdúhadház teach Roma children, few have any training in multicultural education or access to appropriate teaching materials. The principals of both schools also noted prejudices among their teachers. In 1992 the Földi János School principal asked his colleagues to list the three best features of their school. The third most common answer was the segregation of Roma pupils into separate buildings. Some teachers also noted that they viewed having to teach bridging and special classes as punishment. Even when teachers have good intentions, their lack of background and understanding of Roma issues limit their effectiveness. In the Földi János School, one of the teachers learned the Roma language, but teaches a dialect which is not spoken in the settlement.

The majority of Roma parents interviewed in both the Földi János and Bocskai schools expressed dissatisfaction with the segregated schooling system in Hajdúhadház. From the Földi János School, 13 families reported that they had protested against the poor school conditions and teaching quality, but their children were never admitted to the central building. Nearly 70 percent of Roma families who were interviewed indicated that they felt that their children should be allowed to study in mixed classes. Similar sentiments were expressed at the Bocskai School.

Financing Separate Education

Hungary's system of intergovernmental transfers reinforces the separate education of Roma students. As the subsidies are earmarked for bridging and special classes, schools have a financial incentive to maintain these programs, regardless of their usefulness. Both schools have expanded their Roma sections. At the Földi János School, a storeroom was recently converted into another Roma classroom.

While schools have an incentive to retain their subsidies, local governments use the provision of additional resources to the schools as an excuse to decrease their contributions to the schools' budgets. In other words, the local governments reduce their support to the schools in proportion to the subsidy amount. This squeezes the schools fiscally, as the bridging and special schools cost more than the regular classes. The Földi János School principal estimated that the Roma program cost three times as much per student as the subsidy provided by the state.

There is little monitoring of the use of the subsidies. However, the Ministry of Education undertook a national survey of their use in 2001. The ministry, through a research center, contacted more than 900 mayors, of whom 370 did not respond. Those mayors who did respond acknowledged that there were no bridging classes in their schools, although they did receive the subsidies.

The challenges of addressing Roma education in Hajdúhadház are evident elsewhere in Hungary. Recent studies indicate that the implementation of "catch-up" classes in Hungary is widespread. As of 1995, catch-up programs were in 433 schools (Radó 1997). While initially envisaged as a temporary solution, in many cases bridging classes have resulted in long-term institutional segregation, in part due to inadequate facilities, the quality of education in the segregated classes, and the growing resistance by teachers and parents in the mainstream schools to register Roma students at all. Analyses of catch-up programs have revealed that they generally are of low quality, and sometimes exist "in name only" (i.e., not following the specified curriculum) (Radó 1997; Havas et al. 2001). Further, in many areas exclusionary practices persist, including the continued practice of placing Roma in special schools for the disabled.

Case Study # 2: Roma Employment Project in Bagamér[79]

A common sentiment among policymakers and others interested in expanding opportunities for Roma in Hungary and in other countries is that agricultural programs can provide opportunities for self-sufficiency, particularly for Roma in rural areas. In reality there has been very little experience with agricultural programs, and even less evaluation of whether such projects yield their intended results and mitigate rural Roma unemployment. A horseradish project in Bagamér provides a glimpse of how such a project can play out in practice.

The village of Bagamér is situated near the Romanian border, 30 kilometers from Debrecen. In 1999, it had a population of 2,580. There are 186 Roma families in Bagamér, or approximately one-third of the population. Between 1989 and 1992, the majority of Roma employed in state-owned enterprises lost their jobs. In 1999, 80 percent of the heads of Roma families were without legal and permanent work. Restructuring and unemployment affected the entire labor force. The agricultural cooperative in the area, which primarily employed non-Roma, was privatized. These developments led to the emergence of a number of private farms, which rely on more temporary, seasonal labor, rather than on permanent employees. This increased competition for employment and heightened ethnic tensions in the village.

Horseradish cultivation has a long tradition in Bagamér. The plant is processed for use in the food industry and as an ingredient in some pharmaceuticals. Growing horseradish is labor intensive and requires special knowledge. During the socialist period, some private farms and agricultural cooperatives specialized in cultivating horseradish. As a result, at the outset of the transition, a market existed with a network of producers who processed and sold the product on domestic and foreign markets. Although Roma participated in horseradish cultivation as seasonal workers, they were left out of the privatization process because they did not own land or had not been members of the local cooperative. As a result, they were not eligible to become landowners and independent horseradish farmers.

In 1996 Miklós Rózsás, an energetic and prominent member of the local Roma community and chairman of the Local Association of Roma Leaders, and Sándor Zsákai, another leader of the same association, came up with the idea to help Roma become horseradish farmers. They tried to raise money and sent a proposal to the Autonómia Foundation and the Public Foundation for Hungarian Gypsies. Their initiative was rejected at first, but in 1997 they received 1.5 million forints (about US$7,000) from the Autonómia Foundation under the condition that half of the sum would be repaid to the foundation after the harvest. After that they received support from the foundation every year for their horseradish-growing program, and in 2000 and 2001, the total subsidy was provided as a grant.

During the first phase of the project, 1997–99, resources were requested for plowing, fertilizer, pesticides, spraying, irrigation, harvesting, and transportation. The association also requested money for leasing land, while pledging that part of the profit would be spent on future land purchases. The Autonómia funds were transferred in several installments and linked to progress in the project. The association paid providers directly for services such as plowing, while individual producers paid other services. The contract between Autonómia and the association defined the upper limit of what could be paid to each household and for each phase of work, but the beneficiaries themselves could decide when to withdraw the money.

During the first project phase, all participating households but one repaid the loans after the harvest. In 2000 financing conditions changed significantly. The project cycle was extended to two years, and the subsidy became a non-refundable grant. From 2000 onwards the Autonómia Foundation focused its efforts on projects that could become self-sustaining over time. The aims were to support entrepreneurial initiatives and Roma who could become primary producers. The majority of the participants in the Bagamér project in 2000 and 2001 already owned land and were ready to continue farming.

A weakness of the Bagamér project is its small scale. While the nominal value of the financial support from Autonómia has essentially remained the same since 1997, cultivation costs have significantly increased and that has deterred many households from participating in the program. In 2000, 13 families were included in the program, down from 19 in 1997. Another criticism of the project was its lack of targeting and lack of transparency in selecting beneficiaries. The association's main concern was to repay the grant to Autonómia, therefore it sought families that were most likely to succeed in the project, rather than making need a priority. This practice has led to charges of "elitism" from households left out of the project.

Despite these criticisms, the project remained viable. The project demonstrates that even given favorable market conditions, success requires a fortuitous combination of circumstances, including enthusiastic leadership, a profound knowledge of the production process, conducive environmental conditions, and a sponsor that is ready to take risks.

Case Study # 3: The Social Land Program in Zsadány[80]

The Zsadány case study provides another example of an agricultural project. Zsadány is a village in Békés County. Of its 1,882 inhabitants, from 100 to 150 are Roma. The village has been struck by widespread unemployment, agricultural crises, and rural poverty. It has an exceptionally high unemployment rate. Out of the 670 working-age inhabitants, 300 are registered as unemployed. Despite this, the population has been stable for many years, with amicable relations between Roma and the majority population. Roma in Zsadány are relatively well integrated into the larger community, they work and live together with non-Roma, and mixed marriages are not uncommon. Rather than succumbing to economic decline, the mayor and the local government have actively sought to rejuvenate the village, including applying successfully for public work programs from the central government and initiating the social land program.

The Social Land Program

Since 1990, relevant ministries have financed social land programs across Hungary, and mostly the Ministry of Social and Family Affairs has supported these programs. The main objective of these programs is to alleviate rural poverty by providing financial assistance, services, and support to poor households that lack the means and capacity to engage in small-scale farming or animal-breeding projects (see table 5.8). Nearly 75 percent of the programs offer assistance in production and services and are aimed at increasing self-sufficiency and income levels. The program is open to Roma and non-Roma families and is means-tested to reach the poorest households. Roma comprise 51 percent of the beneficiaries of the program throughout the country, while regionally the rates vary from 29 percent (Békés County) to 70 percent (Jász-Nagykun-Szolnok County).

The Zsadány Program

The local government started the social land program in Zsadány in 1995. While the primary program goal is to improve the living conditions and prospects of the poor, other aims include stimulating

TABLE 5.8 PROGRAM AND ACTIVITIES SUPPORTED UNDER THE SOCIAL LAND PROGRAM

Program Types	Activities
1. Assistance in production and services (means tested)	Use of land; leasing of land, seeds, machinery, and chemicals; support for animal breeding
2. Organization and integration of production	Organization of production and marketing; assistance in processing, storing, and transportation of crops; securing tools
3. Services directed at the participants	Technical assistance; training courses, events; community development; self-aid groups; setting up organizations for more effective production

Source: Ministry of Social and Family Affairs of Hungary.

community involvement in local development, providing public works, promoting inclusion of poor and excluded groups, and reducing prejudices against Roma and other vulnerable groups.

The Ministry of Social and Family Affairs has supported the Zsadány initiative every year since 1995, with the exception of 1997, when the Autonómia Foundation filled the gap. The Public Foundation for Hungarian Gypsies also provided support. Ministry assistance resumed between 1998 and 2000. While the amount of financial support remained relatively stable, the content of the program has changed considerably over the years. The project initially focused on growing tomatoes; however, because of unfavorable environmental and market conditions, in 1998 cultivation shifted to corn and mixed vegetables, along with rabbit breeding. Over the years, significant investments have been made in agricultural assets (machines and land).

Of the 40 families participating as of 1999, 20 were Roma. The turnover of participants is relatively high; only half continued in the program for a second year. There are various reasons for the high turnover, including better employment opportunities elsewhere. As of 1999, only three people were excluded from participating in the program.

By most accounts, the program is considered to be important in its attempts to address problems such as poverty, unemployment, and social exclusion. Program profitability is modest at best. According to the rough estimates of the local government in 1998, every forint of assistance generated an income of 1.3 forints. A benefit of the program is that the long-term unemployed become eligible for unemployment benefits after six months of program participation.

Given the kinds of environmental and market conditions that plague agricultural production, as well as local challenges related to the lack of arable land and the small scale of production, small projects supported under the social land program rarely become sustainable. Nevertheless, the program has demonstrated adaptability and flexibility. Investments in assets have improved program efficiency and effectiveness, which contributed by providing relatively stable sources of legal income to beneficiaries, easing the poverty of rural families and increasing community acceptance and inclusion of both Roma and non-Roma families.

Case Study # 4: Is Nyíregyháza Building a "Roma Town"?[81]

Between 1998 and 2000, the local government of Nyíregyháza worked hard to develop one of the largest Roma settlements in Hungary. The city invested significant resources of its own into the development of the settlement, named "Gusev," as well as funds received from the central government and donors. City officials organized public work programs, developed the sewage system, replaced the water pipes, and opened a Roma community center. The results of these investments are significant. However, if the entire program is implemented, it will further separate Roma in Nyíregyháza from the rest of the population.

Nyíregyháza is located in Szabolcs County. It has two large Roma settlements: the Orosi Street settlement, which is located at the eastern gate of the city in a prosperous area, and the Gusev settlement, which is one of the largest Roma settlements in Hungary. Gusev is located on the city outskirts, separated from the majority population by a railway station, military barracks, and an industrial zone. The city's plans are to remove the Orosi settlement and rehabilitate the Gusev settlement to accommodate both populations.

The Orosi settlement was built in the 1960s as a temporary housing settlement. By the 1980s, urban sprawl around the impoverished settlement had grown substantially, prompting the municipality to demolish half of the houses and relocate the families to Gusev. In the 1990s, pressures to remove the remainder of the settlement increased, prompted in part by increasing property values and dynamic development in the surrounding area, including several new shopping malls and plans to build a foreign-funded exhibition center adjacent to the Roma settlement. According to a 1993 survey, there were approximately 510 Roma still living in the settlement.

In contrast, the Gusev settlement was created in the late nineteenth century and served as barracks of the monarchy's cavalry regiment. In the 1950s, it was used to house Soviet officers, and later it became a residence of the local party and administration elite. In the 1960s, the appeal of the settlement declined as more affluent families moved to new high-rise housing estates. By the 1970s, the settlement became a "penal colony" within the public housing system. Families in debt, evicted families, and many Roma who had moved into the city were provided with housing in Gusev. A survey conducted in the early 1990s indicated that there were about 830 registered residents living in Gusev. Current estimates place the population at more than 1,000. Over the years, the settlement's infrastructure and reputation have deteriorated, and the population has become predominantly Roma.

In the 1990s, the city of Nyíregyháza undertook a wide range of urban development projects aimed at cleaning up the inner city and fostering investments in industry and services. Investors interested in the city's development potential have pressed for the removal of the Orosi Street settlement. In response, the municipality agreed that Gusev be rehabilitated and more housing be built to accommodate new residents, including those from Orosi Street. Moving the large number of Orosi Roma into other neighborhoods in Nyíregyháza was deemed too politically risky.

In 1998, the local government established a corporation to oversee local housing development, including new housing and rehabilitation, the management of the meager public rental housing stock, collection of debts, and relocations. The city council approved 60 million forints for the program and received an additional grant of 25 million forints from the central government for public works. Staircases of the apartments were repainted, basements cleaned, and sidewalks constructed in the narrow streets. Water pipes were replaced throughout the settlement, and water meters were installed in the single-room units. The Roma Community Hall was refurbished. Special programs for children, job clubs, art clubs, and various competitions were introduced to reduce the exclusion in the settlement and reinforce local trust in municipal institutions, programs, and resources. A wide range of further improvements is planned, including a homeless shelter, additional sewage, and the installation of district heating in all apartments.

Improving the living conditions and access to services in the Gusev settlement seems to be a move in the right direction. Yet, rehabilitation of the settlement and the relocation of Roma families from Orosi will further isolate the Roma population by increasing their geographic and educational segregation from the rest of the population in Nyíregyháza. Further, it ignores the strong potential for increased interethnic tensions among Roma. The two Roma communities are opposed to the idea of living together. This has further heightened tensions within the Roma community and increased suspicion of the local government among Roma.

PROJECT EXPERIENCE: LESSONS LEARNED

Despite the diversity of the projects reviewed in the case studies, some general issues and conclusions emerged that have implications for future projects in Hungary and elsewhere

Tradeoffs in Managing Project Objectives

The success of many projects depends on how project objectives are interpreted and managed. In many cases, project objectives entail difficult tradeoffs and the negotiation of multiple—often conflicting—interests of donors, implementing organizations, beneficiaries, and majority communities.

Targeting Beneficiaries

Beneficiary selection involves tradeoffs in objectives. For example, the Bagamér horseradish project selected participants based on their capacity for success in farming and did not necessarily seek the families in greatest need. This approach can be controversial because of the high poverty level among Roma communities. However, in the long run this approach may improve the welfare of the community. Targeting households with the greatest potential can help ensure that the project gets sufficiently established and that it can be expanded to those in greater need. However, perceptions of inequality, a lack of transparency, and increased ethnic tensions (through the inclusion of non-Roma families) may also jeopardize project objectives. In the Bagamér case, further information is needed to assess whether the households that did participate in the project benefited from it, and whether they would have succeeded without project assistance.

Risks of Decentralization

The Roma resettlement program in Nyíregyháza demonstrates some of the potential risks of decentralized project that are overseen by local governments. In Hungary, housing policies and programs are determined exclusively at the local level. While this will allow projects to be tailored to local conditions, it raises the risk of their being "captured" by local interests if they are designed and implemented without incorporating the needs and concerns of local minority self-governments, other civil society groups, or Roma themselves. National monitoring and evaluation would allow for more inclusive criteria to be applied and could help ensure that beneficiaries are included in decision-making processes and in project implementation.

Improved Conditions: Segregation or Integration?

The Nyíregyháza case study shows how the interpretation of project goals may serve some—but not all—interests. Significant efforts were made to improve the living conditions of the Gusev Roma settlement, yet in the long run, these efforts and the relocation of Roma families from Orosi into this community will exacerbate the social exclusion of Roma through explicit geographic and educational segregation. Alternative programs aimed at facilitating greater integration of Roma and non-Roma communities were either not considered or were deemed politically too risky. These issues echo the challenges described in the previous chapter on Roma settlements in Slovakia. While it is urgent to improve living conditions in settlements, such changes are investments in the future separation of the settlements from the majority population.

Desegregation efforts in Hajdúhadház have come up against similar barriers. Both primary schools in the town have made significant efforts to improve the conditions for Roma students. However, both are concerned about becoming known as the local "gypsy school" and risk losing the children of the local elite to the other school. There is intense competition between these two schools for resources, better students, and reputations. While it is in the interest of both schools to retain the state subsidies for special education classes, they have been reluctant to challenge the strong opposition to desegregation expressed by non-Roma parents and education officials.

Organizational Leadership and Experience

A number of the case studies demonstrate the importance of linkages with established and respected organizations and the benefits of capable and committed leadership. The experience and reputations of leaders and implementing organizations affect their abilities to secure support from donors and manage projects.

A key factor in the success of the Bagamér horseradish project was its leadership. The head of the association is a charismatic leader who was formerly the head of the local MSG and has had significant leadership experience in Roma civil society. He received project management training and was effective in raising resources for the horseradish project and other activities from a wide range of public and private sources. He is widely accepted by the community, and his staff observed that he "speaks the language of the donors." In addition to funds from the Autonómia Foundation, the association received resources from the Public Foundation for National and Ethnic Minorities in Hungary, the Soros Foundation, the Ministries of Youth and Sports and of Social and Family Affairs, and PHARE. Over time, the association's experience and credibility have grown, in part due to its leader's personality and the association's involvement in a number of other community programs in social welfare, education, health promotion, and crime prevention.

The dominance of personality in project leadership also has its risks. The Bagamér case illustrates that while a strong leader can motivate and move a project forward, such leadership can also limit transparency if the leader relies on inside connections and networks in securing resources and selecting project participants and staff. In Bagamér this has led to resentment and tensions within the community.

Leadership also played an important role in the Zsadány case. The local government, headed by Mayor Árpád Dudás, has worked hard to secure a variety of public works programs and the social land program for reducing rural poverty. Dudás is widely perceived as the engine of the social land program. His combination of relevant experience and commitment has contributed to the program's relative success, ongoing support from the Ministry of Social and Family

Affairs,[82] and the general social cohesion between Roma and non-Roma participants.

Local Economic Environment

The broader economic context within which projects are undertaken also has important implications for project success. For example, the horseradish project in Bagamér was able to draw on existing resources—a previously developed network and market, cultivation experience, and expertise of workers—which contributed to its relative success. However, agricultural projects tend to be particularly vulnerable to outside shocks and, as a result, may be more risky than other initiatives. In Bagamér, the 1998 market collapse created significant difficulties for many producers in the area. Agricultural crises and market vagaries also significantly affected the profitability and self-sufficiency of the social land programs in Zsadány. In neither case would the projects have survived without significant outside support.

Lack of Guidelines and Monitoring and Evaluation

Finally, most of these projects highlight the need for clear guidelines and rigorous monitoring and evaluation mechanisms. Programs financed from budgetary and private sources are not coordinated and often appear to be randomly selected. The majority of projects have no mechanisms for monitoring or evaluation. The Public Foundation for Hungarian Gypsies has been the only public sponsor to set up a monitoring system in addition to strictly collecting loan installments for the self-employed. The Autonómia Foundation is the only non-governmental sponsor that regularly monitors its programs. While Autonómia's monitors are prohibited from giving advice or practical assistance to beneficiaries, they follow the progress of the projects to completion and have at least one clear criterion for success, namely the proportion of loans repaid. In most other cases, supervision of the programs and the utilization of funds are, at best, irregular. These issues are discussed further in the final chapter.

CONCLUSIONS

The proliferation of Roma policies and projects in Hungary is impressive. The government has made significant strides in creating and establishing the institutional framework for the protection of minorities in general and of Roma in particular. This includes the establishment of the MSG system, a Hungarian initiative unique in Europe. These efforts have been supported and supplemented by a large and growing amount of project activity undertaken by a wide variety of community-based organizations. Nevertheless, barriers remain to the more effective functioning of this growing network of government and non-governmental entities.

Responsibility for policy development on Roma issues, coordination, and implementation has been distributed among a number of government bodies, leading to challenges in transparency, accountability, and coordination. For example, the implementation of the Medium-Term Package for the integration of Roma has been hampered by a lack of clarity over institutional mandates, ongoing difficulties in coordination across government agencies, and insufficient funding for all the programs included. Further, while many general policies aimed at assisting marginalized and minority groups do benefit Roma, much of Roma policy itself remains poorly integrated into broader social policy in Hungary. Further, because of the high degree of decentralization in Hungary, significant challenges remain in translating national policy into local implementation, in large part due to a lack of effective monitoring, evaluation, and enforcement.

The MSG system has had mixed results. It has helped to raise the profile of Roma issues in Hungary and has increased access to national and local policymaking in areas concerned with minority education and culture. Moreover, many Roma MSGs have become active politically and socially in important ways within their communities. Despite this, the capacities of both the national and local Roma MSGs have been limited by a combination of insufficient finances, weak political competencies and influence, and a general lack of authority and legitimacy. Some observers cite their relatively limited mandate to "cultural issues" as insufficient in addressing the real needs and concerns of Roma communities.

Despite these challenges, the substantial policy and project experience in Hungary provides a rich foundation from which considerable lessons have been derived. Efforts to improve monitoring and evaluation will further translate this learning into policy and project development and implementation that are better able to meet Roma needs and facilitate societal integration. To these ends, the Hungarian government remains committed to improving and expanding its efforts as indicated by its plans for the future adoption of a long-term strategy for the integration of Roma, accompanied by comprehensive anti-discrimination legislation.

Chapter 6
Roma in Spain

The situation of Roma in Spain provides a useful counterpoint to the analysis of Roma in the Central and Eastern European countries discussed so far, with both important similarities and differences. Sizable Roma communities live in many of the existing EU member countries, but the largest population lives in Spain. Thus, Spain has a wide range of project experience, both positive and negative, from which to draw. Spain's experience in accessing EU institutions to support Roma, including Structural Funds, also illustrates opportunities for new member states. This chapter explores the Spanish policy approaches to place developments in Central and Eastern Europe in an emerging European context.

To frame this discussion, it is important to recognize some significant differences in the experience of Roma on both halves of the European continent. Exclusion from the labor market and economic opportunities has been a long-term phenomenon for many Roma in Western Europe. In contrast, Roma in Central and Eastern Europe had jobs during the socialist period. As a result, many have high expectations that the government will step in to provide jobs and services. This sentiment lies behind much of the frustration expressed by Roma in Central and Eastern Europe.

Levels of integration and relations with non-Roma also differ between Western and Central and Eastern Europe. Socialism required a large, settled labor force without a high level of skills or education. Assimilation efforts thus focused on erasing specific national, ethnic, and cultural identities, while drawing Roma into the formal labor force. In contrast, in Western Europe, with its more diversified labor markets, the integration process has generally been less systematic and sustained. Without the concerted employment campaigns associated with socialist industrialization, many Roma in Western Europe have maintained traditional niche occupations as craftsmen, traders, or seasonal farm laborers. Similarly, although most Roma in Western Europe are settled, there are more nomadic Roma in Western Europe than in the Central and Eastern European countries.

Roma in Western Europe have also not experienced the widespread upheaval in their economic circumstances brought about by the transition in the East. For Roma in Western Europe, economic conditions, including access to social services and employment opportunities, have been relatively stable. At the same time, rising xenophobia and anti-immigration sentiments are causes for concern across Europe. While the majority of Roma are not immigrants or foreigners in the countries where they live, they are often considered as such and bear the brunt of prejudice and discrimination. An overview of Roma living conditions and policies in Spain provides insight into the conditions for addressing Roma poverty in an expanding Europe.

ROMA IN SPAIN: A WESTERN EUROPEAN EXAMPLE

Spanish Roma face many similar issues to their eastern counterparts, particularly in access to opportunities on the labor market and education, housing, and living conditions. Because of Spain's higher level of economic development, levels of poverty and social exclusion among Spanish Roma (*gitanos*) are relatively lower than those faced by many in Central and Eastern Europe. Nevertheless, Roma in Spain have had a long and tumultuous history and currently face many of the same challenges, if to a lesser degree, as do Roma in Central and Eastern Europe in terms of social exclusion, poverty, and discrimination (see box 6.1).

Box 6.1 The History of Roma in Spain

Little is known about the origins of the Spanish Roma, due to their early migrations and the absence of a written history. The historical experience of Roma in Spain is marked by five distinct periods in the evolution of Spanish government policy.[a]

Until 1499: Acceptance
The first Roma to reach Spain were thought to have arrived between 1415 and 1425. Between their arrival and 1499, the Spanish population generally accepted Roma, who were thought to be Christian pilgrims and were valued for their trades and skills.

1499–1633: Expulsion
Persecution of Roma began with the reign of Ferdinand and Isabella of Aragon and Castile in the late 1400s and their efforts to create a homogenous Catholic state. Ethnic and religious minorities, including Roma, who were ordered to either assimilate or leave the country. Non-integrated Roma were branded as highway robbers, thieves, and sorcerers. Although faced with the prospect of expulsion and the loss of their language, many Roma decided to stay in Spain, while at the same time attempting to preserve their traditional way of life.

1633–1783: Forced Assimilation
With Spain's economic growth in the early 1600s, policies toward Roma shifted from expulsion to forced assimilation. Various laws were passed in an attempt to end the nomadic lifestyle of Roma and settle them. The government hoped that Roma would simply seek formal employment and assimilate into the larger population. Again, however, Roma overwhelmingly managed to maintain their traditional way of life outside of mainstream society.

1783–1939: Incorporation and Legal Equity
Following the late 1700s, Spanish Roma experienced a period of formal legal parity, accompanied by considerable discrimination and exclusion

(continued)

Box 6.1 *(continued)*

in practice. In 1783, Charles III signed a decree that formalized legal equality between Roma and non-Roma citizens. The establishment of anti-Roma laws which was forbidden and Roma were not to be singled out as a distinct ethnic group in official texts.[b]

These actions were followed by a period of relative incorporation, when further attempts were made by the government to extend the rights of Roma and to reduce anti-Roma sentiments. For example, the Constitution of 1812 stressed the recognition of legal equality for Roma, granting Roma the full rights and responsibilities of citizenship. At the same time, the government gave little attention to improving their social and economic status within Spain. During this period, there were no government initiatives to assist Roma.

1939–present: From Dictatorship to Democracy
These general trends continued through the Spanish Civil War and the onset of the Franco dictatorship in 1939. Under Franco, Roma were openly discriminated against and prohibited from speaking *caló* in public. The Spanish National Guard classified Roma as a "dangerous group of people" to be dealt with cautiously.

After Franco's death in 1975, King Juan Carlos assumed the throne and began the democratic transition. This marked a shift in government policy toward addressing Roma issues more openly. The transition was a time of general change and reincorporation in Spain, with an emphasis on democratic and human rights for all Spanish citizens. Article 14 of the Constitution guarantees equality and full citizenship and prohibits discrimination on grounds of racial origin, religion, or gender. Formally, the post-1978 policy was one of "assisting in the development of the Gypsy people and the recognition of the fact that the Gypsies have their own culture"(Gamella 1996).

Notes:
a Unless otherwise noted, the historical background is drawn from Gamella (1996), Martín (2000), and Sánchez Ortega (1986).
b This law has made the collection of data on the Roma population extremely difficult, as the 1783 action strongly discouraged the distinction of the Roma community in data collection and lawmaking. However, the collection of data based purely on ethnicity was technically not made illegal until the Constitution of 1978.

The most recent government estimate of the number of Roma in Spain is just over 630,000 (1999). However, as the Spanish Constitution of 1978 prohibits data collection on the basis of ethnicity, these numbers are disputed. Government officials, NGOs, and academics generally agree that the population ranges between 400,000 and 600,000. Spain thus has the largest population of Roma in Western

TABLE 6.1 ROMA POPULATION ESTIMATES IN SELECTED
WESTERN EUROPEAN COUNTRIES

Country	Government Estimate[a]	Council of Europe Estimate[b]	Minority Rights Group Estimate[c]
Austria	N/A	20,000–25,000	20,000–25,000
Finland	10,000 (1998)	10,000	7,000–9,000
France	N/A	N/A	280,000–340,000
Germany	50,000–70,000 (1996)	70,000	100,000–130,000
Greece	150,000–300,000[d]	80,000–150,000	160,000–200,000
Italy	130,000	120,000	90,000–110,000
Portugal	40,000 (1997)	N/A	40,000–50,000
Spain	*630,000 (1999)[e]*	*N/A*	*700,000–800,000*
Sweden	20,000(1996)	40,000–50,000	15,000–20,000
Switzerland	N/A	35,000	30,000–35,000
United Kingdom	90,000	300,000	90,000–120,000

Sources: See footnotes, below.

a Estimates submitted to the UN Committee on the Elimination of All Forms of Racial Discrimination (except Greece, Italy, Spain, and the United Kingdom); see http://errc.org/publications/factsheets/numbers.

b Council of Europe, 2002 (Questionnaire on the Legal Situation of Roma/Gypsies/Travellers in Europe), http://assembly.coe.int/documents/workingdocs/doc02/EDOC9397.htm.

c Liegeois and Gheorghe (1995).

d In 1997, the General Secretariat for Adult Education estimated the number of Roma in Greece to be 150,000–200,000; the year before they were estimated at around 300,000.

e Estimate by the Congress of Deputies (1999a, 1999b).

Europe and one close to the population in Hungary. Following Spain, the largest populations of Roma in Western Europe are in Greece, Italy, France, the United Kingdom, and Germany (see table 6.1).

The majority of Roma in Spain speak Spanish, however, a significant number speak the Roma language, *caló*. It is not known how many Roma speak caló, although estimates range widely between 40,000 and 140,000. The primary distinction between groups of Roma is made between Spanish and Portuguese Roma. Portuguese Roma mostly reside in the western part of the country and speak a slightly different caló dialect.

The Roma communities in Spain are markedly diverse, including along socioeconomic lines and integration levels. In some instances, the long-term residency of Roma in a region has resulted in significant integration between Roma and the majority population. In Andalusia, for example, Roma traditions and customs feature prominently in the traditions of the broader Andalusian population (Gamella 2002). However, while some Roma communities in Andalusia are more likely than other Roma in Spain to exhibit higher levels of integration, they coexist with persistently marginalized groups and a small minority of more affluent Roma (Gamella 2002).

Roma were first recognized as legal citizens in the Spanish Constitution of 1978. The Constitution guarantees the fundamental rights and freedoms on the basis of citizenship and does not formally define or recognize Roma or other ethnic minority groups (*FCNM*) (*Framework Convention for the Protection of National Minorities 1995*). To date, Spain has no specialized state or government bodies responsible for minorities, human rights issues, or racial discrimination; the juridical protection of fundamental rights and freedoms are secured through broad civil, criminal, and administrative guarantees (*FCNM* 1995; OSI 2002).

In 1995, the government estimate of 325,000 to 400,000 Roma was submitted to the UN Committee on the Elimination of All Forms of Racial Discrimination.

THE NATIONAL PROGRAM FOR THE DEVELOPMENT OF ROMA

The situation of Spanish Roma has changed substantially in the post-Franco era. Significant gains have been achieved through the overall improvement in economic conditions throughout Spain. These developments have had a positive impact on the advancement of Roma, through improved access to public housing, education, health services, and social assistance (ASGG [Asociacion Secretariado General Gitano] 2001).

In 1988, the government began implementing the National Program for the Development of Roma (NPDR), which marked an important turning point in recognizing the exclusion of Roma and formulating policy strategies (Villareal 2001). The main goals of the NPDR are to improve the quality of life for Roma, foster equal opportunities, promote the inclusion of Roma in Spanish society, and improve relations between Roma and non-Roma. Despite improvements and government policy efforts, the exclusion and poverty of Roma in Spain persist in many areas, suggesting that continued and specific actions are still needed to further improve their welfare.

The NPDR was endowed with an annual budget of around 500 million pesetas (approximately US$4 million), with matching funds promised from regional and local governments. Between 1989 and 1999, close to one billion pesetas (US$8 million) have been spent annually on projects targeted at Roma (*FCNM* 1995). In addition, starting in 1989, 0.52 percent of the net personal income tax collected has been allocated to supporting the Catholic Church and various NGOs.[83] This program has channeled an additional 200 to 500 million pesetas annually to NGOs, which work with the Roma community. Over 1989 and 1999, these subsidies totaled nearly four billion pesetas (US$36 million)

(*FCNM* 1995). A central administrative body, the Roma Development Program Service Unit, was established to support and coordinate the NPDR within the public administration and to provide technical and financial assistance to NGOs. This assistance includes facilitating participation of Roma in official institutions, organizing training programs for professionals working with Roma, and promoting greater awareness about Roma.

Further program coordination is carried out by three commissions: the Follow-up Commission, responsible for program oversight; the Inter-Ministerial Working Group, responsible for coordinating sectoral initiatives among government ministries; and the Consultative Commission, comprised of Roma and non-Roma representatives, whose aim is to ensure cooperation between government and NGOs in NPDR implementation and to represent the main issues affecting Roma to the other commissions. Responsibility for implementing the program rests at the regional level. Regional governments choose projects (see box 6.2). Once chosen, they are submitted to the Ministry of

---

BOX 6.2 THE ANDALUSIAN PLAN FOR THE ROMA
COMMUNITY

Approximately 43 percent of Roma in Spain live in Andalusia. The region has made additional efforts to improve Roma living conditions. In 1996, the Andalusian government approved a "Comprehensive Plan for the Gypsy Community," which became operational in 1997. The plan's primary task is to coordinate activities concerning Roma.

This function is considered particularly important because of the large number of programs and projects implemented in the region. Andalusia receives the largest share of money from the National Program for the Development of Roma—almost half of the total budget. Andalusia is also the largest beneficiary of the European Social Fund because of its relatively lower levels of development compared to other regions in the country. The majority of initiatives targeted at Roma in Andalusia are small scale and highly localized. The programs are financed by a combination of the following:

- Transfers for the NPDR from the Ministry of Labor and Social Affairs (in 1997, close to 220 million pesetas, or 60 percent of estimated project costs) plus matching funds from the Andalusian government for 40 percent of total project costs;
- Transfers from the 0.52 percent personal income tax for non-profit organizations and/or associations, the majority of which go to the Federacion de Asociaciones Romanies Andaluzas.
- Contributions from various European Social Fund programs. While these programs are open to the broader community, in some cases 80 to 90 percent of the participants are Roma.

Labor and Social Affairs at the federal level, where they must fulfill certain requirements to be considered for funding. Both federal and regional governments make decisions jointly on the selection of projects and funding. National funding must be co-financed by regional and local authorities, which are required to contribute at least 40 percent of the total project cost (Villareal 2001).

Project Activity

According to the 2000 annual report of the Service Unit of the NPDR (Villareal 2001), an average of 100 projects have been implemented annually since 1995, with a peak of 120 projects in 1998. Of the more than 500 employees responsible for the implementation of the projects each year, approximately 22 percent are Roma. There are an estimated 50,000 direct beneficiaries per year, or approximately 12,000 families.

There is considerable diversity in the kinds of projects being implemented.[84] The majority are conducted in the fields of education (including prevention of school absenteeism, extracurricular activities, and adult education); social assistance; housing (including renovations and resettlement support); health education (including courses for young mothers and drug abuse prevention programs); and vocational training courses. A few projects have focused on cultural activities, including Roma language classes or cultural exhibitions.

In addition to sectoral projects, in 1992 the NPDR Unit began sensitivity training programs for regional and local civil servants, aimed at improving the ability of regional and local administrators to address Roma issues. Diversity awareness has also been promoted through infrequent roundtables that bring together Roma representatives and civil servants. The NPDR Unit also lodges frequent complaints against negative portrayals of Roma in the media.

For Spain's Roma population, the NPDR marked a significant milestone because it represented the first time the national government officially recognized the specific issues faced by Roma and established concrete nationwide measures to address them. The NPDR exhibits a number of strengths and weaknesses.

Strengths

Centralized Contact Point. The NPDR Unit provides an important contact point for organizations, individuals, policymakers, and members of parliament working on Roma issues. The unit provides a focal point for information sharing and facilitates meeting a wide range of interests over program goals and project and implementation strategies.

Local Government Involvement. For all NPDR interventions, regional autonomous communities or local administrations must co-finance central government funds. National authorities coordinate, finance, and carry out follow-up activities, but regional and local governments allocate resources and implement the projects. This decentralized system has helped to place the Roma issue on the agenda of regional and local governments.

Roma Participation. Another NPDR strength is its emphasis on fostering Roma participation. This is achieved in two ways. First, where possible, the NPDR recruits Roma personnel to work on the projects and to participate in the training and development of Roma mediators, teachers, and social workers. Second, a portion of the funds is spent on supporting Roma associations that have played an active and important role in project implementation.

Focus on Access to Social Services. In the 1980s, social welfare services became universally available to all citizens of Spain, including access to education, health, general social services, and specialized social services (e.g., for disadvantaged children and the elderly). The program works to integrate Roma more effectively into these mainstream social service and social assistance networks through outreach and specialized programs. For example, in Andalusia, children's vaccination and family planning programs for Roma are part of the mainstream public programs.

Weaknesses

Weak Legislative Status. There are also a number of ongoing concerns related to the ability of the NPDR to effectively carry out its mandate. One concern is that the NPDR does not enjoy the status of a legislated plan. While the NPDR was initially introduced as a bill to parliament, it was never passed. This lesser status may threaten the long-term financial sustainability of the NPDR.

Lack of Monitoring and Evaluation. Another significant concern is the lack of systematic monitoring and evaluation of projects and programs. In the majority of cases, the only documentation available is expenditures or the project implementer's own subjective evaluations of the project's success or failure to meet its expected objectives.

Insufficient Roma Involvement. While Roma participation is encouraged and has been notable in a variety of projects and in the role of Roma associations, concerns remain about the lack of genuine participation of Roma communities, particularly in the design, implementation, and evaluation of NPDR goals and projects (ECRI [European Commission against Racism and Intolerance 2003; OSI 2002]). In some cases, the allocation of funding to Roma NGOs has been seen as a way for state officials to elude responsibility.

Limited Scope of Project Activity. The NPDR marks an important shift in policy attention and resources directed to addressing Roma poverty and exclusion; however, the number of projects and beneficiaries remains relatively small in comparison with the numbers and needs of the Roma population. Further, some critics point to the need for greater project attention to fostering Roma identity, traditions, culture, and language, to combating discrimination, and to facilitating greater participation in political and legal structures (ECRI 2003).

A Spanish NGO to Watch: the Fundacion Secretariado General Gitano[85]

The case of the Fundacion Secretariado General Gitano (FSGG)[86] provides a useful example of the type of project activity that has resulted from NPDR financing. The FSGG is the largest and most prominent Spanish NGO working toward the advancement and integration of Roma. It is an example of a strong NGO with experience working with the Roma community that has successfully promoted the development of collaborative relationships with a range of government, private, and international entities.

The organization began operating during the mid-1960s, but did not become a legal entity until 1982. In keeping with its emphasis on intercultural collaboration, a Board of Trustees, half of whom are Roma, governs the FSGG. In 2001, roughly 40 percent of the 647 members of the total staff were Roma; and 67 percent of the total were women.[87] FSGG activities have been growing steadily over the last 38 years, with significant expansion in the last couple of years. Between 2000 and 2001, the number of projects increased from 30 to 38. Over this same time period, the number of direct beneficiaries grew from 29,000 to 64,000, with a corresponding increase in financing for projects from around 4.6 million euros to 8.4 million euros.

The majority of FSGG financing is from the Spanish central government (roughly 36 percent), European sources (approximately 27 percent), and in particular, the European Social Fund (see box 6.3 on the Acceder Project). Significant financial support also comes from autonomous community and local governments (around 36 percent). In recent years, the FSGG has pursued increasing collaborative initiatives, including co-financing, with close to 60 public and private organizations.

The FSGG is engaged in a wide variety of initiatives in vocational training and employment, education, health, youth issues, women's affairs, and territorially based social interventions. In general, nearly half of the budget goes to employment programs, nearly 20 percent to education initiatives, and just under 12 percent to health, youth, and women's programs. The most prominent initiative to improve Roma inclusion into the labor market is FSGG's involvement in the Acceder Project.

Education. Among the education programs that FSGG has initiated are a series related to educational mainstreaming focused on improving Roma access and integration into the compulsory education system, reducing absenteeism, improving performance, and encouraging positive relations between Roma and non-Roma (see box 6.5, on the School Monitoring Program in Madrid). Extracurricular activities are also offered as well as economic and tutorial support for Roma students interested in university education. The FSGG supports a variety of training programs, including teacher training and vocational training for the socially disadvantaged.

Health. To promote the improvement of Roma health, the FSGG works to improve Roma access to health services through mediation and information. Projects have also been implemented that offer technical assistance to organizations on specific Roma health issues, including HIV/AIDS prevention. Additional actions have focused on the prevention of drug abuse among Roma youth and public drug-abuse health services. The FSGG supports the European Community–funded project entitled "Health and the Roma Community."

Women. In partnership with eight Roma associations, the FSGG has a number of programs focused on advancement and support for the development of Roma women centering on health education, literacy, and integration into the labor market.

Collaborative Efforts. One of the FSGG's most important features and strengths is its active coordination with other NGOs and local governments. For example, the FSGG has developed three territorially based, integrated programs through agreements with the governments of Madrid, Aranjuez, and Castilla. Also, under the auspices of the Acceder Project, the FSGG has been active in joint efforts with 13 autonomous communities. The organization also has worked closely with the European Commission on a series of multicultural pilot projects focusing on integration (identifying good practices in combating discrimination against Roma) and identifying measures to combat social exclusion. In 1999, FSGG (then ASGG) started working in several Central and Eastern European countries, providing technical assistance in the Czech and Slovak Republics and Hungary.

Living Conditions of Spanish Roma

While Roma live throughout Spain, they are geographically concentrated in four regions, or "autonomous communities" of the country (see table 6.2). Almost half of the total Roma population (43 percent) live in the southern province of Andalusia. Madrid has the second highest concentration of Roma with nearly 10 percent, followed by Catalonia and Valencia at close to 9 percent each.

TABLE 6.2 ROMA POPULATION BY AUTONOMOUS COMMUNITY
(Estimates, 1993–99)

Autonomous Community	1993 Estimate	Percent of Total Roma Population in Spain	1999 Estimate
Andalusia	157,097	42.8	286,110
Aragon	10,961	2.7	18,209
Asturias	2,877	0.8	4,780
Balearic Islands	6,877	1.9	5,423
Canary Islands	515	0.1	854
Cantabria	2,320	0.6	4,021
Castile-Leon	20,198	5.5	28,339
Castile–La Mancha	17,072	4.7	33,552
Catalonia	31,881	8.7	52,937
Extremadura	6,811	1.9	11,318
Galicia	7,374	2.0	13,741
Madrid	35,588	9.7	59,082
Murcia	19,877	5.4	33,006
La Rioja	4,433	1.2	7,361
Valencia	31,585	8.6	52,455
Navarra	3,593	0.9	5,954
Basque Country	7,028	1.9	11,675
Ceuta and Melilla	1,222	0.3	2,030
Total	**367,039**	**99.6**	**630,847**

Source: Ministry of Employment and Social Affairs of Spain (El Ministerio del Empleo y Asuntos Sociales de España).

Despite perceptions to the contrary, Spanish Roma generally live in permanently settled communities. In some autonomous communities, 87 percent of Roma have lived in the same municipalities for 15 years or more (Gamella 1996). Nevertheless, for many, the concept of mobility is still an important element of social organization and culture (Gamella 1996). There also has been a trend toward greater urbanization. Many Roma have moved from rural to urban areas in recent decades (Fresno 1994).

Roma in Spain share a similar demographic profile to that of Roma in Central and Eastern Europe. Historically, Roma birth rates are higher than for the majority population. Over the past five centuries, the population has grown to over 30 times its original size. In comparison, over the same period the Spanish population increased 10 times, from 4 million to 40 million.

The Roma population is much younger than the majority population. Approximately 40 to 50 percent of Spanish Roma are below the age of 16 (Giménez Adelantado 1999; ASGG 2001). This can be attributed in part to high birth rates. While the birth rate for Roma in Spain is unknown, in Andalusia, the rate is estimated to be 23.8 per 1,000, compared to 13 per 1,000 for non-Roma Andalusians and 10 per 1,000 for the total population of Spain (Gamella 1996). Roma women marry at a young age, often as early as 13 or 14 years old, and have children between then and age 30. The average size of a Roma family is 5.4 members, in comparison with 3.7 in the average Spanish family (Congress of Deputies 1999a). Roma also have a lower life expectancy than the general population, estimated at 65 years (Vásquez 1980), compared with the much higher national average of 78.

Labor Market Status

As in Central and Eastern Europe, Roma in Spain were historically employed in traditional trades. Since the 1970s more rapid economic development and technological advances have displaced these jobs. New technologies have rendered many traditional Roma workers irrelevant or obsolete (e.g., blacksmiths, horse dealers, farm hands, and peddlers). Many rural Roma have been compelled to move to cities in search of employment.

The labor market characteristics of Roma in Spain differ substantially from those of the rest of the population. Few hold salaried full-time jobs. Most are engaged in independent, part-time, or casual labor. Recent data from a subcommittee of the parliament (Congress of Deputies 1999b; *FCNM* 1995) show that the employment standing of Roma in Spain is characterized by jobs that are low paid and largely in the informal sector. It was estimated that 50 to 80 percent of Roma work in "traditional professions" of peddling, collecting solid urban waste, and performing seasonal work. Another 5 to 15 percent work as antique dealers, shop owners, and in the arts, while 10 to 15 percent work in the "new professions" of construction, public works, and as civil servants.

Other reports indicate that at the beginning of the 1990s, between 10 and 15 percent of Roma were *chatarreros* (collectors of scrap metal, glass, or paper) (Grupo PASS 1991), while the proportion of Roma engaged in selling goods on the street was between 50 and 75 percent (ASGG 1996).

Many of these forms of employment—and particularly street selling—are being threatened by growing restrictions (e.g., increased municipal taxes, stricter eligibility for permits, heightened police surveillance, and increased fines for non-compliance) and competition from public and private companies (e.g., in the collection of recyclable materials) and from new immigrant labor (OSI 2002).

A variety of government and NGO initiatives have been undertaken to improve access to employment for Roma. In particular, job training and related employment services have been provided in conjunction with the European Social Fund job-training initiatives (see box 6.3).

Box 6.3 The Acceder Project: Training and Employment Services

The Acceder project began in 1998 as a two-year pilot project in Madrid and has subsequently expanded to become a national program (ASGG 2000; ASGG 2001). The national program is currently being implemented throughout the principal municipalities in Spain (a total of 34) in 13 autonomous regions. The program is administered by the FSGG, a national, non-profit organization working for the advancement of Roma that receives financial support from the National Program for the Development of Roma via the personal income tax contributions.

The main program objectives are to (i) provide Roma with professional qualifications and access to work contacts by addressing their needs and those of employers; (ii) increase the accessibility of general vocational training and employment services to unemployed Roma; and (iii) raise awareness of discrimination against Roma and work to improve society's view of the community.

The program provides individualized support to participants in identifying and preparing for employment. While the program is open to all interested applicants, 79 percent were Roma in 1999. Roma mediators work closely with job seekers and employers to identify their skills, training needs, and employment opportunities. The mediators provide support to applicants throughout the training and job search process.

In 1999 there were 304 active job seekers enrolled in Acceder, and 63 percent found employment. However, the job retention rate is not known, and cost-benefit analysis of the program is not available. FSGG staff and participants note that the program strengths are its individualized approach in assessing and matching skills and jobs and the use of mediators who can bridge the gap between *gitanos* (Roma) and non-Roma. Challenges include the difficulty of providing adequate and appropriate training for individuals with low education levels, persistent discrimination on the labor market, and incentives. Participants may be reluctant to accept low-paying jobs and risk losing access to social assistance benefits.

Housing

During the 1970s, government housing policy was aimed at eliminating shantytowns and informal settlements. A state housing program was developed to address the housing needs of the dislocated, treating Roma and non-Roma equally. Many Roma were relocated to high-rise apartment buildings. However, these relocation programs did not take into consideration Roma preferences. For example, the new buildings did not allow for large families to live together and did not allow Roma to continue with certain occupations, such as the collection and storage of scrap metals. As a result, a large number soon left their new homes to return to more traditional settlements, and these programs were generally considered unsuccessful (Gamella 1996).

In the 1980s and early 1990s, shantytowns continued to grow, populated mostly by Roma. Government policy toward Roma shifted toward the creation of small towns and housing settlements exclusively for Roma—policies that contributed to greater segregation of many Roma communities. In these towns, they often moved into "transitional housing" or into more open, one- and two-level houses with courtyard areas. However, because these settlements were generally located on the outskirts of cities and towns, where they often lacked basic facilities and were more easily neglected by municipal authorities, the condition of many of these settlements rapidly deteriorated into slums. Insufficient long-term planning has hindered many from making the transition from substandard temporary housing to higher quality, integrated housing arrangements (OSI 2002). Resettlement and desegregation efforts are hampered by resistance from non-Roma residents, restrictive criteria for social housing or housing loans, and among Roma, high illiteracy rates and a lack of access to basic information and trust (Calvo Buezas 1995; ASGG 2000; OSI 2002; ECRI 2003). Anti-Roma sentiment and support for segregation are persistent and increasing. A 1986 poll indicated that 11.4 percent of teenagers would expel Roma from the country if they could; by 1993, nearly 30 percent agreed with that statement (Calvo Buezas 1995).

Since the early 1990s, government policies have evolved to address the specific needs of Roma families. In part, these policies reflect the acknowledgment that the segregation of Roma into isolated communities has inhibited their integration into society and a recognition that the deterioration of rapidly built, low-quality, state-constructed housing has contributed to social deterioration and illegal activities within these communities. Currently, housing issues are evaluated on a case-by-case basis, with the aims of integrating Roma families into more diverse neighborhoods and Roma children into the mainstream schools (see box 6.4). There has also been the formation of a number of new associations and NGOs to work with Roma housing issues.

Efforts in the housing area over the last 30 years have yielded mixed results. While the overall success of programs and Roma participation in them have remained relatively low, an increasing number of Roma are taking advantage of better housing opportunities, and very few exclusively Roma neighborhoods remain.

Box 6.4 Roma Housing Re-Accommodation Program in Madrid

The Institute for New Homes and Social Integration (IRIS) was created in 1998 and is run by the Madrid Regional Community.[a] IRIS funding is provided by the National Program for the development of Roma through the regional autonomous community of Madrid, with some support from the national government.

IRIS has two main objectives: (i) to move slum and ghetto dwellers to improved housing; and (ii) to provide follow-up services for those re-accommodated to facilitate social integration into their new communities. IRIS pursues its objectives by acquiring apartments for Roma families. Along with apartments, IRIS provides follow-up support services.

An estimated 1,550 slum dwellings exist in the city of Madrid, with an additional 305 in the region's municipalities. In 1998, 272 families were re-housed with a similar number in 1999. Subsidies secured in 1998 for these re-accommodations totaled 450 million pesetas.

To date, the program is generally perceived to be a success, in part because of the rapid pace of re-accommodation and the low proportion of program dropouts (less than 2 percent). These successes are attributed to the consensual process of apartment allotment. In addition, the program makes a significant effort to further social integration through the provision of complementary social programs for children's education and for inclusion at school, and employment support.

Notes:
a IRIS was created after the Consortium for Re-accommodation of Slum Dwellers was dissolved. Part of the consortium's competence was absorbed by the Municipal Housing Enterprise and partly by IRIS.

Health Status

As in other countries, in Spain reliable data on the health status of Roma is scarce and limited to scattered surveys. The information that is available paints a worrisome picture. For example, one study reported a high incidence of birth defects among some groups of Roma (Martinez-Frais and Bermejo 1992). A 1995 study reported a nine times higher prevalence of hepatitis A in Spanish Roma children than in the non-Roma population (Cilla et al. 1995). The most serious health problems facing Roma in Spain include inadequate nutrition, congenital diseases, gaps in vaccination coverage, and drug addiction. HIV/ AIDS has also become a concern, however, there is no published data on the actual incidence or trends among Roma.

Education

While the Spanish education system has taken additional measures over the last decade to reach Roma students, access to adequate education remains a challenge. Literacy, enrollment, attendance, and completion rates are all very low among Roma. Illiteracy levels for adult Roma are high, with rates approaching 70 percent (Congress of Deputies 1999b). For the population over the age of 55, illiteracy rates for men and women are around 75 percent and 90 percent, respectively (CIDE [Centro de Investigación y Documentación Educativa] 1999). However, data on younger Roma indicate that illiteracy rates, while still high, are dropping. For the population under the age of 25, illiteracy rates were 20 percent and 45 percent for men and women, respectively (CIDE 1999). One important factor contributing to the lower illiteracy rates for Roma young people is that the law on compulsory education, requiring children between the ages of 6 and 15 to attend school, began to be enforced in 1990.

Despite gains in literacy, the Spanish school system is still not adequately reaching or retaining many Roma children. In a 1993 report, an estimated 25 percent of Roma school-age children were not enrolled in school (Jiménez González 1993). According to the same source, of those 75 percent enrolled, 36 percent did not attend school regularly. A more recent study indicated that between 1994 and 2001, the majority of Roma pupils attended school irregularly (54 percent), and of these, 31 percent missed classes for three or more months per year (FSGG 2002). Other sources report truancy rates that are sometimes as high as 70 percent (Congress of Deputies 1999b). In addition, the school dropout rate is very high, close to 60 percent for boys and 80 percent for girls (Jiménez González 1993). Most dropouts leave school after age 11, although most boys spend more years in school than girls.

Education disparities between Roma and non-Roma start early. While nearly 59 percent of Roma children have access to kindergartens (CIDE 1999), the 2001–02 national average was nearly 94 percent (Ministry of Education 2001). A very small number of Roma finish the required 10 years of education, known as the Educación General Básica (Basic General Education). In 1993, it was estimated that only about 5 percent of Roma pupils completed and only 1 percent of Roma students succeeded in reaching secondary education (university preparation). In 1993, 200 Roma students attended university in Spain. Another study found that up to 80 percent of Roma pupils do not complete basic education and many pupils are two or more years behind the average (Santos 1999).

Roma children in Spain face barriers to education that are similar to those discussed in earlier chapters for Roma in Central and Eastern Europe, including discrimination, cultural perceptions about the role and value of education, and systemic constraints inherent in the educational system.

Schools can be a hostile environment for Roma children. Roma may face discrimination from both non-Roma (*payo*) parents and teachers, as well as from school administrators and local authorities (Jiménez González 1993). Low school attendance and completion rates are often attributed to low demand for education among Roma families (Roma 2000). Low demand may be due in part to the opportunity costs of education and the need for children, and particularly girls, to work at home. As basic education does not guarantee a job upon completion, many Roma students see few incentives to stay in school. Concerns also exist about the negative impact of majority values that are transmitted through the education system on traditional Roma culture (Santos 1999). A recent study suggests that Roma attitudes towards education are shifting, with 77 percent of those families surveyed indicating that children should complete compulsory education and 36 percent indicating that children should continue their studies beyond basic education (FSGG 2002).

Finally, a study identified a number of shortcomings with the government's current education policy in their ability to reach Roma students (Roma 2000). These include deficiencies in the remedial education system, the lack of multicultural education, and insufficient attention to teacher training.

Remedial Education. Under the Spanish education system, disadvantaged students are provided support through "remedial education." To a large degree, remedial programs have evolved into technical and language-training courses to prepare students for (often low-wage) employment. Further, under the program, disadvantaged students are provided with schoolbooks, meals, hygiene programs, and vaccinations. This system has been criticized as perpetuating the segregation of Roma children from their non-Roma peers, as well as limiting their ability to pursue higher education or higher-wage employment.

While efforts in the 1990s largely abolished this system in the attempt to mainstream Roma education, segregation continues *de facto* through the disproportionate concentration of Roma in certain schools due to the withdrawal of non-Roma children by parents and, in some cases, to the selective placement practices of school inspectors. In some districts consisting of 50 percent Roma, Roma children constitute 80 to 90 percent of the student body in neighborhood schools (Fresno in OSI 2002).

Lack of Multicultural Education. School curricula typically do not include materials on Roma. Although efforts are being made to increase educational materials in schools that teach students about Roma in a positive manner, there is still a very long way to go. As of 1993, Roma culture was still largely absent from textbooks. One study examined close to 49,000 pages from texts used in the General Basic Education (primary and middle school), secondary school, and technical training school education and found that only 50 lines made any mention of Roma (Calvo Buezas 1989). The majority of these references to Roma "were either foolish or negative representations of them." The inability of Roma children to identify with their own history and values in school is thought to contribute to lower levels of attendance and academic performance.

Insufficient Teacher Training. Similarly, there continues to be a widespread lack of teacher training on issues of cultural diversity, such as multicultural education and social and cultural anthropology of minority groups within Spain. Although some attempts have been made to provide courses on Roma schooling and multicultural education, there has not been a concerted and organized effort to educate teachers on these issues.

Government efforts to improve educational quality and access for minorities involve two complementary streams: compensatory programs designed to promote equality of education that are targeted towards minority and disadvantaged children; and intercultural programs aimed at promoting diversity and difference in general (OSI 2002). Compensatory programs vary widely across Spain and are generally thought to be valuable and necessary additions to improving the quality of education available to disadvantaged students. Concerns remain about the danger of reinforcing segregation and the lack of attention to Roma identity, culture, and language. Intercultural education programs, which have the potential to include Roma culture in mainstream education, remain "more of a concept than a reality, because there is no legal framework for its implementation" (OSI 2002). Under the auspices of the NPDR, a significant number of NGOs have received funding for Roma education projects.

EUROPEAN UNION SUPPORT FOR ROMA IN SPAIN

The European Commission funds a number of initiatives that support Roma either indirectly, within the framework of its regional development and social exclusion policies, or more directly, through programs targeted at Roma. The two largest funds are the European Regional Development Fund (ERDF) and the European Social Fund (ESF). Initiatives that affect Roma are primarily conducted through the ESF and

Box 6.5 The School Monitoring Program in the Municipality of Madrid

The School Monitoring Program[a] began in three districts in the Municipality of Madrid as a part of the collaborative Plan of Action[b] launched in January 1999 by the Madrid City Council and the Asociacion Secretariado General Gitano (ASGG, now FSGG) (see box 6.3, above).[c] The general program aim is to facilitate the integration of Roma children into the regular school system. The main program objectives are as follows:

- Promote the increased participation of Roma children in pre-primary education (0–6 years).
- Promote the continuation in and completion of compulsory education (6–16 years).
- Develop greater skills in terms of school habits, constructive relationships among classmates, and classroom learning techniques.
- Promote the involvement of the Roma families in the educational process.
- Conduct an ongoing diagnosis of the school situation of Roma pupils.

Four complementary sets of interventions are included in the project. The first involves efforts by Roma mediators/trainers to make contacts with teachers and social workers to identify the main problems encountered by Roma pupils and the school (e.g., absenteeism, school conflicts, under-performance), as well as to increase teacher/staff awareness of Roma culture. The second involves monitoring Roma pupils' attendance and performance, including making home visits to families to encourage greater support and involvement of parents in their children's education. So that they can develop additional skills, motivation, and cultural confidence, children are recruited to participate in a series of complementary extracurricular activities (e.g., dance classes, sports activities, field trips, visits to museums, and training workshops). Finally, efforts are undertaken to increase the number of Roma children in preschool education. Earlier exposure to the education system is expected to increase children's overall skill levels and to improve their familiarity and comfort with formal education.

Results and Challenges

As of 2000, the program has been conducted in 16 state schools that were selected from three districts involved in the plan.[d] In 1999, the program assisted 314 Roma pupils, including making 220 visits to family homes. There were 174 pupils who participated in the formation of 14 workshop groups that focused on traditional Andalusian song and dance.

In 2000, increased attention was given to the problem of continued school attendance of children aged 12–16 years, with particular emphasis on extracurricular courses/workshops that focused on practical vocational skills (e.g., carpentry, bricklaying). In the first three months, the program increased the number of interventions, monitored 136 pupils,

Box 6.5 (*continued*)

made 150 visits to families, and assisted 568 pupils through extracurricular activities.

As of 2000, it was too early to assess results, including educational outcomes. However, there were signs of progress. In addition to the inclusion of an increasing number of Roma pupils in education support initiatives, progress is evident in terms of noticeably lower absenteeism rates and high participation and motivation levels for extracurricular activities. In particular, Roma participation in activities related to Roma culture (e.g., workshops on traditional Andalusian song/dance) is reportedly high. Moreover, this program has increased constructive contact between Roma and non-Roma, as well as improved awareness of Roma issues within the educational system.

The program reported a number of ongoing challenges, including an inability to conduct home visits to all those families in need. Initially, interventions with families were conducted in an unstructured, ad hoc manner by the mediator/trainers, and in some cases was ineffective at generating greater parental understanding and involvement. As a last resort for children not attending school until the legal age of 16, education authorities may open a file on the pupil and impose fines on the families. However, in the Municipality of Madrid, families reportedly rarely pay, and collection is rarely enforced. Program efforts have been taken to improve on these aspects of this process. In addition, proposals have suggested the need for individual tutorials for children with greater learning needs, special training for teaching staff in Roma culture, and the production of educational materials that better reflect Roma culture and interests.

Notes:
a This program is also known as the "Program of Support and School Monitoring of Infants and Gypsy Youth."
b The general aim of the Plan of Action is to facilitate the effective integration of the Roma population through a series of initiatives including the School Monitoring Program; the Program for the Monitoring and Follow-up of Rehoused families by the Municipal Housing Enterprise; the Basic Care Program to promote and facilitate the "normalization" of Roma access to public social services; the Program for the Promotion of Roma Women; and the Program of Social Participation and Cultural Promotion, the last of which was not operational as of 2000.
c Centers to conduct the plan's implementation were set up in the districts of Carabanchel (Pan Bendito), Villaverde/Usera (El Espinillo), and Puente de Vallecas (Adali Cali), with an additional responsibility for overall coordination and management located in the FSGG headquarters in Carabanchel.
d The schools were chosen on the basis of a set of criteria including a minimum percentage of Roma pupils, school proximity to the Plan of Action centers, and acceptance on the part of the teachers and administrators.

the Equal Community Initiative. Additional projects for Roma are supported through the Socrates, Youth for Europe, and the Community Action Program to Combat Discrimination.

ERDF finances are primarily used to promote the development and structural adjustment of less-developed regions within countries. These regions include those whose per capita GDP is below 75 percent of the EU average. Nearly 73 percent of Spanish Roma live in regions identified as lagging behind.[88] Since 1994, Spain has received a total of 26,300 million euros (1994–99) and 38,096 million euros (2000–06) for this purpose.

ESF funds are directed towards measures to improve employment prospects. Since 1994, ESF funds have supported both geographic and thematic objectives in Spain, with the latter targeted towards vulnerable groups in society, including Roma. These include initiatives aimed at groups facing difficulties in the labor market, including youths, the long-term unemployed, those suffering from social exclusion, and under-skilled workers, as well as people suffering from discrimination and inequalities in the labor market (Equal Community Initiative).[89] Between 1994 and 1999, the ESF contributed nearly 8,600 million euros towards these aims. For the 2000–06 funding cycle, 2,240 million euros was allocated to education, training, and employment objectives, while 485 million euros is being directed toward combating all forms of labor market discrimination and inequalities, both of which are important areas for Roma.

Under these broader objectives, some programs are targeted more specifically toward Roma. For example, since 1999, the Integra program has promoted measures to improve access to the labor market and the employability of marginalized groups, including the long-term unemployed, the homeless, and Roma. The 2000–06 Acceder Project, aimed at fostering access to employment for groups in danger of exclusion, including Roma (see box 6.3), is funded under the Equal Community Initiative with an emphasis on combating discrimination.

CONCLUSIONS

The Spanish experience provides an interesting Southern European counterpoint to the experiences of Central and Eastern European countries. Direct attention to the advancement of Roma integration in Spain started relatively late. Roma were not considered legal citizens until the 1978 Constitution. In post-Franco Spain, education was common through the 1980s, but compulsory education laws were not actively enforced until 1990. Improving economic conditions, better social services, European integration, and a democratic system, all opened opportunities for tackling poverty across the country and for

Roma in particular. The National Program for the Development of Roma provides a framework for the involvement of regional and local governments and NGOs—and many Roma themselves—in Roma issues. The European Social Fund—an instrument that will soon be available to the accession countries—has also been involved in project development and finance.

This context has promoted innovative projects, which aim to overcome exclusion in education, housing, employment, and other areas. While further evaluation is needed, programs such as the Acceder Project, which provides Roma with support for entering the mainstream labor market, are useful project experiences for the Central and Eastern European countries. In fact, the NGO that runs the Acceder Project, has consulted in Slovakia and Hungary.

The experience of Roma projects in Spain has not been wholly positive. Lessons from failed housing projects and the challenges faced in fostering greater inclusion of Roma in the labor market and school systems provide cautionary examples. These projects and policies suffer many of the same weaknesses as those in other countries, including a lack of sustainability, insufficient funding, and an absence of monitoring and evaluation.

While these projects are positive steps towards poverty reduction and greater integration of Roma, the scale of efforts remains small relative to the size and condition of Roma communities in Spain. However, continued efforts through the National Program for the Development of Roma, the robust NGO community, attention to Roma participation in projects, and a positive track record of initiatives in key social areas constitute a promising base for further progress.

Chapter 7
The Road Ahead

The plight of Roma in Central and Eastern Europe has not gone unnoticed. During the 1990s, initiatives by governments, NGOs, and international organizations addressed various issues related to Roma, from human rights to racial stereotyping in the media to education and employment. This book was designed to advance these efforts by providing detailed information about the nature of Roma poverty, the course of project experience thus far, and future policy avenues. This chapter suggests some lessons learned—first, about the nature of Roma poverty and the policy context in Europe; second, about general policy approaches for addressing Roma poverty; and finally, about specific policies.

Improving conditions for Roma is closely linked to the overall success of each country's economic and social development strategies. In this context, policymakers need to make it a priority to implement policies that promote and sustain growth while trying to boost social welfare and ensure the overall inclusiveness of government policies. But the extent and characteristics of Roma poverty indicate that these sector-wide policies will not be sufficient. Some areas will require targeted interventions to ensure that Roma are able to participate fully in the labor market, public services, and society in general.

THE NATURE OF ROMA POVERTY AND POLICY CONTEXT

The unique characteristics of Roma poverty mean that certain issues must be addressed at the country level. But some common lessons and implications cut across national borders. In particular, policies to address Roma poverty must respond to three main aspects of the policy environment: the multidimensional roots of Roma poverty; the diversity of Roma populations; and the context of European integration.

Aspects of Roma Poverty

Roma poverty is strikingly high in Central and Eastern Europe. Poverty rates for Roma in Bulgaria, Hungary, and Romania are as much as 10 times that of non-Roma. Poverty among Roma is highest among families where the household head has little education or is unemployed and among families with three or more children. These characteristics are also found among the non-Roma poor, but for Roma, the chances of being poor are higher than for their non-Roma neighbors, irrespective of education level and employment. The conclusion is clear: Roma poverty is partly related to low educational attainment, limited labor market participation, and larger family sizes, but it also stems from factors associated with being Roma, including the multiple dimensions of exclusion.

Qualitative case studies of Roma poverty showed that many causes of Roma poverty are interrelated. For instance, access to health care and to waste collection is limited in remote Roma settlements. Roma parents sometimes enroll their children in special schools for the mentally handicapped after suffering discrimination in regular schools. The interconnections between the different aspects of Roma social exclusion uncovered in this study suggest that Roma poverty cannot be addressed by projects that focus on a single issue. Instead, the Roma poor need comprehensive policy approaches that address all sides of their plight.

Another important finding of this study—highlighted in the case of Slovakia—is that the marginalization of a Roma settlement correlates to its level of poverty. Roma living in more remote and segregated neighborhoods have fewer chances to participate in the mainstream economy, access social services (including education and health care), and tap into social networks and information about economic opportunities, such as jobs. In other words, geographic and social exclusion are important correlates of poverty. In contrast, Roma living in integrated areas are more likely to interact with non-Roma, leaving them better positioned to spot and seize economic opportunities.

Multidimensionality of Roma Poverty

Roma poverty extends far beyond relative income deprivation. Instead, it relates to a complex set of phenomena, including a poor labor market, limited education status, inadequate housing, the legacies of past policies, and a long history of troubled relations between Roma and majority populations in Central and Eastern Europe. All these factors combine to make it hard to address individual problems in isolation.

For instance, as the country case studies show, deep-seated mistrust and poor communication between Roma and public officials make even a seemingly simple immunization program difficult to implement. Roma parents sometimes refuse immunizations, distrusting the intentions of doctors. Indeed, health officials in Romania resorted to intimidation to press Roma women to immunize their children. But such coercion was, at the very best, a partial, stop-gap solution that helped a few children's health even as it deepened underlying social divisions. Key, interrelated features of Roma social exclusion include the following:

- *Poor labor market status.* As detailed in chapter 2, one of the primary reasons Roma have been slower to benefit from the transition to market economies has been their difficulty in securing employment.
- *Geographic exclusion.* As chapter 3 highlights, Roma poverty is often closely related to the geographic separation of Roma

settlements. In Slovakia, such remote towns were legacies of World War II–era discrimination. Roma living in such far-flung communities were poorer and more cut off from basic social services.

- **Poor relations with majority communities and a legacy of discrimination.** Chapter 2 showed that, correcting for factors such as educational attainment and age, there was still an undefined "Roma factor" in poverty rates. All other considerations and explanations aside, Roma were simply more likely to be poor. This probably reflects both discrimination and the aftermath of poor relations between Roma and the majority communities in Central and Eastern Europe—a heritage of intolerance that itself results in part from past state policies and deep societal prejudices.

Attention to Diversity

While demonstrating the distinctive nature of Roma poverty, this volume also emphasizes the diversity of the Roma themselves. Roma are not all alike; neither are their social conditions. Indeed, the ethnic, occupational, religious, and economic diversity among Roma populations is tremendous. The proportion of Roma-language speakers differs greatly from country to country, as does the proportion living in cities, integrated neighborhoods, or segregated rural settlements. These differences deeply affect welfare. Efforts to create, define, or represent a single Roma community will founder on the rocks of internal diversity. Roma tend to have distinctive problems of integration and access, but the situations of vastly different communities and individuals cannot be shoehorned into a single, simple set of answers.

The European Dimension

Policies for addressing Roma poverty also must be framed within the context of European enlargement, the recent accession of eight countries in Central and Eastern Europe to the EU and the candidacy and aspirations of other countries. The timing of the publication of this book and other reports on Roma is hardly coincidental. Roma poverty has gained attention because of the rapid process of European integration. To meet the EU's accession criteria, Central and East European countries built institutions and passed legislation to address Roma issues. However, this marks only the beginning of the process. Even following enlargement, tackling Roma poverty requires a long-term approach that remains part of each country's overall economic and social development program.

The European Commission's involvement in Roma issues is evolving, and accession has accelerated this process. With the May 2004 enlargement, Roma became the largest and most vulnerable minority in Europe. The implications of accession for EU policy toward Roma have been in flux. While the Directorate General for Enlargement handled Roma issues for candidate countries, institutional responsibility for Roma in member states within the commission has not been determined. While the commission has engaged in Roma-specific activities, these are spread across different directorate generals, including education, health, and employment and social affairs. There has been increasing demand from some members of the European Parliament and from Roma groups to appoint a focal point for Roma issues within the commission.

The European Commission's involvement in Roma issues has focused on three areas: the legal framework, including protection against discrimination; financial support through structural fund resources provided to member states for specific objectives; and through policy coordination and cooperation. The EU provides support for the protection of fundamental legal rights. This was most prominent during the accession process through work on anti-discrimination legislation. Roma stand to be among the main beneficiaries of EU legislation banning discrimination on grounds of racial or ethnic origin in employment, education, social security, health care, housing, and access to services.

The EU takes a coordinated approach to employment and social inclusion policies called the "Open Method of Coordination" (OMC). This approach was adopted following the decision of the Lisbon Council in March 2000.[90] OMC involves member states working towards agreed goals and objectives, including policies to promote the inclusion and participation of minorities. The European Commission monitors the progress made by both current and new member states through a set of 18 "Laeken indicators," covering income, employment, education, and health. Member states prepare annual "National Action Plans," which report progress on the indicators and lay out a program for tackling poverty and exclusion. These reports are a potential mechanism for developing approaches toward addressing Roma poverty. The commission has already recommended that some new member states make specific mention of Roma in their national plans.

On the financing side, new member states are transitioning from EU support that is provided through the enlargement process to general support mechanisms that are available to all member states. The PHARE program has been the main channel for EU support for Roma-related activities in candidate countries.[91] Between 1993 and 1999, 20 million euros were allocated to Roma-linked projects across six candidate countries (European Commission 1999). The total amount of PHARE funding allocated for financing Roma projects in candidate

TABLE 7.1 PHARE-FUNDED PROGRAMS FOR ROMA IN CENTRAL
AND EASTERN EUROPE, 1993–2001
(European Community Grants, in thousands of euros)

	1993–97[a, b]	1999	2000	2001	*Total*
Bulgaria	1,565	500	3,500	6,350	11,915
Czech Republic	1,778	500	2,850	3,000	8,128
Hungary	1,919	6,900	2,500	5,000	16,319
Romania	2,661	0	1,000	7,000	10,661
Slovak Republic	1,935	3,800	3,800	10,000	19,535
Total	**9,858**	**11,700**	**13,650**	**31,350**	**66,558**

a Includes funds in support of Roma communities channeled through the Civil Society
Development Foundations (funded under the PHARE National Program), the Democracy Program, the Lien Program, and the Access Program.
b Includes both macro and micro projects: macro projects are large partnership projects
intended to promote sustained activities for up to 24 months and which may
continue after the EU grant has ended; micro projects are intended to contribute to
citizens' initiatives and locally inspired activities.
Source: European Commission, Directorate General for Enlargement, 2002.

countries has risen from 11.7 million euros in 1999 to 31.4 million in
2001 (European Commission 2002; see table 7.1).[92] The European Initiative for Democracy and Human Rights (EIDHR) has also provided
EU financing.[93] In the 4 years after the initiative's establishment in
1994, approximately 4.5 million euros were allocated to Roma projects. The Directorate General for Education and Culture also manages
programs to encourage cooperation between EU member states and
candidate countries in the fields of education, training, and youth.
Roma projects are also supported through the Socrates and the Youth
for Europe programs.[94]

With accession, the new member states have access to the Structural and Cohesion Funds. While Roma are not explicitly mentioned
in programming criteria for these funds, Roma communities will
receive resources through the instruments to achieve social exclusion
and local development objectives. Structural Funds are targeted to
underdeveloped regions and include objectives such as combating
inequalities and discrimination in the labor market and rural development through local initiatives. The Acceder Project in Spain, mentioned in the previous chapter, is financed through the European
Social Fund, one of the four Structural Funds. Resources are significant. For 2004–06, the total amount programmed through the Structural Funds for all objectives for the 10 new member states was 15 billion euros. Bulgaria and Romania will continue to have access to
PHARE resources through their expected accession in 2007.

A major challenge for the new member states and for Roma communities in particular will be building the capacity of local communities

to identify and propose successful projects for funding and to implement them according to EU procedures and processes. Some training programs have been initiated, but this process will take time. In Slovakia, the Social Development Fund mentioned in chapter 3 aims to build the capacity and experience of Roma settlements and other marginalized communities to successfully compete for resources from the European Social Fund. Similar projects in Bulgaria and Romania share similar objectives.

The European dimension of the Roma poverty issue provides a useful framework for policy. First, Roma are not poor only in Central and Eastern Europe. Chapter 6 examined the situation in Spain, which has also faced issues of integration and Roma poverty. Second, the process of European integration offers a unique opportunity for addressing Roma poverty at a cross-national level. It also lets countries learn from one another throughout the accession process. Third, since the ongoing project of creating an integrated Europe will not be completed when the latest accession treaties are ratified, the accession process offers both an opportunity to institutionalize a long-term approach to reducing Roma deprivation in Central and Eastern Europe and a chance to reflect on the shortcomings of Roma policy further west.

POLICY IMPLICATIONS AND APPROACHES

The multidimensional roots of Roma poverty, the diversity of Roma communities, and the European context suggest several policy implications. Only a comprehensive policy approach can simultaneously address multiple causes of poverty. Moreover, with full respect for their heritage and deep involvement by their leaders, Roma must be better integrated into European societies. Here, some useful lessons can be drawn from other countries with similar experiences. Finally, any policies that are tried must be carefully implemented, meticulously evaluated, and anchored in participation by Roma. The following section addresses these policy lessons, before discussing more specific interventions.

Links with Systemic Reform

Better access to quality social services for Roma is linked to the overall effectiveness of each country's education, health, and social protection systems. Throughout the region, countries have embarked upon complex systemic reforms to improve the efficiency, equity, and relevance of public services. In many ways, the socialist systems were ill suited to the realities of a market economy. One way in which they have proven ineffective is in their inability to reach vulnerable groups, including the Roma. But this is hardly just a minority issue. Systemic reform, improved access, and higher-quality social services will improve conditions for the entire population.

Reducing unemployment is a critical step toward mitigating poverty and improving living standards. This requires a multi-pronged approach. It is necessary but not sufficient to maintain macroeconomic and political stability and advance financial sector reform. Increasing employment opportunities hinge on a better environment for job creation—including measures to support small and medium-sized enterprises—and easier credit for small business owners. Many of these measures can encourage self-employment and entrepreneurship.

Another national-level issue that would help unskilled Roma workers is lowering the non-wage costs of labor. High payroll taxes and non-wage-labor costs in many countries discourage employers from hiring unskilled laborers, who are proportionately more expensive than workers with higher skills. Studies in numerous OECD countries show that the unskilled are often hurt the worst by such non-wage-labor costs (Blanchard et al. 1995; World Bank 2001b).

Education reform is also particularly relevant for Roma. Comprehensive reforms of both general and vocational education are needed to better prepare workers for the labor market. Secondary school programs and curricula must be reviewed to ensure that they properly position young people for the labor market by shifting away from narrow vocational and technical training to more general, rigorous, and academic programs. Improved vocational education, which expands elements of the general education curriculum, could attract young Roma and help them secure marketable skills.

Social assistance reforms can improve work incentives and reduce the risk of dependency on cash benefits. Many countries have worked to ensure that social assistance benefits provide a meaningful safety net for the poor. Benefits must not inadvertently discourage able-bodied people from working even as they help low-income working families.

In addition to improving the effectiveness of cash benefits, social assistance reforms should also enhance the roles of social workers working with poor communities. Social workers in most countries in the region function largely as administrators, instead of fully using their capacities to work with individuals and households. For many Roma in the most isolated settlements, social workers are the main contact point with the outside world. These workers should refer their clients to other social services, provide information about employment opportunities, and counsel and support households in a variety of ways.

An Inclusive Approach

Since Roma poverty is rooted in broad-based social exclusion—economic, social, and geographic—ameliorating it will require an inclusive approach that is designed to expand and promote Roma involvement and participation in mainstream society, while maintaining their cultural and social autonomy. Only policies that let Roma take advantage of national and European labor and housing markets, education and health systems, and social and political networks have a chance of reducing poverty over the long term. Therefore, existing policies should be made more accessible to Roma, and new initiatives should specifically reach Roma. Policies of inclusion would complement the rights-based approaches discussed in chapter 1 by tackling the economic and social barriers that Roma face.

A central policy goal should be the multifaceted inclusion of Roma into institutions and mechanisms that create economic and social opportunities. The emphasis here should be placed on incentives, not coercion. Interventions that reduce Roma isolation and exclusion can help improve their living conditions over the longer term. An inclusive approach must support Roma empowerment and include them in the projects and programs that affect them. Several successful projects use Roma mentors to bridge between Roma and non-Roma communities. Roma teachers' assistants who work with parents or Roma peer advisors who help with job placement can facilitate social integration while strengthening the Roma community. These objectives were behind the initiative of nine countries of Central and Eastern Europe to launch a "Decade of Roma Inclusion" beginning in 2005 (see box 7.1).

Box 7.1 The Decade of Roma Inclusion, 2005–15

The Decade of Roma Inclusion grew out of the June 2003 conference "Roma in an Expanding Europe: Challenges for the Future" hosted by the government of Hungary. The Open Society Institute, the World Bank, and the European Commission organized the conference with the support of UNDP, the Council of Europe Development Bank, and the governments of Finland and Sweden.

At this high-level conference, prime ministers and senior government officials from eight countries—Bulgaria, Croatia, Czech Republic, Hungary, Macedonia, Romania, Serbia and Montenegro, and Slovakia—made a political commitment to close the gap in welfare and living conditions between Roma and non-Roma and to break the cycle of poverty and exclusion. The Decade will run from 2005 to 2015. The

(continued)

Box 7.1 (*continued*)

objective is to take steps to speed up and scale up social inclusion and the economic status of Roma by:

- Setting a limited number of quantitative national goals for improvements in education, employment, health, and housing and the establishment of the necessary information base to measure progress toward these goals;
- Developing and implementing national action plans to achieve those goals; and
- Regular monitoring of progress against the goals, and adjusting action plans as necessary over the Decade.

An inclusive approach also should overcome divisions between Roma and non-Roma. Such policies build trust and help develop social capital. In most cases, inclusive policies should target everyone in a community, rather than just Roma, although there may be exceptions where explicit attention to ethnicity is necessary, as in overcoming language barriers. Multicultural education and curricula that include the history and culture of Roma and other minorities are also critical for overcoming cultural barriers. Training teachers, local government officials, and other social service personnel can reduce discrimination by public service providers. Finally, public-information campaigns can promote multiculturalism and raise general awareness about discrimination. In this vein, policies that expand opportunities include the following:

- Reducing segregation in housing, particularly by alleviating problems associated with isolated rural settlements;
- Integrating Roma students into mainstream educational systems by establishing preschool programs and providing food, clothing, and transportation subsidies to make it easier for poor students to attend;
- Increasing outreach to Roma communities by social service providers, including health and social workers;
- Involving Roma as liaisons between communities and public services; and,
- Providing job training and programs that increase Roma participation in formal labor markets.

An inclusive approach rejects the coercion implicit in assimilationist and exclusionary policy approaches towards Roma, while remaining compatible with rights-based approaches. Nevertheless, a policy approach based on social inclusion centers on improving opportunities and social and economic welfare. Often, rights are necessary but not sufficient to create opportunities. One reason for this is that rights are often exercised vis-à-vis the state, while economic opportunities arise from the market. Participation in market activities often cannot be mandated. Thus an inclusive policy must be comprehensive, creating incentives for inclusion across a range of market, state, and social networks and institutions, for example, by providing job training and programs that increase Roma participation in formal labor markets.

Learning from Examples

When considering future policy directions, ideas may be found in the policy experiences of other countries' and regions' minority policies, particularly in the West. North and South American countries provide interesting counterpoints to European experiences, in part because the histories of African and indigenous peoples in the Americas offer more parallels to Roma than to other national minorities in Europe. While all ethnic groups have distinct features, minority-majority relations share important similarities everywhere, and much can be learned from the policy experience of countries that have confronted these issues in the past and still face them today. These issues deserve further exploration.

To be sure, Roma in Europe have endured centuries of exclusionary and assimilationist policies without being absorbed into majority societies. They remain stateless and have founded no movement for statehood. In this regard, their closest parallel may be with Native Americans, a separate ethno-linguistic community that has often preferred preserving its own traditions and way of life to integration. These general characteristics underline both the challenges facing an inclusive approach to Roma poverty and the long-term nature of the policy responses required. They also underscore the stakes.

Attention to Evaluation and Implementation

The development of a comprehensive national policy response to Roma poverty must be combined with attention to monitoring, evaluation, and implementation. The range of Roma projects in Central and Eastern Europe has provided much experience in implementation. Still, despite the high level of activity, very few initiatives have been evaluated or monitored, making it extremely difficult to identify lessons for the future. As countries move forward, they must examine this ever-growing body of experience. A related priority is the need to build monitoring and evaluation mechanisms into new and ongoing initiatives and to provide opportunities for exchanging information within and across countries.

Filling Information Gaps

The first step toward increasing monitoring and evaluation capacity—and, hence, improving project design—is making more and better information available. This volume has highlighted the critical lack of basic information about Roma. To remedy this, countries need to examine their statistical instruments and administrative data to find out how they can better capture policy-relevant information on Roma and other minorities. Multilateral coordination, advice, and guidance can help ensure data comparability. Still, more information on international practices is needed, particularly in addressing privacy issues about ethnic identification. On a related note, the outcomes of targeted public policies and NGO initiatives require close monitoring, and the results of program evaluations should be used for ongoing policy development. The lessons should be disseminated across regions and countries.

Gaps in information on poverty and welfare persist at both the country level and in particular subject areas. In particular, more information is needed on the conditions of Roma in the countries of the former Yugoslavia. The review of the western literature on Roma undertaken for this report found little data on Roma in these countries, despite the large estimated Roma population in countries such as FYR Macedonia. From a sectoral perspective, regular and comparable information on Roma household welfare and living conditions—in addition to data on education and health status—are needed across countries to identify community needs and develop policy strategies. Of the main policy areas, health (particularly reproductive health) has perhaps been the most neglected to date, and instruments for monitoring health status and communicable diseases are sorely needed.

While privacy concerns about data collection must be respected, policymakers need up-to-date information to design programs and monitor outcomes. Such data collection should benefit Roma in the long run through better-designed and -targeted interventions. To protect privacy, declarations of ethnicity should be voluntary, and periodic sample surveys, rather than national administrative data, should be used to collect information on specific topics. Roma groups must also be involved in the development, implementation, and analysis of surveys, as happened during the 2001 census in Slovakia. Qualitative assessments can also provide valuable information for project design.

Increasing harmonization of European practices in conducting surveys and censuses should facilitate the availability of better data. EU approaches focus on the protection of human and minority rights and transparency in confidentiality.[95] Adoption of consistent EU safeguards should be helpful to dispel concerns and help governments to persuade Roma communities about the benefits of data collection and to improve the quality of responses to ethnicity questions in censuses.

Direct involvement of Roma in data collection and surveys can go a long way to improving their relevance and quality. A 2003 household survey of Roma and refugees conducted by the Institute for Strategic Studies and Prognoses and UNDP in Montenegro made a concerted effort to involve Roma in the preparation, implementation, and analysis of the data. Roma survey team members were able to provide valuable information and clarifications on the survey results. The process also gave the Roma participants and their communities greater ownership and confidence in the results, and they have been active in the dissemination of the findings and discussion of policy implications (ISSP [Institute for Strategic Studies and Prognoses and UNDP] 2003).

Monitoring and Evaluation

The importance of building monitoring and evaluation mechanisms into projects and policies cannot be overstressed. To ensure accountability, monitoring should be an integral part of all projects (see box 7.2). Evaluations to assess a project's impact and outcomes are equally important. This entails collecting baseline data at the start of a project to use for comparison once the project has been completed. For example, an intervention designed to improve school enrollment should measure enrollment before the project began and then assess whether participants stay in school longer and perform better with the new program in place. The time horizon for outcome evaluation should also be enough to assess the longer-term impact. Again, in the case of education, the evaluation should consider not just whether children are in school at the end of the project, but what they have learned, whether they graduate, whether they continue their education, and how the project affected their chances for higher education and employment.

Ensuring Participation

Regardless of whether policies are explicitly designed for Roma, Roma must be involved. The track record of programs directed at Roma— during both the socialist and transition periods—clearly showed that including Roma in the design, implementation, and evaluation of programs is essential for success. The recent past is littered with projects and programs, however well-intentioned, that failed because they were designed and implemented without the participation of the future beneficiaries. Take for example housing projects that built apartments that were unsuitable for Roma or social-assistance programs that gave Roma goods they would rather have sold.

Roma involvement in policy and project development rests on the existence of effective mechanisms for participation. While Roma have

Box 7.2 Monitoring and Evaluating School Success for Roma Children

The Step-by-Step Special Schools Initiative of the Open Society Institute provides a useful example of how project evaluation can improve the success of a project and contribute to policy development. This project aimed to address a particularly troubling problem: the shunting of Roma children into "special schools" intended for the mentally and physically handicapped. It also sought to formulate policy recommendations that would improve the chances for Roma children in mainstream schools.

The project operated in Bulgaria, the Czech Republic, Hungary, and Slovakia. Roma students in special schools in each of the countries were taught the mainstream curriculum instead of the slower special-school curriculum. Teachers and administrators were trained in anti-bias education, second-language learning, and the Step-by-Step methodology. Additional support was provided in the form of classroom materials. A Roma assistant teacher was assigned to each site to help in the classroom and work with students and their families outside of school.

Evaluation was built into the project from the start. Local researchers were hired to collect data in each project site, as well as several control sites; an international researcher coordinated their efforts and ensured data comparability. Data were collected on process indicators, such as student attendance and parental involvement, as well as on educational outcomes. Students were also tested at the end of each academic year, and interviews were conducted with students and parents. *Monitoring* was integral to the project to keep it on track. Master teacher-trainers at the national and international levels worked closely with project staff to provide support and ensure consistency across project sites.

The results after the second year of the project were heartening. On aggregate, the project found that 64 percent of Roma second-graders in the project sites did not belong in special schools. In other words, these Roma pupils were able to meet national standards for the mainstream curriculum with the support of the project. These powerful results make the case for interventions to get Roma children out of special schools and into mainstream classes. The empirical analysis makes a compelling case that investments in education for Roma students—including teacher training, language support, and parental involvement—can pay off over the longer term; graduates of mainstream schools have far more employment and education opportunities than graduates of the special schools. Similarly, the ongoing monitoring let project managers make course corrections and distill lessons for follow-on projects.

Source: Rona and Lee 2001.

been increasingly involved in civil society and policymaking, significant challenges remain. Some of these have been discussed earlier, including lingering prejudices, mistrust between Roma and non-Roma, low education levels, and widespread illiteracy that shrink the potential pool of Roma leaders and voters. Policymakers must continue to expand opportunities for Roma to participate in civil society and public service at the local and national levels. Non-Roma involvement is also crucial. The example of Slovakia in chapter 3 highlights the perils of segregation. Roma who do not interact with wider society, including other Roma communities and non-Roma, are cut off from social services, the labor market, education, and—all too often— prosperity. More contacts and partnerships between non-Roma and Roma will ease the mistrust and miscommunication that limit local and community development.

Across the region, post-Soviet political liberalization created a proliferation of civil society organizations, including NGOs, political parties, religious organizations, and community associations. Many groups have been formed to address particular issues related to ethnic minorities, including a wide range of Roma organizations, many of them financed by external sources. Chapter 6 discussed the range of NGOs working on Roma issues in Hungary. Similarly, a 1996 survey by the Union of Bulgarian Foundations and Associations identified more than 1,300 organizations that addressed ethnic issues and put Roma among their priorities (Iliev 1999).

Roma NGOs, like Roma communities themselves, are diverse and often fragmented. In some cases, this limits the effectiveness of Roma in their dialogue with government officials and other potential partners. Roma organizations disagree frequently and struggle to reach consensus. This may reflect several issues, including the groups' relative political inexperience, divisions between Roma subgroups, and some characteristics of Roma social organization, such as the rather common absence of hierarchical structures within Roma groups.

Local governments are also important. Throughout the region, the role of local governments has changed substantially during the transition as decentralization replaces communist centralization. The decentralization process is reinforced by the EU's principle of "subsidiarity," by which services should be delivered at the lowest possible level of government. The process of building effective, accountable, responsive local governments has not been an easy one—with particularly unfortunate consequences for society's most vulnerable, including Roma. Roma participate in local governments by running for elective office, using public services, and interacting with local officials. Local governments are also potentially important sources of support for Roma communities, individuals, and associations. But, as the Nyíregyháza case study from Hungary in chapter 5 illustrated, local governments can also further marginalize Roma. Even where national policies do not discriminate, local-level, biased implementation can derail original intentions.

Roma participation in politics and political affairs is generally limited. Few Roma are members of political parties, and parties rarely reach out to them. While recent local government elections increased the number of Roma in government, their presence is far from widespread. Roma political parties have traditionally been weak and fail to attract substantial blocs of Roma voters. A 2003 National Democratic Institute assessment of Roma political participation identified a wide range of barriers that limit the political involvement of Roma. These include poverty and illiteracy, competing ethnic identities, lack of political experience, and lack of interest and will on behalf of political parties to engage with Roma. However, the assessment found substantial interest and potential for capacity building to facilitate greater political participation of Roma (National Democratic Institute 2003).

In recent years, all countries in the region have introduced institutions for integrating Roma into policymaking at the national and local levels. Perhaps the most ambitious approach was taken in Hungary, which in 1993 introduced a system of minority self-governments, as discussed in chapter 5. Other countries, including the Czech and Slovak Republics and Romania, have established national consultative bodies to shape policymaking related to minorities.

In the Czech case, a new Inter-Ministerial Commission comprised of Roma and non-Roma representatives of government agencies now advises the parliament. In Romania, the Council for National Minorities, tied to the parliament, includes representatives from minority organizations. The strength of these bodies varies, however, and some even lack budgets. In most cases, it is too early to gauge how representative and effective these institutions are.

Many countries have also recently adopted national policy strategies on Roma issues. Such a plan is currently under discussion in Serbia and Montenegro. In Bulgaria, the government adopted "The Framework Program for Equal Integration of Roma in Bulgarian Society" in March 1999—the culmination of an unprecedented process of consultation and consensus building both between the government and Bulgaria's Roma community and among Roma NGOs themselves. The program, which 75 Roma NGOs endorsed, offers strategic guidelines in the areas of anti-discrimination policy, economic development, and social services (OSCE 2000).

While it is too soon to judge the impact of these strategies and action plans, they have helped elevate dialogue between the Roma community and national governments and have raised core policy issues. Examples from Western European countries—such as Spain, a case discussed in chapter 7—can provide useful insights here.

POLICY DIRECTIONS

Addressing Roma issues will take experimentation, patience, and close collaboration between Roma communities, the international community, NGOs, and national governments. Initiatives need to be designed and adapted to local country circumstances, as well as to the varying needs of Roma groups. Considerations of diversity need to be built in at the outset. Policies should balance three related sets of objectives: first, increasing economic opportunities by expanding employment participation; second, building human capital through better education and health; and third, strengthening social capital and community development through increased Roma empowerment and participation. Implementing these measures will involve collaboration between central government ministries, local governments, Roma communities, NGOs, and international partners.

Employment

The difficulty Roma face in accessing and reentering the labor market is a main contributor to poverty. Long-term unemployment, in addition to leaving people in poverty, leads to a psychology of dependence on social benefits, which makes reentry into the labor market even more difficult. Another reason for widespread unemployment is that many Roma have obsolete skills, which are no longer relevant for the labor market.

Expanding labor market opportunities is a priority throughout the region. Opportunities must be widely shared, and the poorest must have the means to take advantage of new jobs. Without this, a core poor "underclass" will persist. Specific attention is needed to address the additional barriers that Roma face, including lower education status, geographic isolation, and discrimination. A mix of passive unemployment benefits protect the long-term unemployed and stimulate employment. Experiences from Hungary and Spain provide examples of promising projects (see box 7.3). Initiatives that increase opportunities for Roma in the labor market start with improvements in education status.

Improving access to credit makes it easier for Roma and other low-income groups to start their own businesses. NGOs can play an important role in helping communities initiate projects. Partnerships between these organizations and banks are needed to establish credit mechanisms. Regulatory obstacles to the development of income-generating activities and labor force mobility should be identified and removed. On a related note, expanding the availability of microcredit could weaken the grasp of local usurers who currently lend funds at extortionate rates in some Roma settlements.

Another important element is more effective public works programs. Many current programs focus on short-term, low-skilled employment and provide participants with neither enhanced skills nor better long-term

Box 7.3 Promoting Roma Employment

One of the most established programs to promote employment and income-generating opportunities for Roma is Hungary's Autonómia Foundation, which provides grants and interest-free loans to develop employment programs for Roma. Its income-generating initiatives include livestock breeding, agricultural programs, and small-enterprise development.

The success of Autonómia's projects, as measured by its loan repayment rates, has soared since the foundation was established in 1990. In 1998, repayment rates reached nearly 80 percent, compared to 10 percent during Autonómia's first year. Autonómia attributes this improvement to the involvement of trained monitors, some of whom are Roma, who work closely with project teams throughout the implementation process. Autonómia is now expanding its programs to other countries in the region. In 2000, the first group of Roma began training to start small grant and loan programs for Roma in four CEE countries, including Slovakia. Further evaluation of the project should examine the project's impact on participants' welfare.

Sources: Autonómia Foundation; Tanaka et al. 1998.

employment prospects. The quality and training content of public works jobs should be improved so that participants gain transferable skills.

Training programs can also facilitate labor-market reentry for low-skilled and unskilled workers. However, because international experience with such programs is mixed, programs must be carefully tailored to fit labor market conditions—a point particularly relevant to Roma (Dar and Tzannatos 1998). Some initiatives have sought to train Roma in traditional trades that are not in much demand.

At the policy level, anti-discrimination legislation must be in place, complete with effective and accessible mechanisms for appeals. Beyond legislative measures, project interventions can overcome barriers between non-Roma and Roma by building confidence through on-the-job training and employment experience. A successful public works project in Bulgaria showed non-Roma contractors that Roma could be reliable, effective employees—a standing rebuke to deeply held stereotypes about Roma laziness. Another possible approach is offering tax incentives to employers who employ Roma.

Education

Because education is so central to improved welfare and economic status, it has been a priority focus for both governments and NGOs. More project activity has taken place in the education area over the past decade than in any other sector. The review of social sector projects in Hungary presented in chapter 5 found that nearly 30 percent of resources allocated to Roma projects during the past decade were for education.

Education initiatives take various forms and intervene at different points within the education cycle. One key priority is lowering the barriers that prevent Roma children from starting school. Many children are discouraged from attending school because of deprivation at home and cultural differences, including language. Economic constraints can be loosened by coordinating social assistance and education policies to ease the cost of education for poor families—including such tactics as school feeding programs (which boost both nutrition and attendance), linkages between child allowances and school enrollments, and scholarships for low-income students. Social workers can also identify households in need of assistance.

Preschool programs can prepare children for the classroom and surmount language barriers. Several countries have tried targeted preprimary initiatives to facilitate school attendance and performance. In 2002, the Bulgarian government announced its intention to make preschool free and compulsory. For its part, the Slovak government has supported the Zero Grade Program, which expands preschool attendance for Roma children.

NGOs can also play important roles. The Open Society Institute initiated the "Step-by-Step" program, modeled on the U.S. Head Start initiative, in both Roma and non-Roma communities. In 2000, over 8,000 Roma students in 17 countries in Central and Eastern Europe and the former Soviet Union enrolled in Step-by-Step programs. Step-by-Step takes an integrated approach that provides training and support to teachers, while involving parents in the classroom. Parental involvement at all levels of education should be explored and fostered, including bringing parents into the classroom as teachers' aides, parent-teacher associations, and regular parent-teacher interactions.

Initiatives that reduce the dropout rate and smooth the way to secondary and tertiary education are also critical, but there is less experience here. Still, mentoring programs and extracurricular activities that provide tutoring and supplementary educational events have been introduced in some countries. Schools like the Gandhi School in Pécs, Hungary, and the Romani High School for Social Affairs in Kolin in the Czech Republic integrate Romani studies, including language, history, and culture into the curriculum. Successful elements from these schools—including multicultural curricula, teacher training, and parental involvement—can be incorporated into all public schools (see box 7.4).

Better education for Roma students can boost school attendance and educational outcomes. This will require fighting discrimination within school systems and diminishing the role of special schools and institutions for Roma. The practice of unnecessarily channeling Roma

Box 7.4 Alternative Secondary Schools in Hungary

Hungary has experimented with alternative approaches to secondary-school education that aim to help Roma children bridge the gap between basic and secondary school, improve their academic performance, and create future opportunities. Roma are much less likely to start and complete secondary school than other children. A 1993 survey of Roma in Hungary found that only 1 percent of Roma took the final examination for secondary schools and only 13 percent received training as skilled workers.

A World Bank–commissioned review of these alternative approaches looked at six different schools, most of which had been established during the previous five years. All the schools were private and received support from a range of local and international foundations and NGOs, as well as state budget subsidies. While most students were Roma in each school, not all the institutions explicitly targeted Roma children.

The type of education provided by the different schools varies greatly. In some cases, the schools provide vocational training, such as the "Roma Chance" Alternative Vocational Foundation School in Szolnok, the Don Bosco Vocational Training Center and Primary School in Kazincbarcika, and Budapest's Kalyi Jag School. Others, such as the Jószefváros School and the Collegium Martineum in Mánfa, support secondary school students through extracurricular activities and classes and, in the case of the Collegium Martineum, dormitory accommodations in a supportive home environment. Finally, the Gandhi School and Students' Hostel in Pécs is a six-year secondary school (or gymnasium) that prepares students for university.

The schools differ in the extent to which they emphasize the Roma background of their students in their curricula and approach. In most of the schools, strengthening Roma identity and preserving Roma tradition are explicit and integral components of school mission. These schools offer classes in Roma language, history, and art. Others, such as Don Bosco, focus on building the self-confidence of students through professional training.

The schools also take different approaches to the underlying socioeconomic disadvantages of students. Some, such as the Collegium Martineum, target disadvantaged students and provide housing and other support to boost attendance. Most of the schools also involve parents, although this often proves difficult because of low education levels.

Sources: Orsós et al. 2000.

students into special schools in the first place must be reviewed, as should policies that limit the future opportunities of special school graduates. Special education should be reformed to address true learning disabilities and the special needs of at-risk children.

Limiting the use of separate classrooms and schools for Roma can improve education quality and reduce divisions between Roma and non-Roma communities. Within schools, separate classrooms for Roma should be abolished. For geographically remote settlements, other options could be considered, such as the pilot project in Bulgaria that transports Roma children from a Roma settlement to an integrated school (see box 7.5).

Box 7.5 Desegregation of Roma Schools in Bulgaria: The Vidin Model

In Vidin, the Open Society Institute and the Roma NGO known by the acronym DROM have been collaborating on an innovative program to integrate Roma students into the mainstream school system. Vidin is a town of 85,000 in northwest Bulgaria, where 6 percent of the population was identified as Roma in the 1992 census. In the 2000–01 school year, 460 students, or half of the school-age students, were integrated into the mainstream school system; more were expected to follow in the next school year. Under the project, students are bused from the settlement to school and back. In addition to transportation, the project involves Roma monitors who interact with parents and the school to encourage attendance. Low-income students also receive shoes and school lunches; students are given their lunch on the bus to reduce the stigma of receiving it at school.

While preparing the program, DROM went door-to-door in the Roma settlement explaining the project. DROM also sought the support of the schools, the mayor, and the media. The project eventually gained support of all the stakeholders except the mayor, who agreed not to block it. With the agreement of several Roma parents, DROM invited the six mainstream schools in Vidin to participate in a TV program at which each school presented its program, philosophy, and teachers. Roma parents then selected a school for their children. This lessened their concerns and marked the first time that their views had been solicited by the authorities.

At the end of the first semester, the project was a dramatic success, as seen in 100 percent attendance, first-term final-grade averages identical to those of non-Roma pupils, parental and teacher satisfaction, the absence of reported incidents of anti-Roma prejudice, full support from the Regional Directorate of the Ministry of Education,

(continued)

Box 7.5 (*continued*)

and encouragement to scale up in other cities. In addition, 35 Roma parents of the bused children themselves returned to school in adult-education programs, and three teenagers who had dropped out in the third grade asked to join the program, prompting teachers to work extra hours with them. On the negative side, 24 pupils received failing grades in one or more subjects, and three left the program. (One returned to the Roma school, and two functionally illiterate eighth graders dropped out.)

The program's success to date is attributable to three major factors. First, parents feel that their children are protected from prejudice because they are bused and monitored throughout the day by adult Roma; parents also feel that their children can meet the higher scholastic standards. Second, the schools have accepted young adult Roma monitors in the schools who assure that the children are not mistreated. The monitors also follow parental engagement and student participation in extracurricular activities. Moreover, the monitors help the teachers and ease cultural differences. Third, the children are happy to be in schools where real learning takes place. Ongoing assessment of project outcomes will be essential to understand the longer-term implications of the highly encouraging Vidin project.

Source: Open Society Institute.

Teachers define the quality of education and must be trained to meet the challenges of a multicultural environment. Ongoing support mechanisms that help teachers on the job are also critical. Particular training should include Roma history and culture, conflict resolution, and classroom management. Some countries have also experimented with Roma teachers' assistants and mediators who can assist in the classroom environment and link Roma communities and schools. In Romania, the Ministry of Education has appointed Roma education inspectors in each of its 41 counties to monitor the quality of Roma education.

Health Care

Relative to the other policy areas, much less is known about the health issues facing Roma communities. This calls out for better monitoring. In particular, more effective observation of communicable diseases, such as tuberculosis, hepatitis, and HIV/AIDS, is critical. Health services must also be available in isolated Roma communities. Policies that can expand such access to remote rural areas and segregated urban communities would include providing incentives for physicians, community health workers, and social workers to work with communities would to address problems and teach prevention.

Public health interventions can be designed to overcome cultural barriers to care. Some countries have experimented with using Roma mediators to promote health activities within Roma communities and to facilitate interactions between Roma and health care professionals—especially around overcoming Roma resistance to such basic care measures as immunizations. Information campaigns are also critical for addressing many emerging health risks, including substance abuse, sexually transmitted diseases, and conditions associated with poor nutrition and housing. Other initiatives can include better dissemination of public health information through the media and schools, as well as better coordination with organizations such as churches and Roma NGOs.

Health services need particular attention. Outreach can raise awareness about a range of issues, including women's health. Attention to reproductive and family health care issues can help overcome cultural taboos, such as the fear of screening for cervical cancer. Some of the PHARE projects are addressing women's health issues in different ways. In the Slovak Republic, for instance, a team of NGOs organized a hygiene and child development course for Roma mothers. Countries in other regions have launched successful initiatives for improving women's health through community groups and education.

Housing

Because Roma live in such different conditions, housing is a complex sector that requires close coordination between governments and communities. Effective legislation and enforcement mechanisms are needed to prevent housing discrimination and clarify property ownership. In many slum areas and settlements, unresolved questions about building ownership and residency rights have blurred the responsibilities for upgrading and maintenance to the point where no one is responsible. Similar dynamics block incentives for residents to invest in and maintain properties. A UNDP program in Bucharest worked towards legalizing apartments for households in a neighborhood where ownership was not clear. The municipality assumed the management of the properties and let residents apply for rental contracts.

Adequate mechanisms for community involvement and choice are equally important. The legacy of failed housing programs and projects during the socialist era has made this particularly critical, but there are still few experiences from which to draw. Some promising facilities have emerged recently that let communities and households apply for resources for community development and better housing, including microcredit arrangements and social funds. Finding out whether these instruments can reach Roma communities will take careful consideration and monitoring.

Measures to alleviate poor conditions in some of the most disadvantaged Roma settlements include (i) clarifying property rights; (ii) resolving disputes over the ownership of land and buildings that are stopping residents and local governments from investing in and maintaining rundown properties; (iii) simplifying procedures for obtaining building permits to allow residents to upgrade their property; and (iv) providing clear information to the public on procedures for applying for construction permits and acquiring property.

Outlying Roma settlements need expanded coverage of utilities and public services. One option would be bringing isolated settlements into mainstream service networks. While inhabitants should still be charged for utilities, subsidies may be needed for low-income households, particularly to cover the cost of public goods, such as sanitation. Local governments and communities can be given incentives to provide services in settlements, possibly through a central fund. Finally, opportunities within public works programs can improve basic infrastructure and services in Roma communities.

Social Assistance

Safety net programs that provide cash assistance to the poor are an important source of income for many Roma families. Many countries in the region are reforming cash benefits to make them more effective and more capable of reaching the poor. Such programs need to meet the needs of poor households without discouraging those who can from working—which would leave them in a "poverty trap," dependent on social benefits. The Slovak case, in particular, highlighted the perils of this reliance on social benefits.

Work incentives can be built into social assistance programs through time limits, work requirements, and other mechanisms. Benefits should be phased out so that low wage workers— the working poor—will still be entitled to benefits but at a level that will not discourage them from working. This would improve work incentives for those at the margins and increase income among low-income working families. Social workers should also shift their role to act as employment facilitators who can help the unemployed find work. Work-related programs, such as support for childcare and transportation subsidies for low-income workers, can also make it easier to find jobs and break the dependency cycle. Lessons from the U.S. welfare reform experience of the 1990s are illustrative here (see box 7.6).

Box 7.6 Lessons from U.S. Welfare Reform

During the 1990s, as concerns grew about the increasing number of welfare caseloads, the U.S. government introduced substantial legislative changes in programs that are designed to assist low-income families. In particular, the federal government granted a growing number of waivers early in the decade, allowing states to experiment with alternative rules for the Aid to Families with Dependent Children (AFDC) and Food Stamps programs. These changes were followed in 1996 by the Personal Responsibility and Work Opportunity Act, which fundamentally changed the public assistance system in the United States. The act abolished AFDC, which required states to match federal welfare funds, and replaced it with Temporary Assistance to Needy Families (TANF), which granted unconditional, fixed amounts of funding to states and allowed them to set their own rules for eligibility and benefits.

In the light of these changes, several states started using "diversions" (one-time assistance, rather than enrollment in ongoing TANF-funded programs) and benefit programs that let recipients keep more public assistance benefits after returning to work, thus increasing both work incentives and income among low-income families. Some states also worked to transform public assistance offices into employment assistance offices, where applicants were given constant incentives to seek and find work. Moreover, several states imposed more penalties on those who did not respond to these work incentives. Finally, individual states spent more money on work-related programs relative to cash benefits.

To what extent was welfare reform responsible for these trends? To be sure, the U.S. economy enjoyed tremendous prosperity during the 1990s. As a consequence, employment growth was high, unemployment was low, and wages have grown significantly among workers of all skill levels starting around 1996. These factors influenced the welfare of less-skilled workers and are therefore important in explaining the trends described above. In fact, between one-third and two-thirds of the caseload change can be attributed to the economy's overall performance.[a]

Unfortunately, a strong economy affects not only poverty but also economic policy, which makes it hard to measure the effect of welfare policy changes independently of the business-cycle effect.[b] But while the overall effect of welfare reform is difficult to pin down, both Canada and the United States have experimented with particularly innovative types of welfare reform programs in ways that permit some form of evaluation.

These programs combined financial incentives with work mandates. In particular, the Minnesota Family Investment Program substantially decreased the benefit-reduction rate for public assistance recipients (thus allowing them to keep more public assistance income when they went to work), while also mandating participation in work/welfare programs. Striking a similar note from north of the U.S. border, Canada's

(continued)

Box 7.6 (*continued*)

Self-Sufficient Program (SSP) provided substantial financial support to long-term public assistance recipients who worked 30 hours or more per week. These programs' results showed that employment, earnings, and family income increased for program participants even as poverty fell.

Although these programs are not money-savers in the short run—indeed, they actually provide more assistance to low-income families than did traditional welfare programs—it is important to consider their long-run effects, particularly since studies of people leaving welfare suggest that most of them (55–85 percent) become employed at a future date and about one-half to two-thirds report higher incomes after they get off welfare (Brauner and Loprest 1999).

Moreover, such programs can be improved through good design. For instance, employment is associated with extra expenses in the form of childcare, transportation, and more. So in some states, public support for those items was included as part of their welfare policy, together with health insurance coverage through the Medicaid system.[c] At the federal level, the Earned-Income Tax Credit program served a similar function.

In sum, in the U.S. case, a confluence of events seemingly came together—a strong expanding economy, substantial revisions of public assistance programs that emphasized work and reduced benefit eligibility, and major policy changes that increased the numbers of people returning to work and the subsidies to support work, particularly among vulnerable groups. This seems to have created the right environment for the decline in poverty rates and welfare caseload observed in the data. Moreover, because many of the programs described above rely strongly on the availability of jobs, it is not clear how sustainable these welfare policy changes are in the long run—or how dependent their success has been on a booming U.S. economy. Still, the fact that the SSP managed to succeed, despite a Canadian economy that did not do as well as the United States in the 1990s, shows that programs can work in less favorable environments with high unemployment, if they are designed correctly.

Notes:
a Different studies provide different measures. See Figlio and Ziliak (1999), and Schoeni and Blank (2000).
b There is some crude evidence that such changes had a substantial effect on caseloads, but there has been significantly less research relating TANF changes to work behavior or poverty rates. In this respect, the best evidence comes from the fact that participation rates are increasing among vulnerable groups (e.g., single mothers with young children).
c Most low-skilled jobs do not offer health insurance, and this could act as a deterrent for employment.

Sources: Blank 2000; Peterson 2000; Schoeni and Blank 2000.

CONCLUSIONS

Roma poverty remains one of the foremost policy issues for Central and Eastern European states given the context of EU integration. With enlargement, Roma now represent the largest minority group in Europe, and their dire living conditions cannot be ignored. By going deeper into the nature of Roma communities and providing a more complete picture through both quantitative and qualitative data, this report finds that Roma poverty is a multifaceted problem that can only be addressed by an inclusive approach—involving government, civil society, and other partners—that addresses all dimensions of Roma social exclusion simultaneously. The dominant policy approach since 1989 has tended to be the opposite, relying on a fragmented set of projects, often delivered by local NGOs with limited assistance from the state. So the potential to make a difference through a comprehensive change of direction is large and bright.

The current level of activity and interest in Roma issues in Central and Eastern Europe provides a promising start. The next step is to integrate the lessons of these experiences into policy. The mechanisms to facilitate this have been put in place. Most countries have now formulated strategies for improving the conditions of Roma and built institutions to develop, coordinate, and administer policies and projects. But the road ahead is long and winding. Improvements will not come overnight. Indeed, the debilitating poverty among Roma communities in some West European countries highlights the scope of the challenge for their neighbors to the east. Effective policy responses will require a multilayered approach, involving cross-country partnerships among Roma and international organizations, national and local governments, NGOs, and communities. With sustained leadership, both by Roma and by those who recognize how much Roma can contribute to an enlarging EU, Roma can look forward with real hope.

Notes

1. OSCE (2000); OSI (2001); Save the Children (2001a, 2001b); UNDP (2003).

2. Europe and Central Asia refers to the former socialist countries of Central and Eastern Europe and the former Soviet Union.

3. There is substantial international evidence that welfare and socioeconomic status can have an ethnic dimension, including analysis on the disparities in welfare between blacks, whites, and Native Americans in the United States, the conditions of indigenous peoples in Latin America, and the status of ethnic minorities in other parts of the world. For a review of the literature, see Psacharopoulos and Patrinos (1994).

4. This differs significantly across subgroups, ranging from 14 to 85 percent (Tomova 1998).

5. The European Roma Rights Center has extensively documented discrimination and human rights violations of Roma. Regular updates and country reports can be found at www.errc.org.

6. Article 6 of the Treaty on European Union refers to the European Convention for the Protection of Human Rights and Fundamental Freedoms, which all European states have ratified. The protection of individuals belonging to minorities is considered to be "an inherent part" of the EU policy on human rights. The convention's Article 14 states that the rights and freedoms laid down in the convention should "be secured without discrimination on any ground such as sex, race, colour, language, religion, political or other opinion, national or social origin, association with a national minority, property, birth or other status." See http://europa.eu.int/comm/external_relations/human_rights/rm.

7. The Copenhagen Document is sometimes referred to as the "European Constitution of Human Rights." It was adopted in 1990 by the conference on the Human Dimension of the Conference on Security and Cooperation. While legally non-binding, it explicitly recognizes the importance of national minorities.

8. The framework convention, developed by the Council of Europe in 1995, entered into force in February 1998; it is legally binding under international law

and contains principles that each contracting party must implement through national legislation and government policies.

9. The EU Charter on Fundamental Rights lays down the equality before the law of all people (Article 20), prohibits discrimination (Article 21), and requests the EU to protect cultural, religious, and linguistic diversity. See http://europa.eu.int/comm/external_relations/human_rights/rm.

10. The Council of Europe's European Charter for Regional or Minority Languages (1992) contains provisions, which may be applied to "nonterritorial" languages such as the Roma language.

11. The European Court of Human Rights recently noted that while there was an "emerging international consensus . . . recognizing the special needs of minorities and an obligation to protect their security, identity and lifestyle . . . [the divided Court itself is] not persuaded that the consensus is sufficiently concrete for it to derive any guidance as to the conduct or standards which Contracting States consider desirable in any particular situation" (from *Chapman v. United Kingdom*, UCHR, Judgment of 18 January 2001 [No. 27238/95], in OSI [2001]).

12. For more on measuring poverty, see Ravallion (1994).

13. For example see the Luxembourg Income Study.

14. The official World Bank poverty rates are US$1 and US$2 per day, but because of higher heating costs in the Europe Central Asia region, the higher rates of US$2.15 and US$4.30 are used for the countries analyzed in this book.

15. Further information on the methodology used in this analysis can be found in Revenga et al. (2002).

16. As discussed above, the dataset allows for multiple definitions of Roma ethnicity. For the analysis that follows, the broadest definition of Roma is used. If either the individual or the interviewer indicated that the individual was Roma using any of the criteria included in the survey, all household members are assumed to be Roma for the purposes of the analysis.

17. The U.S. and European literature on poverty and social exclusion finds that socially or economically excluded groups may often adopt behavior patterns that differ from the majority population, which affect the return to productive endowments and the overall welfare of the excluded population (Loury 1999; Silver 1994).

18. This issue is discussed further in the next chapter on Slovakia.

19. A highly publicized attempt was made in the Slovak Republic by the city of Kosice, which sought to move people who were not paying rent (largely Roma) to the Lunik IX neighborhood, a housing development on the outskirts of the town (OSCE 2000).

20. Results are from the Romania Integrated Household Survey, 1998.

21. This reflects the fact that more Roma in the Bulgarian sample live in Roma settlements, where housing conditions are generally poorer than in more integrated neighborhoods.

22. For a discussion of labor market dynamics in the early transition see Allison and Ringold (1996) and Commander and Coricelli (1995).

23. Employment rates are not comparable across countries because of differences in the definition of the working-age population (see box 2.3).

24. Birthrates are not ideal measures, as they do not account for the age distribution, however, fertility rates were not available.

25. The Romania case study of Babadag found a high rate of intermarriage (Rughinis 2000).

26. For a more detailed discussion of the history of Roma in Slovakia see Crowe (1994).

27. Estimates differ, but approximately 6,000–8,000 Czech Roma are thought to have been killed.

28. Roma were officially allowed to form organizations during the Czechoslovak Republic (1918–38), but none did. The first Roma organization was established in 1948 and was banned soon after by the communists.

29. This figure is based on a loose definition of settlements, including integrated areas in towns and villages; as a result, it is unclear to what extent the higher number of settlements in 1998 reflects an actual increase or whether it is due to changes in the way in which settlements were counted.

30. Housed in the Office of the Plenipotentiary for Roma Communities, the database from which this information is gathered, provides only a rough estimate of the number of settlements and their conditions. The fieldwork conducted for this study found significant errors in the database regarding the number and location of settlements.

31. *Gadjo* (plural *gadje*) is a Roma word for non-Roma.

32. Based on information collected during the qualitative survey.

33. The amount differs from one municipality to another, depending on the wealth of the municipality. For instance, in a better-off neighborhood close to Bratislava, the annual collection fee is 1,000 crowns (about US$21). In other areas it is much less.

34. According to respondents in one village it can cost up to 47,000 crowns for a gas connection (close to US$1,000).

35. Based on 1996 Microcensus data, refer to World Bank (2001b).

36. The practice of collecting information based on ethnicity was discontinued in 1998 after protest from Roma and Hungarians. One reason for these criticisms was that ethnicity was being judged by labor office staff, a practice inconsistent with Slovak legislation aimed at protecting basic individual rights.

37. Primary education in Slovakia includes grades 1–9 and generally covers children from 6 to 16 years old.

38. Fees are set regionally and vary based upon the economic situation of the region. For example, in 2000 fees ranged from 600 crowns in Bratislava, to 20 crowns per month in Rimavská Sobota.

39. There are approximately 380 special schools throughout the Slovak Republic for mentally and physically disabled children. A total of 30,583 students study in special schools, which amounts to about 3 percent of the total

number of students at kindergartens, primary schools, and secondary schools.

40. The minimum class size is four. The maximum number of students is 8 for grade 1; 10 for grades 2–5; and 12 for grades 6–9.

41. In Slovakia, textbooks are free of charge. Children keep their books at home. However, in some—especially segregated—settlements, teachers keep the books in the classroom explaining that children do not have a place to keep the books at home and as a result, they are damaged throughout the course of the year.

42. For example, in 1461–62, the Wallachian ruler Vlad IV Tepes (the Impaler) brought 11,000–12,000 Roma from Bulgaria, while in 1471, the Moldavian ruler Stephen the Great is reported to have brought 17,000 Roma to use as slave labor (Crowe 1994).

43. Such laws were passed to restrict the freedom of movement of Roma slaves, to forbid interethnic marriage, and to discourage escape attempts and the illegal trade in slaves (Crowe 1994).

44. By some accounts, official policy was not to annihilate the Roma per se, but to ensure that they were removed from tainting the Romanian nation. However, according to the War Crimes Commission established by the Romanian People's Court, 36,000 Roma died during the war, constituting the highest absolute number of Roma deaths in any European country. Those who survived are reported to have lived in relative freedom, with some even serving in the Romanian national army (CEDIME-SE 2001).

45. Ceaușescu's "systemization" program uprooted many Roma and non-Roma communities.

46. Based on a poverty line of US$4.30 per capita per day.

47. For example, according to an "Ethnobarometer" survey taken in 2000, it was reported that 38–40 percent of non-Roma Romanians would prohibit Roma from settling in Romania; 23 percent of ethnic Romanians and 31 percent of ethnic Hungarians would refuse to accept Roma in their city, town, or village in Romania. Another recent poll (2000) found that 67 percent of the population feel resentment toward the Roma (OSI 2001).

48. According to the 1993 study, only a small proportion of the Roma population (7 percent of adult men) practiced traditional Roma trades. While a larger proportion of the population (35 percent of adult men) acquired "modern" skills, the large majority of the sample—58 percent of men and 85 percent of women—report having no trade (either traditional or modern) (Zamfir and Zamfir 1993).

49. The description of income levels is based upon the observations of the field researchers and provides only a rough indication of relative welfare in the different communities.

50. Data from the 1998 Romania Integrated Household Survey.

51. This study, cited in Save the Children (2001), was conducted by OSI and the Central European University Centre for Policy Studies for their forthcoming country report entitled *EU Accession Project: Roma Minority in Romania.*

52. Since this study was conducted, social assistance reforms have improved in effectiveness and coverage. Positive effects for Roma have been noted, including (i) greater access to ID cards; (ii) improved targeting of the unemployed through a workfare requirement; and (iii) increased social capital generated by the participation of Roma and non-Roma in workfare activities.

53. Data are from the 1998 Romanian Integrated Household Survey.

54. In addition to difficulties in accurately identifying the exact number of Roma in villages, towns, and cities, even reliable estimates indicate that the Roma population is unlikely to reach 20 percent in most or all territorial administrative units (OSI 2001).

55. Under the department's supervision, a limited number of initiatives were undertaken within the Framework of the Strategy for the Integration of the Roma. For example, the Ministry of Labor and Social Solidarity formulated a special program for professional guidance at the level of the local departments for labor and social protection, through Roma agents. In parallel, the General Police Inspectorate implemented some programs for preventing violence in localities and communities with the participation of Roma organizations and associations (UN 2001).

56. A list of Romanian Roma NGOs, compiled by the Resource Center for Roma Communities, is available at http://www.romacenter.ro.

57. See http://europa.eu.int/comm/enlargement/hungary (Bilateral Relations: EU-Hungary, as of January 26, 2003).

58. See http://europa.eu.int/comm/enlargement/hungary (Pre-Accession Assistance).

59. More recently, it has been estimated that there are currently some 50,000 registered NGOs in Hungary (http://www.autonomia.hu/english/indexen .html).

60. For a list of Roma and other NGOs dealing with issues related to sustainable development and advocacy, see the Non-Profit Information and Training Center (NIOK), *NGO Onarckep* at http://www.niok.hu/indexe. htm.

61. The other recognized minorities are Armenians, Bulgarians, Croats, Germans, Greeks, Poles, Romanians, Ruthenians, Serbs, Slovaks, Slovenes, and Ukrainians (PER 1998).

62. As this chapter was prepared as the Roma Office was being set up, it focuses on the previous structure.

63. See the "Summary of Measures Taken by the Government Affecting the Roma Minority over the Past Two Years," http://www.meh.hu/nekh/Angol/ roma_summary.htm.

64. In 1994 the Gandhi Foundation—a joint government and private initiative—established a high school and dormitory, the Gandhi High School, at Pécs that was primarily aimed at educating talented Roma youth. The school is managed by the foundation but financed through the Ministry of Education.

65. As the new coordinating body for the Mid-Term Package, the new Inter-Ministerial Committee for Gypsy Affairs was given greater power to appoint subcommittees. In addition, it provides greater consultative access to Roma social organizations that, by invitation, may attend up to four of the committee's sessions per year. The Parliamentary Commissioner for Minority Rights and the director of the Gandhi Foundation have standing invitations to all committee deliberations (Kállai and Törzsök 2000).

66. See also the "Summary of Measures Taken by the Government Affecting the Roma Minority over the Past Two Years," http://www.meh.hu/nekh/Angol/roma_summary.htm.

67. See the Minorities Ombudsman home page at http://www.obh.hu/nekh/en/index.htm

68. Concerns about the accountability of NMSG representatives have been raised due to the lack of formal mechanisms and the electoral college style of representation by which neither members of the minority nor the Hungarian populace more generally have any direct say in the NMSG composition (Kováts 2001b).

69. According to Article 27 of the Minorities Act of 1993, by law, the NMSG independently may take responsibility for the establishment and maintenance of institutions to support the development of national identity and culture, including the establishment of a theater, museums, an institute for the arts/sciences, and a minority library. They also may take responsibility for the maintenance of secondary and higher educational institutions with countrywide coverage and the establishment/operation of legal advisory services.

70. For example, the first Roma NMSG set up its own form of intermediary representation (23 regional offices as of 1997) from its own resources to facilitate the link between the NMSG and the 477 Roma MSGs. Research from 1998 indicated that these actions were of mixed success, in part due to the unofficial status of these offices (Kováts 2001b).

71. See www.meh.hu/nekh/Angol/data2_2000.htm.

72. The team was led by János Zolnay and included Gábor Bernáth, Angéla Kóczé, József Kolompár, Katalin Kovács, and Zsolt Zádori.

73. Of the total projects in the inventory, 93 percent could be mapped.

74. According to Labor Force Survey Data (World Bank 2000).

75. Housing expenditures do not include home construction subsidies.

76. These figures are considered to be under-representative of the total activity of ministries on Roma projects; however, more detailed and comprehensive information on these projects was difficult to obtain.

77. Drawn from original case study by Gábor Bernáth (2000).

78. Throughout Hungary, a disproportionate number of students are designated as mentally disabled. According to a 1996 OECD report, 35 children in 1,000 were labeled mentally disabled. This was in comparison with two in Turkey, four in Finland, and nine in Italy. In the small villages in Borsod-Abaúj-Zemplén County, Roma students are automatically sent to special

classes for the disabled. This has been the practice for years. In that county, 90 percent of Roma students attend special classes.

79. Drawn from an original case study by Zsolt Zádori (2000).

80. Ibid.

81. Drawn from an original case study by János Zolnay (2000).

82. The ministry has supported the Zsadány initiative every year since 1995, except in 1997 when, for reportedly politically motivated reasons, the subsidy was halted. In 1997, the Autonómia Foundation stepped in with financing of 1.7 million forints, which allowed the agricultural initiative to continue. Ministry financial aid was resumed again for 1998, 1999, and 2000.

83. Taxpayers decide how to allocate their money.

84. Due to a lack of systematic monitoring and evaluation of projects, data on the specific kinds of projects that are being implemented, the allocation of resources, and the relative weight of spending on different sectors were not available.

85. Information drawn primarily from ASGG (2001) and www.fsgg.org.

86. Prior to 2001, the FSGG was known as the Asociación Secretariado General Gitano (ASGG). For convenience, this chapter refers only to the FSGG, while any actions and programs prior to 2001 were undertaken through the ASGG.

87. In 2001, of the 657 staff, 457 were salaried workers and 190 were volunteers or interns. Community mediators and educators comprised 42 percent of the staff; administrators responsible for the coordination and management of programs and teams accounted for 39 percent of the staff.

88. In Spain, the following regions were eligible between 1994 and 1999: Andalucia, Asturias, Canary Islands, Cantabria, Castile-Leon, Castilla–La Mancha, Ceuta and Melilla, Extremadura, Galicia, Murcia, and Valencia. These same regions are eligible for 2000 to 2006, with the exception of Cantabria, which lost its eligibility in January 2000, when it achieved a per capita GDP level above 75 percent of the community average.

89. Groups included by the Equal Community Initiative include women, ethnic minorities, people with disabilities, older workers, refugees, ex-offenders, and people with drug and alcohol problems; it also includes actions to help the social and vocational integration of asylum seekers.

90. Council of Ministers decision (2000) final on June 28, 2000.

91. Since 1989, the EU has provided support for Central and Eastern European countries. The main instrument through which this assistance is provided is the PHARE program, under the responsibility of the Directorate General for Enlargement. In 1993, PHARE support was reoriented to focus more on the needs of countries applying for EU membership, including an expansion in support to infrastructure investment. In 1997, PHARE funds were again reoriented to focus entirely on the pre-accession priorities highlighted in each country's Accession Partnership agreements. PHARE funding is distributed as grants rather than as loans.

92. While having a special focus on Roma issues, some projects are not targeted solely at Roma and may include other ethnic minorities or disadvantaged groups. As a result, these figures do not represent the amount spent *exclusively* in support of Roma. For a more detailed breakdown of PHARE-funding for Roma by sector and project title, for Bulgaria, the Czech Republic, Hungary, Poland, Romania, Slovakia, and Slovenia, see European Commission 2002.

93. The Directorate General for External Relations manages the EIDHR. For more information on the EIDHR and its projects, see http://europa.eu.int/comm./europeaid/projects/ddh_en.htm.

94. The Directorate General manages the Socrates and Youth programs for Education and Culture. For more information on the Socrates Program, see http://europa.eu.int/comm/education/socrates.html and for the Youth Program, see http://europa.eu.int/comm/education/index_en.html.

95. These are outlined in the European Convention on Human Rights, the European Charter on Fundamental Rights, and the European Commission Directive on equal treatment of persons regardless of racial or ethnic origin.

References

Ainscow, M., and H. G. Memmenasha. 1998. The Education of Children with Special Needs: Barriers and Opportunities in Central and Eastern Europe. Innocenti Occasional Paper No. 67, UNICEF-ICDC, Florence.

Allison, C., and D. Ringold. 1996. Labor Markets in Transition in Central and Eastern Europe: 1989–1995. World Bank Technical Paper No. 352, World Bank, Washington, DC.

ASGG (Asociación Secretariado General Gitano). 2000. Proyecto ACCEDER: Informe Final, Acceder integra. ASGG, Madrid.

————. 1996. Situation and Normalisation of Street-Selling in Spain. ASGG, Madrid.

————. 2001. The Roma Community in Spain and Slovakia: A Guide to Action Strategies. ASGG and Ministerio de Asuntos Exteriores, Madrid.

Bárány, Z. 2000. The Poverty of Gypsy Studies. *NewsNet: The Newsletter of the American Association for the Advancement of Slavic Studies* 40 (3).

————. 2002. *The East European Gypsies: Regime Change, Marginality and Ethnopolitics.* Cambridge: Cambridge University Press.

Basurto, P. 1995. Children: Victims and Symbols. In *Children of Minorities: Deprivation and Discrimination.* Innocenti Insights Series. Florence: UNICEF International Child Development Centre.

Beck, S. 1984. Ethnicity, Class and Public Policy: Tsiganii/Gypsies in Socialist Romania. In *Papers for the Fifth Congress of Southeast European Studies* (Belgrade, September 1984), eds. Kot Shangriladze and Erica Townsend. Columbus: Slavica Publishers.

————. 1985. The Romanian Gypsy Problem. In *Papers From the Fourth and Fifth Annual Meeting of the Gypsy Lore Society*, North American Chapter, ed. Joanne Grumet. New York: Gypsy Lore Society.

————. 1989. The Origins of Gypsy Slavery in Romania. *Dialectical Anthropology* 14 (April 1989): 53–61.

Beissinger, Margaret H. 2001. Occupation and Ethnicity: Constructing Identity among Professional Romani (Gypsy) Musicians in Romania. *Slavic Review* 60:1 (Spring): 24–49.

211

Blanchard, O., et al. 1995. *Spanish Unemployment: Is There a Solution?* London: CEPR.

Blank, R. M. 2000. Fighting Poverty: Lessons from Recent US History. *Journal of Economic Perspectives*, 12 (2) (Spring 2000).

Brady, David. 2003. Rethinking the Sociological Measurement of Poverty. *Social Forces* 81:3 (March), 715–751.

Braham, M. 1993. The Untouchables: A Survey of the Roma People of Central and Eastern Europe. A Report to the Office of the United Nations High Commissioner for Refugees, Switzerland.

Brauner, S., and P. Loprest. 1999. Where Are They Now? What State's Studies of People Who Left Welfare Tell Us. The Urban Institute, Washington, DC.

Cahn, C. 2001. Smoke and Mirrors: Roma and Minority Policy in Hungary. *Roma Rights 4*. ERRC.

Calvo Buezas, T. 1995. Racism Increases, Solidarity as Well. Technos, Junta de Extremadura.

———. 1989. Los racistas son los otros: Roma, minorías y derechos humanos en los textos escolares. *Editorial Popular*. Madrid.

Cartner, H. 1994. Romanian Lynch Law: Violence Against Roma in Romania. *Human Rights Watch Newsletter, November 1*. New York: Human Rights Watch.

CEDIME-SE (Center for Documentation and Information on Minorities in Eastern Europe—Southeast Europe). 2001. Minorities in Southeast Europe: Roma of Romania. Report prepared by CEDIME-SE in cooperation with EDRC (Ethnocultural Diversity Resource Center), Cluj, Romania.

CIDE (Centro de Investigación y Documentación Educativa). 1999. *Las desigualdades en la educación en España*. Madrid: Ministerio de Educación y Cultura, CIDE.

Cilla, G., E. Perez-Trallero, J. M. Marimon, S. Erdozain, and C. Gutierrez. 1995. Prevalence of Hepatitis A Antibody among Disadvantaged Gypsy People in Northern Spain. *Epidemiology and Infection* 115: 157–61.

Commander, S., and F. Coricelli, eds. 1995. *Unemployment, Restructuring and the Labor Market in Eastern Europe and Russia*. Washington, DC: World Bank.

Commission of the European Communities. 2000. *2000 Regular Report from the Commission on Hungary's Progress*. Brussels: Commission.

———. 2001. *2001 Regular Report from the Commission on Hungary's Progress Toward Accession*. SEC (2001) 1748. Brussels: Commission.

———. 2002. *2002 Regular Report from the Commission on Hungary's Progress Toward Accession*, SEC (2002) 1404. Brussels: Commission.

Conclusions of the Copenhagen European Council. 1993. *Bulletin of the European Communities* 6, point I.13.

Congress of Deputies. 1999a. *Informe de la Subcomisión, creada en el seno de la Comisión de Política Social y empleo, para el estudio de la problemática del pueblo gitano*. Madrid: Congreso de los Diputados, Comisión de Política Social y Empleo (December).

————. 1999b. *Informe de la Subcomisión para el estudio de la problemática del pueblo Gitano*. Madrid: Congreso de los Diputados, Comisión de Política Social y Empleo.

————. 2002. *Legal Situation of the Roma in Europe*. Document 9397 (26 March), http://assembly.coe.int/Documents/WorkingDocs/doc02/EDOC9397.htm.

Crowe, D. 1991. The Gypsy Historical Experience in Romania. In *The Gypsies of Eastern Europe*, eds. David Crowe and John Holsti. Armonk, NY: M. E. Sharpe, Inc.

————. 1994. *A History of the Gypsies of Eastern Europe and Russia*. New York: St. Martin's Press.

Dar, A., and Z. Tzannatos. 1998. *Active Labor Market Programs: A Review of the Evidence from Evaluations*. Washington, DC: World Bank.

Denkov, D., E. Stanoeva, and, V. Vidinsky. 2001. Roma Schools. Open Society Institute, Sofia.

De Witte, B. 2002. Politics versus Law in the EU's Approach to Ethnic Minorities. In *Europe Unbound: Enlarging and Reshaping the Boundaries of the European Union*, ed. J. Zielonka. New York: Routledge.

Doncsev, T., ed. 2000. *Measures Taken by the State to Promote the Social Integration of Roma Living in Hungary*. Budapest: Office for National and Ethnic Minorities (NEKH).

Dunai, M. 2002. Political Battles Heat Up in Hungary. *Time Europe Daily* (February 15).

ECOHOST (European Centre on Health of Societies in Transition). 2000. (Draft) Health Needs of the Roma Population in the Czech and the Slovak Republics: Literature Review.

The Economist. 2001. Europe's Spectral Nation (May 10).

ECRE (European Committee on Romani Emancipation). 2001. The Social and Economic Inclusion of the Roma—Annual Progress Report. Document ECRE (2001) 003, Brussels, 20 October.

ECRI (European Commission against Racism and Intolerance). 2003. *Second Report on Spain*, CRI (2003) 40. Strasbourg: Council of Europe.

Erlanger, S. 2000. The Gypsies of the Slovak Republic: Despised and Despairing. *The New York Times* (April 3): A10.

ERRC (European Roma Rights Center). 1996. *Sudden Rage at Dawn: Violence Against Roma in Romania*. Budapest: ERRC.

————. 1999. *A Special Remedy: Roma and Schools for the Mentally Handicapped in the Czech Republic*. Country Reports Series 8. Budapest: ERRC.

————. 2000. *Campland: Racial Segregation of Roma in Italy*. Country Reports Series 9. Budapest: ERRC.

Esman, M. 2001. Policy Dimensions: What Can Development Assistance Do? In *Carrots, Sticks, and Ethnic Conflict: Rethinking Development Assistance*, eds. Ronald J. Herring and Milton J. Esman. Ann Arbor: University of Michigan Press.

European Commission, Directorate General for Enlargement. 1999. EU Support for Roma Communities in Central and Eastern Europe—Enlargement Briefing. Enlargement Information Unit.

————. 2002. EU Support for Roma Communities in Central and Eastern Europe—Enlargement Briefing. Enlargement Information Unit, May 2002.

Figlio, D., and J. Ziliak. 1999. Welfare Reform, the Business Cycle, and the Decline in AFDC Caseloads. In *Economic Conditions and Welfare Reform*, ed. S. Danziger. Kalamazoo: Upjohn Institute for Employment Research, 17–48.

Framework Convention for the Protection of National Minorities. (FCNM) 1995. European Treaty Series 157. Strasbourg: Council of Europe.

Fraser, A. 1995. *The Gypsies*. Oxford: Blackwell.

Fresno, J. M. 1994. Análisis socioantropológico sobre la situación actual de la Comunidad Gitana en Espana. Documentos Técnicos 2, ASGG, Madrid.

FSGG (Fundación Secretariado General Gitano). 2002. Evaluation of Educational Normalization of Romani Children. FSGG, Madrid.

Galloway, R., C. Rokx, and L. Brown. 2000. (Draft) Nutrition Status and Issues in ECA. World Bank, Washington, DC.

Gamella, J. F. 1996. *La Población Gitana en Andalucia: Un Estudio Exploratorio de Sus Condiciones de Vida*. Sevilla: Consejería de Trabajo y Asuntos Sociales, Junta de Andalucía.

————. 2002. Social Exclusion and Ethnic Conflict in Andalusia. Analysis of a Cycle of Mobilization and Anti-Gypsy Collective Action (1976–2000). *Gazeta de Antropologiá*, No. 18, Text 18–MO7.

Gay y Blasco, Paloma. 1999. *Gypsies in Madrid: Sex, Gender and the Performance of Identity*, Oxford: Berg.

Gheorghe, N. 1983. The Origin of Roma's Slavery in the Romanian Principalities. *Roma* 7 (1): 12–27.

Gilberg, T. 1974. Ethnic Minorities in Romania Under Socialism. *East European Quarterly* 7 (January): 435–464.

Giménez Adelantado, A. 1999. Contexto sociopolítico y cultural: los espanoles Roma. *Roma* 1 (June), (ASGG biannual magazine).

Goldston, J., and R. Guglielmo. 2001. Shared Standards. *Transitions On-Line* (October 11).

Government of Romania. 2001. Strategy of the Government of Romania for Improving the Condition of Roma, 430/2001, Ministry of Public Information, Bucharest.

Government of Slovakia. 1997. *Statistical Yearbook of the Slovak Republic*.

Grupo PASS. 1991. Map of Roma Settlement in Spain for the Ministry of Social Affairs. Grupo PASS, Madrid.

Hancock, I. 1997. The Struggle for the Control of Identity. *Transitions* 4 (4/September).

————. 2003. The Concocters: Creating Fake Romani Culture. In *The Role of the Romanies: Images and Self-Images of Gypsies/Romanies in European Cultures*, eds. Nicholas Saul and Susan Tebbutt. Liverpool.

Havas, G., I. Kémeny, and I. Lisko. 2001. (2nd draft) Segregation in the Education of Roma Children. Final Research Study. MNEKK, OM, Soros Foundation, and OTKA, Budapest.

Hernandez, A. B. 2002. Member State Reports: Spain. In *Racism and Cultural Diversity in the Mass Media: An Overview of Research and Examples of Good Practice in the EU Member States, 1995–2000*, ed. Jessika ter Wal. Vienna: ERCOMER (European Research Center on Migration and Ethnic Relations).

Iliev, I. 1999. (Draft) Some Approaches at Measuring Social Capital among Roma Communities in Bulgaria: Preliminary Notes.

Implementation Report. 1999. Implementation of the Council of Europe Framework Convention for the Protection of National Minorities, Government Resolution 2023/1999 (II. 12), Office for Ethnic and National Minorities, Budapest.

ISSP (Institute for Strategic Studies and Prognoses) and UNDP. 2003. Household Survey of Roma, Ashkaelia and Egyptians, Refugees and Internally Displaced Persons. Podgorica, Montenegro.

Jenkins, R. 1999. The Role of the Hungarian NGO Sector in Postcommunist Social Policy. In *Left Parties and Social Policy in Postcommunist Europe*, eds. Linda J. Cook, Mitchell A. Orenstein, and Marilyn Rueschemeyer. Boulder: Westview Press.

Jiménez González, N. 1993. Schooling of Gypsy Infancy in Spain. Paper presented at the seminar on Integration and Education of Gypsy Children, Snekkersten and Elsinore, Denmark.

Kabachieva, P., and I. Iliev. 2002. Background Paper for the World Bank Bulgaria Poverty Assessment. World Bank, Sofia (photocopy).

Kádár, A., L. Farkas, and M. Pardavi. 2002. *Hungary: A Comparison of the EU Racial Equality Directive and Protocol 12 with National Anti-Discrimination Legislation*. Brussels: ERRC, Interights, and MPG.

Kalibova, K. 2000. The Demographic Characteristics of Roma/Gypsies in Selected Countries in Central and Eastern Europe. In *The Demographic Characteristics of National Minorities in Certain European States*, eds. W. Haug, P. Compton, and Y. Courgage. Population Study 31, Vol. 2. Council of Europe Publishing.

Kállai, E. 2000. The Roma and Research on the Roma, Caught in the Trap of Integration: Roma Problems and Prospects in Hungary. For an International Conference, June 22–23 1999, Bureau for European Comparative Minority Research, Budapest.

Kállai, E., and E. Törzsök, eds. 2000. *A Roma's Life in Hungary*. Budapest: Bureau for European Comparative Minority Research.

Keating, M., and J. McGarry. 2001. *Minority Nationalism and the Changing International Order*. Oxford: Oxford University Press.

Kémeny, I., G. Havas, and G. Kertesi. 1994. The Education and Employment Situation of the Gypsy Community: Report of the 1993/4 National Sample Survey. Working Paper 17, ILO/Japan Project on Employment Policies for Transition in Hungary, Budapest.

Kertesi, G. 1994. The Labor Market Situation of the Gypsy Minority in Hungary. Working Paper 14, ILO/Japan Project on Employment Policies for Transition in Hungary, Budapest.

Konstantinov, Y. 1999. Case Study of Roma Heroin Users: Maksouda Quarter, Varna. Background Paper for the Bulgaria Consultations with the Poor Study (unpublished).

Kováts, M. 2001a. The Emergence of European Roma Policy. In *Between Past and Future: The Roma of Central and Eastern Europe*, ed. Will Guy. Hertfordshire: University of Hertfordshire Press.

————. 2001b. The Political Significance of the First National Gypsy Self-Government. *Journal on Ethnopolitics and Minority Issues in Europe* (Autumn). European Center for Minority Issues, http://www.ecmi.de.

Ládanyi, J. 1993. Patterns of Residential Segregation and the Gypsy Minority in Budapest. *International Journal of Urban and Regional Research* 17 (1): 30–41.

Ládanyi, J., and I. Szelényi. 2001. The Social Construction of Roma Ethnicity in Bulgaria, Romania and Hungary During Market Transition. *Review of Sociology* 7 (2): 79–89.

Lewy, G. 2000. *The Nazi Persecution of the Gypsies*. Oxford: Oxford University Press.

Liegeois, J-P. 1994. *Roma, Gypsies, Travellers*. Strasbourg: Council of Europe Press.

Liegeois, J-P., and N. Gheorghe. 1995. *Roma/Gypsies: A European Minority*. London: Minority Rights Group.

Livezeanu, I. 1995. *Cultural Politics in Greater Romania: Regionalism, Nation-Building, Ethnic Struggle, 1918–1930*. Ithaca: Cornell University Press.

Loury, G. C. 1999. Social Exclusion and Ethnic Groups: The Challenge to Economics. Paper presented to the Annual Bank Conference on Development Economics, World Bank, Washington, DC (photocopy).

Lovatt, C., and D. Lovatt. 2001. News from Romania: Hungarian Status Bill. *Central Europe Review* 3 (18/21 May), http://www.ce-review.org.

Macura, V., and M. Petrovic. 1999. Housing, Urban Planning and Poverty: Problems Faced by Roma/Gypsy Communities with Particular Reference to Central and Eastern Europe. Document of the Council of Europe, MG-S-Rom (99) 1.

Marko, J. 2000. Equality *and* Difference: Political and Legal Aspects of Ethnic Group Relations. In *Vienna International Encounter on Some Current Issues Regarding the Situation of National Minorities*, ed. F. Matscher. Kehl: Engel Publishers: 67–97. (Web version published 2000.)

Martin, F. A. 2000. Roma in Spain. Background paper prepared for the World Bank (unpublished).

Martinez-Frais, M. L., and E. Bermejo. 1992. Prevalence of Congenital Anomaly Syndromes in the Spanish Gypsy Population. *Journal of Medical Genetics* 29: 483–6.

Marx, K. 1985 *The Communist Manifesto*. Harmondsworth, England: Penguin Books.

McDonald, Christina. Roma Education Policies in Hungary. In *The Roma Education Resource Book*, eds. Christina McDonald, Judit Kovacs, and Csaba Fenyes. Budapest: Open Society Institute.

Ministerio de Trabajo y Asuntos Sociales. 1999. *Secretaría General de Asuntos Sociales, Dirección General de Acción Social, del Menor y de la Familia, Programa Para el Desarollo del Pueblo Gitano*. Madrid: Ministerio de Trabajo y Asuntos Sociales (March).

————. 2000. *Servicio Programa de Desarrollo Gitano, Memoria del Programa de Desarrollo Gitano 1988*. Madrid: Ministerio de Trabajo y Asuntos Sociales.

Ministry of Education. 2001. Basic Data on Education in Spain for the Year 2001/2002. Madrid.

Ministry of Education of Romania (Ministru de Educativ de România). 1998. Ministerul Invatamantului—Institiutul de Stiinte Ale Educatiei. Bucuresti.

Ministry of Labor, Social Affairs and Family of the Slovak Republic. 1997. Conceptual Intents of the Government of the Slovak Republic for Solution of the Problems of Romany Population under Current Social and Economic Conditions. Bratislava.

Minorities Act. 1993. *Act LXXVII of 1993 on the Rights of National and Ethnic Minorities*. Budapest: National Assembly, Republic of Hungary.

Mulcahy, F. D. 1988. Material and Non-Material Resources, or Why the Gypsies Have No Vises. *Technology in Society* 10: 457–67.

Murray, R., ed. 2002. *Improving the Roma Situation: Successful Projects from Romania . . . and Lessons Learned*. Bucharest: European Commission, EU PHARE Programme RO9803.01.

National Democratic Institute for International Affairs. 2003. Roma Political Participation in Bulgaria, Romania, and Slovakia. Assessment Mission Report.

Nord, M. 1988. Poor People on the Move: Country-to-Country Migration and the Spatial Concentration of Poverty. *Journal of Regional Science* 38: 329–352.

Orentlicher, D. F. 1998. Citizenship and National Identity. In *International Law and Ethnic Conflict*, ed. David Wippman. Ithaca: Cornell University Press: 296–325.

Organisation for Economic Co-operation and Development (OECD). 1996. *Education at a Glance: OECD Indicators*. Paris: Centre for Educational Research and Innovation, OECD, 1996.

Orsós-Hegyesi, E., K. Bóhn, G. Fleck, and A. Imre. 2000. Alternative Schools and Roma Education: A Review of Alternative Secondary School Models for the Education of Roma Children in Hungary. World Bank Regional Office Hungary, NGO Studies No. 3.

OSCE (Organization for Security and Co-operation in Europe), High Commissioner on National Minorities. 2000. Report on the Situation of Roma and Sinti in the OSCE Area. OSCE, The Hague.

OSCE ODIHR (Office of Democratic Institutions and Human Rights). 1996. Situation of Roma and Sinti in the OSCE Region: Background Material for the Review Conference. ODIHR, Warsaw.

————. 1997. ODIHR Background Report. OSCE Human Dimension Implementation Meeting, November 12–28.

OSI (Open Society Institute). 2001. *Monitoring the EU Accession Process: Minority Protection—Country Reports on Bulgaria, Czech Republic, Estonia, Hungary, Latvia, Lithuania, Poland, Romania, Slovakia, Slovenia.* Budapest: Central European University Press.

————. 2002. *Accession Monitoring Program, 2002: Monitoring the EU Accession Process. Minority Protection.* Vols. 1 and 2. Budapest, Hungary.

————. 2002. Research on Selected Roma Education Programs in Central and Eastern Europe: Final Report. Education Sub-Board of the Open Society Institute, Budapest, http://www.osi.hu/iep/equity/roma_report_part1.pdf.

Pace, E. 1993. The Making of Minorities. In *Children of Minorities: Gypsies,* ed. Sandro Costarelli. Innocenti Insights Series. Florence: UNICEF International Child Development Centre.

Panaitescu, P. N. 1941. The Gypsies in Wallachia and Moldovia: A Chapter of Economic History, trans. Doris Hardman. *Journal of the Gypsy Lore Society* 20 (2/April/Third Series): 58–72.

Pejic, J. 1997. Minority Rights in International Law. *Human Rights Quarterly* 19 (3): 666–685.

PER (Project on Ethnic Relations). 1997a. The Roma in the Twenty-First Century: A Policy Paper. PER, Princeton.

————. 1997b. The Media and the Roma in Contemporary Europe: Facts and Fictions. PER, Princeton.

————. 1998. Self-Government in Hungary: The Gypsy/Romani Experience and Prospects for the Future (May 9–11 1997). PER, Budapest.

Peterson, J. 2009. Welfare Reform and Inequality: The TANF and UI Programs. *Journal of the Gypsy Lore Society* 20 (2/April/Third Series): 58–72.

Pogany, I. 1999. Minority Rights in Central and Eastern Europe: Old Dilemmas, New Solutions? In *Minority and Group Rights in the New Millennium,* eds. Deirdre Fottrell and Bill Bowring. The Hague: Martinus Nijhoff Publishers.

Poulton, H. 1991. *The Balkans: Minorities and States in Conflict.* London: Minority Rights Group.

Psacharopoulos, G., and H. A. Patrinos. 1994. *Indigenous People and Poverty in Latin America: An Empirical Analysis.* Washington, DC: World Bank.

Puporka, L., and Z. Zádori. 1999. The Health Status of Roma in Hungary. World Bank Regional Office Hungary, NGO Studies, No. 2. Budapest.

Radó, P. 1997. *Report on the Education of Roma Students in Hungary.* Expert Study for the Office of National and Ethnic Minorities (ONEM). Budapest: ONEM and the OSI Institute for Educational Policy.

————. 2001. Roma Education Policies in Hungary. In *The Roma Education Resource Book,* eds. Christina McDonald, Judit Kovacs, and Csaba Fenyes. Budapest: Open Society Institute.

Ravallion, M. 1994. *Poverty Comparisons.* Philadelphia: Harvard Academic Publishers.

Report Submitted by Spain Pursuant to Article 25, Paragraph 1 of the Framework Convention for the Protection of National Minorities (FCNM). 2000. ACFC/SR (2000) 005. Madrid: Council of Europe.

Revenga, A., D. Ringold, and W. M. Tracy. 2002. *Poverty and Ethnicity: A Cross-Country Study of Roma Poverty in Central Europe.* Washington, DC: World Bank.

Ringold, D. 2000. *Roma and the Transition in Central and Eastern Europe.* Washington, DC: World Bank.

Rodgers, G, C. Gore, and J. Figueiredo. 1995. *Social Exclusion: Rhetoric, Reality, Responses.* Geneva: International Institute for Labor Studies, United Nations Development Programme.

Roma. 2000. El pueblo Gitano y la educación. *Biannual Magazine of the General Gypsy Secretariat Association (ASGG)*, Number 7/8, December.

Rona, S., and L. Lee. 2001. School Success for Roma Children: Step-by-Step Special Schools Initiative Interim Report. Open Society Institute.

Rughinis, C. 2000. Romania: Local Service Delivery Module on Roma Communities. Background paper prepared for the World Bank.

Sanchez-Paramo, C. 2001. *Unemployment, Skills, and Incentives. An Overview of the Safety Net System in the Slovak Republic.* Washington, DC: World Bank.

Santos, Montserrat. 1999. Cultural Diversity: Equal Opportunities? *European Journal of Education* 34 (4/December): 437–448.

Save the Children. 2001a. *Denied a Future: The Right to Education of Roma/Gypsy and Traveller Children in Europe.* Vol. 1: *South-Eastern Europe.* London: Save the Children Fund.

————. 2001b. *Denied a Future? The Right to Education of Roma/Gypsy & Traveller Children in Europe.* Vol. 2: *Western & Central Europe.* London: Save the Children Fund.

Schafft, K. 1999. Local Minority Self-Governance and Hungary's Roma. *The Hungarian Quarterly* XL (155/Autumn).

Schafft, K., and D. Brown. 2000. Social Capital and Grassroots Development: The Case of Roma Self-Governance in Hungary. *Social Problems* 47 (2): 201–219.

————. 2002. Social Capital, Social Networks, and Social Power. Paper prepared for the Cornell University Workshop on Social Capital and Civic Involvement, Ithaca, NY, September 13–14.

Schoeni, R. F., and R. M. Blank. 2000. What Has Welfare Reform Accomplished? Impacts on Welfare Participation, Employment, Income, Poverty and Family Structure. NBER Working Paper, No. 7627.

Shuinéar, S. 1993. Growing Up as a Gypsy: Insights from the October 1992 UNICEF ICDC Workshop. In *Children of Minorities: Gypsies*, ed. Sandro Costarelli. Innocenti Insights Series. Florence: UNICEF International Child Development Centre.

Sierra, M. M. 2002. *Anti-Discrimination Legislation in EU Member States: Spain.* Vienna: EUMC (European Monitoring Center on Racism and Xenophobia).

Silver, H., 1994. Social Exclusion and Social Solidarity: Three Paradigms. *International Labor Review* 133 (5–6): 531–578.

Staines, V. 1999. *A Health Sector Strategy for the Europe and Central Asia Region. Human Development Network.* Washington, DC: World Bank.

Stewart, M. 1997. *The Time of the Gypsies.* Boulder: Westview Press.

Tanaka, J., A. Bíró, N. Gheorghe, and H. Heuss. 1998. Toward a *Pakiv* European Roma Fund: Income Generating Programmes for Roma in Central and Eastern Europe. Report commissioned by the Council of Europe and Freudenberg Foundation, MG-S-ROM (98) 10, Council of Europe, Strasbourg.

Tomova, I. 1998. Ethnic Dimensions of the Poverty in Bulgaria. Report Commissioned for the Bulgaria Social Assessment, World Bank, Sofia.

———. 2000. (Draft) Fiscal Decentralization: Ethnicity Module. World Bank, Sofia.

Ulč, O. 1991. Integration of the Gypsies in Czechoslovakia. *Ethnic Groups* 9: 107–117.

UN (United Nations). 2001. *Joint UN/Romanian Government Seminar on the Improvement of the Situation of the Roma in Romania.* Summary of Seminar Proceedings, 2–3 November. Bucharest: The Senate of Romania.

UNDP (United Nations Development Programme). 1999. *National Human Development Report: Bulgaria 1999.* Sofia: UNDP.

———. 2003. *The Roma in Central and Eastern Europe: Avoiding the Dependency Trap.* Bratislava: UNDP.

UNICEF. 1995. *Children of Minorities: Deprivation and Discrimination.* Innocenti Insights Series. Florence: UNICEF International Child Development Centre.

———. 1998. Education for All? Regional Monitoring Reports 5, UNICEF International Child Development Centre, Florence.

———. 1999. Women in Transition. Regional Monitoring Reports 6, UNICEF International Child Development Centre, Florence.

Van der Walle, D., and D. Gunewardena. 2001. Source of Ethnic Inequality in Viet Nam. *Journal of Development Economics* 65: 177–207.

Vašečka, M. 1999. *The Roma.* Bratislava: Institute for Public Affairs.

———. 2000a. Analysis of the Situation of Roma in Slovakia. Draft prepared for the World Bank.

———. 2000b. *Roma—The Greatest Challenge for Slovakia on its Way into the European Union.* Bratislava: Institute for Public Affairs.

Vásquez, J. M. 1980. *Estudio sociológico sobre los Roma españoles.* Madrid: Instituto de Sociología Aplicada.

Villareal, F. 2001. Spanish Policy and Roma. *ERRC Notebook 2.* ERRC.

Walsh, N. 2000. Minority Self Government in Hungary: Legislation and Practice. *Journal on Ethnopolitics and Minority Issues in Europe* (Summer). European Center for Minority Issues, Germany, http://www.ecmi.de.

Wheeler, A. 1999. Gypsies in Eastern Europe—Issues and Possible Actions. Draft discussion paper, World Bank, Washington, DC.

Wippman, D. 1998. Introduction. In *International Law and Ethnic Conflict*, ed. David Wippman. Ithaca: Cornell University Press.

World Bank. 2000a. Balancing Protection and Opportunity: ECA Social Protection Strategy Paper. World Bank, Washington, DC.

————. 2000b. *Making Transition Work for Everyone: Poverty and Inequality in Europe and Central Asia.* Washington, DC: World Bank.

————. 2000c. The Road to Stability and Prosperity in South Eastern Europe: A Regional Strategy Paper. World Bank, Washington, DC.

————. 2000d. *Romania Local Social Services Delivery Study.* Vol. 1 and 2. Report No. 23492-RO. Washington, DC: World Bank, Human Development Sector Unit, Europe and Asia Region.

————. 2001a. *Attacking Poverty: World Development Report 2000/2001.* Washington, DC: World Bank.

————. 2001b. Slovak Republic: Living Standards, Employment and Labour Market Study. Report 22351-SK, World Bank, Washington, DC.

————. 2002. Poverty and Welfare of Roma in the Slovak Republic. World Bank, Washington, DC.

————. 2004. Roma in an Expanding Europe: Challenges for the Future. A Summary of Policy Discussions and Conference Proceedings, June 30–July 1, 2003. World Bank, Washington, DC.

World Bank and National Commission for Statistics. 1998. *From Poverty to Rural Development.*

World Bank, Foundation SPACE, INEKO, and the Open Society Institute. 2002. Poverty and Welfare of Roma in the Slovak Republic. Bratislava.

Zamfir E., and C. Zamfir. 1993a. *Gypsies: Between Ignoring them and Worrying About Them.* Bucharest: Editura Alternative.

————. 1993b. *The Romany Population.* Social Policy Series 8. Bucharest: Bucharest University and the Institute for the Quality of Life.

————. 1996. Children at Risk in Romania: Problems Old and New. UNICEF Child Development Center, Florence.

Zang, T., and R. Levy. 1991. *Destroying Ethnic Identity: The Persecution of Gypsies in Romania.* New York: Helsinki Watch.

About the Authors

Dena Ringold is a senior economist at the World Bank in Washington, DC. She has been involved in analytical and operational work on poverty and social policy in the transition countries of Central and Eastern Europe. Her research has focused on poverty, social exclusion, and ethnic minorities, particularly the Roma population, social protection, and the linkages between fiscal decentralization and local social service delivery. In 2000, she published the Bank's first study on the Roma minority, the first to examine Roma poverty and human development status across countries.

Mitchell A. Orenstein is an associate professor of political science and director of the Center for European Studies at the Maxwell School of Syracuse University in Syracuse, New York. Dr. Orenstein has published extensively on the political economy of policy reform in Central and Eastern Europe, including *Out of the Red: Building Capitalism and Democracy in Postcommunist Europe* (Michigan, 2001). His recent work has focused on reform of post-communist welfare states.

Erika Wilkens is a Ph.D. candidate in political science at the Maxwell School, Syracuse University in Syracuse, New York. Before coming to the Maxwell School, she earned masters' degrees in international relations and the sociology of development and taught at Vytautas Magnus University and Vilnius University in Lithuania. Her current research interests include race/ethnic/minority relations, political incorporation, and the politics of immigration.

Index

Note: n = note